THE INVERTING PYRAMID

THE INVERTING PYRAMID

*Pension Systems Facing Demographic Challenges
in Europe and Central Asia*

Anita M. Schwarz
Omar S. Arias
Asta Zviniene
Heinz P. Rudolph
Sebastian Eckardt
Johannes Koettl
Herwig Immervoll
Miglena Abels

THE WORLD BANK
Washington, D.C.

Contents

Boxes

Figures

Tables

Foreword

The pension and old age security systems that originated in Europe in the nineteenth and twentieth centuries have been effective in sharply reducing poverty rates among the elderly throughout Europe. However, in many countries of the Europe and Central Asia (ECA) region, these systems now comprise the single largest expenditure item in the government budget. As these countries faced fiscal consolidation in the aftermath of the transition, many of them already substantially reformed their pension systems. Current demographic trends in the region, however, suggest that further reforms will be needed.

This book presents the historical evolution of pension systems in Europe, showing how policy makers were able to use the expanding population pyramid, with large younger cohorts and small older cohorts to expand the coverage and increase the generosity of pension systems. Levels of benefits were increased and the duration of retirement increased over time, making pension systems more expensive, with each generation receiving more generous benefits than the generation before. This book focuses on the impact of the break in this demographic evolution, whereby the prognosis for the future population structure is likely to resemble a column or even an inverting pyramid, with smaller cohorts of working age population expected to support larger cohorts of elderly retirees. This change in the demographic structure calls into question the traditional financing mechanisms for old-age support, which relied on the labor taxes on the working age population to finance benefits for the elderly.

The good news is that, despite the demographic challenges, ECA countries do not have to roll back the progress they have made in reducing poverty among the elderly. If the generosity of the pension systems pension promise were rolled back only to where it was in the 1970s, when most of Europe had already achieved substantial poverty reduction among the elderly, the pension systems would be fiscally sustainable. Going back to the promise of the 1970s would involve adjusting the retirement age in line with rising longevity to ensure that average life expectancy after retirement is 15 years, thereby encouraging the elderly to spend their increased healthy years in the labor force rather than in retirement. As the working age population begins to shrink, keeping older workers in the labor force will become important, not just for financing the pension system, but also for maintaining overall economic growth.

Changes in pension policy will need to be accompanied by policies to increase labor market flexibility so as to encourage older workers to remain in the work force. Such policies include incentives for employers to provide lifelong learning and training specifically geared to older workers, and make workforce adaptations which allow older workers to retain a high level of productivity. In some countries, benefits will need to be streamlined to provide workers with basic benefits that ensure that they do not fall into poverty, but may not be sufficient to fully maintain the living standard they enjoyed while working. Tax and social protection systems need to encourage workers to save for a more generous level of retirement benefits than can be provided by the public system, if they desire more benefits in retirement. To that end, governments can encourage the financial sector to provide relevant savings instruments, while ensuring adequate transparency and regulation so that individuals have the opportunity to undertake additional savings without exposing themselves to unknown risks. Governments may also need to re-examine the efficiency of their revenue administration systems to help finance not just pensions, but all other societal needs. This book goes into each of these accompanying policies, but concludes that none of these by itself can address the impact of the demographic challenges that are underway. A combination of policies will be required to effectively face the challenges.

The book concludes that the inverting population pyramid clearly presents challenges to the provision of old age security, but consistent policy choices to return the pension system to parameters similar to those in the 1970s can result in sustainable systems of old age security. But this means that governments need to communicate to the population at large that the growth in generosity experienced in the past 100 years will not be able to continue and will in fact need to be rolled back somewhat. *The Inverting Pyramid* provides a wealth of statistics and analysis that will enable a better understanding of the changes that are needed and illustrates the possible trade-offs when policy makers or voters consider who they want to protect through their countries' pension systems, how much, and when.

Laura Tuck
Vice President
Europe and Central Asia Region
The World Bank

Acknowledgments

This study was prepared by a multisectoral team co-led by Anita M. Schwarz and Omar S. Arias and including Miglena Abels, Sebastian Eckardt, Herwig Immervoll, Johannes Koettl, Heinz P. Rudolph, and Asta Zviniene. The team is grateful for the guidance, support, and technical inputs of Indermit Gill, Kathy Lindert, Andrew Mason, and Ana Revenga. The work was carried out under the overall supervision of Philippe Le Houérou as Vice President of the Europe and Central Asia Region of the World Bank. The team is also grateful for the financing and support they received from the Social Protection and Labor Practice at the World Bank.

Chapter authors are as follows. Chapter 1: Anita Schwarz, with substantive contributions from Omar Arias, Asta Zviniene, Heinz Rudolph, Sebastian Eckardt, and Miglena Abels; chapter 2: Asta Zviniene and Anita Schwarz, with contributions from Miglena Abels and Heinz Rudolph; chapter 3: Anita Schwarz and Asta Zviniene, with contributions from Miglena Abels; chapter 4: Heinz Rudolph; chapter 5: Sebastian Eckardt; chapter 6: Omar Arias, Johannes Koettl, and Herwig Immervoll; chapter 7: Anita Schwarz, with contributions from Asta Zviniene and Miglena Abels.

Thomas Davoine, Christian Keuschnigg, and Philip Schuster of the Institute for Advanced Studies in Vienna prepared background analysis on overlapping generations modeling under the supervision of Omar Arias and Herwig Immervoll. Andrew Reilly and the pensions team at the Organisation for Economic Co-operation and Development applied the OECD's Pensions at a Glance methodology to the pension systems of transition countries of Europe and Central Asia. The author team is also grateful to Otar Dzidzikashvili, Melis U. Guven, Emily Sinnott, Oleksiy A. Sluchynskyy, Manami Suga, and Victor Sulla for their substantive contributions to the development of the report.

Cathy Sunshine edited the full final report, and Jennica Larrison edited preliminary drafts. Marta Helena Reis de Assis, Anahit Poghosyan, and Solange Van Veldhuizen provided invaluable logistical and administrative support.

The team is grateful for the insightful advice and recommendations received from members of the Advisory Board for the report: Anna d'Addio (OECD), Axel Börsch-Supan (Germany), Agnieszka Chłoń-Domińczak (Poland), Mikhail Dmitriev (Russian Federation), Per Eckefeldt (European Commission, DG ECFIN), Elsa Fornero (Italy), Peter Holtzer (Hungary), Gordana Matković (Serbia), Insan Tunali (Turkey), and Fritz von Nordheim (European Commission, DG Employment). Peer reviewers were Gordon Betcherman, Robert Palacios, Roberto Rocha, and Carlos Silva-Jáuregui. The authors also acknowledge useful comments from Mamta Murthi, Martin Raiser, and Michal Rutkowski of the World Bank, as well as from many other colleagues at the concept review and subsequent stages.

Finally, the team received valuable comments and suggestions from government officials who participated in country consultations in Croatia and Georgia; participants in the Pensions Practice Seminar series at the World Bank; staff at the International Monetary Fund; and members of the Europe and Central Asia Regional Leadership Team of the World Bank.

Executive Summary

One of the greatest social achievements in Europe has been the rapid reduction of old-age poverty. This took place in the context of both an expanding pension system and an expanding population. Beginning with the first pension systems in the late nineteenth century, an ever-growing number of workers made contributions to finance the old-age benefits of a relatively small number of pensioners. Both the population and the pension system resembled a pyramid in shape, with a large, youthful population at the base and a small number of elderly at the peak. This arrangement made it possible to provide relatively generous benefits to qualifying elderly. Now, more than a hundred years later, both pension system dynamics and overall demographics have changed, and Europe's pension systems face an uncertain future.

To begin with, pension systems are now mostly "mature," with little room to expand the number of contributors by drawing in larger cohorts of new workers. Initially covering only a subset of formal sector workers, pension systems gradually widened to embrace all formal sector workers, as well as the self-employed, farmers, and women. Few workers now remain outside the pension system in the largest European countries.

Second, while population—and more importantly, working-age population—expanded throughout the twentieth century, both overall population and working-age population are expected to decline in Europe in the twenty-first century. At the same time, in almost all countries in the region, people are living longer. These changes have been magnified in the transition countries of Europe and Central Asia, where labor force participation rates have dropped, and sharp declines in fertility, along with increasing emigration, have resulted in a rapidly declining labor force. In some countries with especially low fertility and high outmigration, the population pyramid has started to resemble an inverted pyramid, with younger cohorts smaller than the cohorts preceding them for the first time. These changes call into question the continuing feasibility of financing old-age support for a growing elderly population from taxes on the wages of a shrinking number of wage earners.

Technical experts throughout Europe are well aware of the challenges ahead and have been busy devising mechanisms that will automatically adjust benefits and retirement ages to the coming reality. The transition countries, in particular, faced huge fiscal challenges in the 1990s as they moved from centrally planned to market-based economies. These countries undertook innovative pension reforms, experimenting with variations on the traditional financing systems while also allowing individuals to set aside part of their own wages as future retirement savings for themselves. These reforms, had they been allowed to unfold as originally envisaged, would have helped pension systems face the upcoming demographic challenges.

The reforms were undertaken as countries attempted to recover from the massive dislocations caused by the transformation of their economies. During the transition, people expected to tighten their belts, and they did. However, when the economies started to recover and grow again, the expectations of the past returned. For a century, every generation of elderly had received more generous benefits than the previous generation of elderly, and once the transition economies stabilized, people expected this pattern of increases to resume. The population at large seemed unaware that the increased benefits of the past had been made possible by a growing population of workers, not by the generosity of benevolent politicians or by a fair return on contributions. Nor was there widespread understanding of the sober implications of changing demography: not only was increasing generosity no longer affordable, but a portion of past increases might need to be given back. When people saw benefit reductions going hand in hand with a growing economy, they demanded rollbacks in the reductions. Politicians often complied, throwing out the elegant designs that technical policymakers had devised.

This book was written not for the pension technician but to provide the average reader a convincing explanation of why the increasing generosity of the past is no longer possible. No one expects generosity to increase during a downturn, such as the one Europe has experienced in recent years, but the past pattern of increases will not be able to rebound even when Europe recovers. The structural demographic shift, in which working-age populations are stagnant or declining, makes future increases in generosity unaffordable.

But the message of the report is not all somber: countries have a number of options. The concept of retirement age is key.

The history of pension systems shows an evolution of pension eligibility, from the first German system, in which pensioners were older than 70 and had limited work capacity, to today's systems, which allow people in good health to retire after only 30 years of work, at ages as young as 55. As health and life expectancy have improved, retirement ages have actually fallen. As a result, pensioners may end up collecting benefits for as long as they paid into the system or even longer. At the same time, as noted, benefit levels have risen. The earliest pensions were meant to supplement the lower earnings that an individual with limited work capacity might earn, but they rapidly expanded into something more, providing healthy individuals an income almost commensurate to what they would have received had they continued working.

As recently as the 1970s, when the grandparents of the baby boom generation retired, retirement typically lasted about 15 years. Benefits were modest and kept the elderly out of poverty, but they did not provide elderly cohorts with higher incomes than working-age cohorts. If countries could now raise retirement ages until life expectancy at retirement is 15 years, as it was in the 1970s, most could afford today's benefit structure even with the future challenging demographics. Alternatively, countries could choose to reduce benefits to a more basic level, comparable to what was provided in the 1970s, but retain the right to retire at age 65. Or they could do both, that is, raise the retirement age while reducing benefits, which would mean less drastic changes on both counts. Encouraging immigration could keep the labor force growing and mitigate some of the changes needed, but immigrants will also get old and require pensions. Immigration reforms can provide time to allow the economy to adjust to a more basic level of old-age support, but they do not prevent the need for adjustment unless a country envisages steadily increasing the number of immigrants forever.

If the future problem is coming from the declining number of wage earners relative to pensioners, might it be possible to supplement the financing of old age from wage taxes with other sources of government revenue? While a few countries might be able to find additional sources of revenue, in most European countries revenue collection is already quite high, and the decline in the number of wage earners is likely to negatively affect other revenue sources as well. One option might be to move away from labor taxes and toward a broader-based consumption tax. But this would imply restructuring the pension system away from a contribution-based benefit system to a general-revenue financed system, which would tend to provide more basic benefits to the elderly.

If workers are to spend more of their healthy lives working, rather than retiring at some age that in the past was considered appropriate for retirement, the labor market will need to accommodate older workers. Attitudes will need to adapt, with both employers and employees recognizing that older workers are not taking jobs from younger workers but instead offer complementary skills. Simple and relatively cheap physical modifications to the workplace can also help make older workers more productive. And while older workers might not appear to learn as quickly as younger workers, training specifically aimed at their learning styles has been found to be quite effective. A legal framework that provides more flexibility, allowing older individuals to draw part of their pensions while working part-time, can also encourage people to stay in the workforce.

As pension systems downsize, the role of personal savings for retirement becomes even more important. Savings allow workers more flexibility in choosing when they retire; they also allow workers to spread their consumption across their lifetime as they wish, choosing whether to consume more when young or when older. Savings systems that encourage personal savings will be an integral part of any pension system in the future.

The bottom line is that while the demographics look grim, it is possible to retain benefits similar to those provided today if people are willing to work as long as they stay healthy and rely on a pension for only the last 15 years of life. Alternatively, a more basic benefit might be provided earlier. Countries need to think about and choose which path they wish to follow. But making these choices is not a simple election-year decision. It must be a long-term strategy, grounded in broad societal consensus, to be followed for decades into the future. The authors hope that this volume will contribute to a public dialogue that enables each society to safeguard its future prosperity by deciding how much old-age security it will provide, and when, and to whom.

CHAPTER 1

The Inverting Pyramid

One of the spectacular achievements of European social policy in the twentieth century has been a significant reduction in old-age poverty. This has been achieved largely through the introduction and development of pension systems, most often based on social insurance policies, with social assistance programs often used to protect those few elderly who do not have access to the pension programs. Over time, however, these pension systems have become one of the largest expenditure items in government budgets. And these expenditures are set to rise even further as people live longer, healthier lives.

The primary financing source for these pension systems has been labor taxes, often labeled contributions, which are levied on the wages of the employed working-age population. Projections suggest that the working-age population will shrink in Europe over the next few decades, calling into question the financing for the increasing pension expenditures. Even general budget revenues will be pressured as the labor force shrinks and the growth rate of government commitments keeps pace or increases.

While the primary source of the pressure on pension systems is the aging of the population and declining fertility rates, additional pressure comes from the previous expansion of coverage within the pension system and the lack of opportunities for further coverage expansion. In the historical evolution of a typical country, the age structure starts out looking something like a pyramid, with few elderly at the peak and large numbers of children at the base (figure 1.1a). Within this population pyramid, as explained in chapter 2, the pension system produces its own pyramid. Initially, few elderly collect pensions, while only a part of the working-age population contributes. As more and more working-age people join the pension system over time, each generation of pensioners is followed by a generation with higher coverage in the pension system. As long as the pension system keeps expanding, the number of pensioners remains lower than the number of contributors and the pension pyramid remains a pyramid, even if the age structure of the population changes.

In Europe, the age structure has indeed changed: it has moved toward a column rather than a pyramid, primarily due to lower fertility rates. In some countries with especially low fertility rates and high outmigration, it has even started to resemble an inverted pyramid, in which younger cohorts are smaller than the cohorts preceding them for the first time. The age structure of the pension system, instead of remaining a pyramid, has also moved toward a column, albeit for slightly different reasons. As long as the percentage of the working-age population covered by the pension system kept growing, the system maintained its pyramid shape. But once the majority of the working-age population became contributors, the pension system became bound by the population age structure (figure 1.1b).

The transition countries, those moving from centrally planned to market economies, have had a slightly different experience. Coverage of the working-age population in the pension system was complete at a much earlier date. For example, while many nontransition countries still had limited women's labor force participation in the 1960s, most of the transition countries already had close to 100 percent of women in the labor market. While fiscal pressures on pension systems have been slowly building everywhere, they were felt most strongly in the early 1990s in the transition countries of Central Europe, the Balkans, and the former Soviet Union (FSU), where sharp losses in formal employment occurred during the transition. So these countries are experiencing an inverted pyramid in their pension systems, with large numbers of elderly being supported by a relatively small working-age population (figure 1.1c).

Buckling under this pressure, most of the transition countries significantly reformed their pension systems in the 1990s and

FIGURE 1.1

Population and Pension System Dynamics in Europe and Central Asia

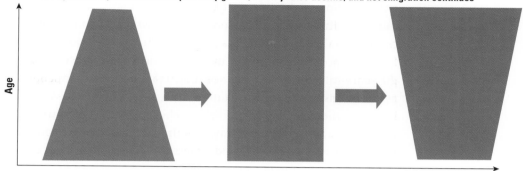

a. Population dynamic as life expectancy grows, fertility rates decline, and net emigration continues

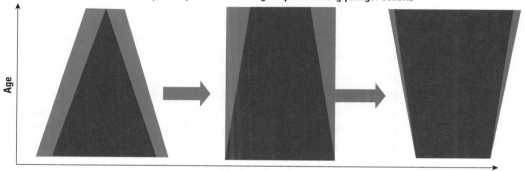

b. Pension system dynamic as coverage expands among younger cohorts

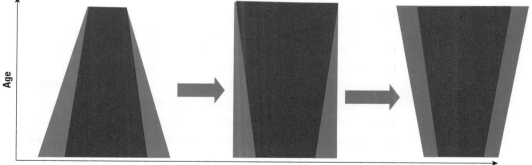

c. Pension system dynamic as formal sector employment declines

early 2000s. They introduced a multitude of parametric and structural reforms, often with World Bank support. The urgency of the reforms subsided in the mid-2000s as the region enjoyed high growth in gross domestic product (GDP). Some countries relaxed their pension reform efforts and even reversed prior reforms,

offering more generous benefit indexation, legislating new pension supplements, and straying from the plans to build pension
system assets and reduce liabilities. As fiscal pressures returned
with the financial crisis of 2008, however, many countries had to
make painful cuts in other programs in order to continue paying
the elevated pension benefits promised during the boom years.

This report evaluates the pension reform experience of the last
20 years in Central Europe and Central Asia. It asks whether the
assumptions made at the start of the reform period were valid,
whether the reform paths initially chosen by the countries were
preferable and remain so today, whether the speed of reform implementation was sufficient, and whether these reforms have so far
delivered on their expectations.

Reversals and revisions of the pension reforms raise questions
about whether the reforms have been sufficiently discussed outside
the relatively narrow circles of pension experts. The report is
intended to initiate pension reform debate more broadly among
policy makers, the media, and social organizations. There is an effort
to broaden the debate to include the linkages of pension systems to
economic growth, fiscal policies, and the functioning of labor and
capital markets. The political economy questions of how pension
expectations are built and how pension reforms are agreed upon are
also considered. The breadth of the discussion inevitably means sacrificing some depth, which the report attempts to partially remedy by
referencing numerous publications by experts in the areas of
pensions, macroeconomics, fiscal policy, labor markets, financial
markets, and political science.

While the report has been written primarily for the benefit of policy
makers in the developing countries of Europe and Central Asia, it also
provides comparative information where possible on all the European
Union (EU) member countries and on Switzerland, Iceland, and
Norway, as well as other non-EU countries of Europe. Due to constraints of data availability, not all analysis is carried out for all countries, but efforts were made to include as many countries as possible.

Five Country Clusters

The report groups the countries in clusters based on the analysis
presented in figure 1.2. The grouping takes into account three main
characteristics that determine pension system sustainability. The
horizontal axis of the figure indexes pension benefit generosity, measured as a ratio of average pension to GDP per capita. The vertical

axis shows the average expected number of years in retirement. Therefore, the countries with high values on both axes currently tend to spend a large proportion of their GDP on pension programs.

The size of the bubbles in figure 1.2 shows the expected growth of the working-age populations in these countries over the next four decades. Countries marked by large bubbles expect their working-age population to grow; assuming a contribution-based, pay-as-you-go financing model, this allows them to afford higher benefit levels and longer retirement spans over this period. On the other hand, countries represented by smaller bubbles expect the working-age population to contract, and they will have to make painful choices if they hope to sustain their pay-as-you-go pension systems.

Five distinct clusters of countries are shown in figure 1.2 and will be discussed separately throughout the report:

- *High-Income Generous Spenders* consist of Belgium, Cyprus, France, Greece, Italy, Luxembourg, Malta, Slovenia, Spain, and Switzerland. They are distinguished from the rest of the countries by long retirement spans of 20 to 23 years. These countries also tend to pay generous benefits of around 50 percent of GDP per capita or higher. The demographic prospects of these countries are quite challenging, which puts the sustainability of their generous pension systems at risk.

FIGURE 1.2

Pension Benefit Generosity and Working-Age Population Growth in Europe and Central Asia

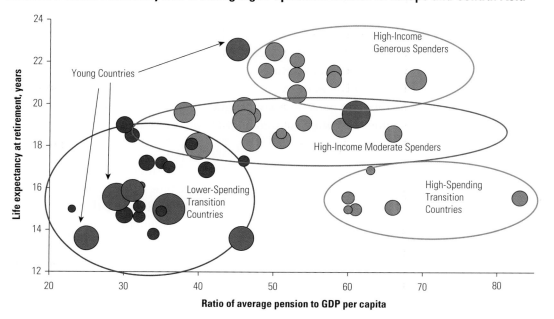

- *High-Income Moderate Spenders* include Austria, Denmark, Finland, Germany, Iceland, Ireland, the Netherlands, Norway, Portugal, Sweden, and the United Kingdom. Retirement spans in these countries range from 18 to 20 years. While benefit levels among this group of countries vary substantially, the average is around 50 percent of GDP per capita. Except for Portugal, which faces very challenging future demographics, the countries in this cluster are projected on average to maintain the current size of their working-age populations, often with the help of significant immigration.

- *Lower-Spending Transition Countries* include Albania, Armenia, Belarus, Bulgaria, Croatia, the Czech Republic, Estonia, Georgia, Hungary, Latvia, Lithuania, Moldova, Poland, Romania, the Russian Federation, and the Slovak Republic. In this report, "transition countries" are those that have recently moved from centrally planned economies to market-based economies. Fiscal strains associated with this transition have induced a diverse set of pension reforms in these countries, resulting in retirement spans of 14 to 19 years and benefit levels averaging around 35 percent of GDP per capita. Unfortunately, these countries also face extremely challenging demographic realities, raising issues of sustainability even at lower benefit levels.

- *High-Spending Transition Countries* include Bosnia and Herzegovina, the former Yugoslav Republic of Macedonia, Montenegro, Serbia, and Ukraine. This cluster of countries faces demographic realities just as challenging as those of the Lower-Spending Transition Countries, if not more so, but they have not yet reduced their benefits to more sustainable levels. Life expectancy at retirement is also relatively low among countries in this cluster, from 14 to 17 years. (The country of Bosnia-Herzegovina comprises two entities, the Federation of Bosnia-Herzegovina and Republika Srpska. They have separate pension systems, and both provided data for the study; therefore, they are sometimes treated separately in this report.)

- *Young Countries* consist of Azerbaijan, Kazakhstan, Kosovo, the Kyrgyz Republic, Tajikistan, Turkey, Turkmenistan, and Uzbekistan. They are shown in figure 1.2 as large blue bubbles, and their placement appears somewhat random. This is because the generosity of pension spending in these countries, where the elderly population is still small, has a much smaller impact on overall government expenditure than in the other country clusters. Therefore, pension spending generosity is influenced much more by cultural and historic factors than by fiscal considerations.

While the analysis is largely based on the country clusters, the report also refers to the geographic-political subregions of Western Europe; Central Europe (including the Baltics); the former Soviet Union (FSU) countries (excluding the Baltics); and the Balkans. Countries in these subregions often share similar historic and economic contexts and exhibit some similarities in their policy choices. Dividing countries into these subregions was found more illuminating when discussing the historic development of pension systems, while the cluster approach is used in discussing pension system outcomes and future prospects. Finally, the report frequently refers to "transition countries," meaning the Central European, FSU, and Balkan countries, all of which have moved from primarily centrally planned to market-based economies in the last two decades.

Organization of the Report

Chapter 2 looks at the birth and development of pension systems and the accompanying societal expectations. This discussion is set primarily in Western Europe, the birthplace of the social insurance model. The story is also relevant to the broader set of European and Central Asian countries, as the goals for their pension systems are often modeled on the poverty reduction and income replacement targets already achieved by the pension systems of Western Europe.

Chapter 3 discusses the pension reforms implemented over the last two decades and their impact on ensuring financial sustainability and poverty reduction. Chapter 4 suggests ways to increase private and public savings to supplement retirement income when the current pension financing model comes under strain in the next few decades. Chapter 5 looks for the fiscal room to supplement labor tax financing with other revenues, while chapter 6 considers the possibilities for stemming the decline in the labor force. The final chapter sums up lessons from two decades of pension reform and presents options for countries facing demographic and fiscal pressures going forward.

CHAPTER 2

The Evolution of Public Pension Programs

Introduction

Over the past century, public pension programs in Europe have successfully reduced poverty among the elderly and provided a mechanism for replacing wage income during old age, when the elderly no longer work. The initial goals for these programs were much more modest, however. They set out to deliver some supplemental income to low- and middle-income industrial workers who were not able to work full-time due to their advanced age. Over time the programs were expanded to include most elderly, other kinds of benefits were added, pension levels rose significantly, and the average period of benefit receipt grew much longer.

The societal expectations of what public pension programs should deliver grew accordingly, and the modest beginnings were quickly forgotten. Public pension programs today are often perceived to be static institutions that have always delivered and will always deliver standards of living to the older population similar to those enjoyed by the employed, especially in countries with earnings-related benefit design. New societal norms about the "right" time to retire have also become strongly entrenched. Furthermore, a strong public perception exists that the current level of benefits and long retirement spans are fully paid for by contributions and taxes collected during the active period of workers' lives.

After the collapse of the centrally planned economic systems, the transition countries of Central Europe, the former Soviet Union (FSU), and the Balkans started rebuilding their pension systems, hoping to meet the same social goals achieved by the pension programs of the developed countries of Europe. The transition countries also tried to improve on the Western European model by introducing new combinations of pension system components. These innovations were expected to help insulate the pension structures from political interference, add to their financial robustness, improve incentives for labor market participation, and increase economic growth.

However, under the prevalent pay-as-you-go (PAYG) financing model, the generosity of a pension program can only depend on the contribution revenues per pensioner. After growing rapidly for a century, these revenues per pensioner are stabilizing and even starting to decline as the number of contributors begins to fall and the number of elderly increases, both in Western Europe and in the broader region. As illustrated in chapter 1, both the population pyramid and the pension pyramid are starting to invert. This is the most important structural change in the financing mechanism of the PAYG pension programs to date, and it cannot be overemphasized. Consequently, public pension programs have to change and adapt to this new reality, just as they adapted to the more favorable environment of the past. The short public memory of the history of pension programs and the perceived stability that has become associated with them are obstructing necessary reforms.

So far, pension programs in Western Europe have easily delivered increasingly generous benefits to increasingly large numbers of people. A continuously growing contributor base from the expanding pyramid along with rising contribution and tax rates have guaranteed a strong source of financing. In fact, at just over 100 years of age, many of the European pension systems are still not fully mature, meaning that the oldest residents, especially women, do not yet necessarily have a right to their own pensions or at least do not yet have full contribution histories resulting in full pension benefits. This reduces pension expenses compared to what might be expected given current demographics if the pension system were fully mature, and temporarily allows for increased benefit generosity.

However, the current generosity of benefit packages cannot be sustained in the future. This chapter reviews the history of the pension systems in Western Europe to aid in understanding the evolution of pension programs and reform agendas in Europe and Central Asia.

While the reforms demanded by the demographic changes and maturation of the pension systems are far from trivial, history shows that a "new" interpretation of retirement, required by the new circumstances, was in fact the accepted social norm just a few decades earlier.

Beginnings of Pension Systems in Western Europe

Prior to the late nineteenth century, extended families and small local communities provided old-age support. People working in small-scale agriculture could continue to provide some work effort until very late in life while also receiving support from family members as their ability to work declined. Since people typically did not move far from their birthplace, most elderly were lifelong members of close-knit communities. In the event that an old person had no surviving family members, churches and neighbors often provided basic support.

As industrialization proceeded, people were drawn from their local communities into the newly developing cities, where they lived and worked among people with whom they had few family or social ties. Urban industrial jobs did not provide the flexibility of a reduced work pace for older individuals that agricultural communities had offered. Moreover, with continuously changing technology, the human capital of older workers was quickly depleted. Small occupational savings societies developed to address some of these needs, but participation was voluntary, and many people remained unprotected from important risks. People increasingly felt the need for a safety net to protect themselves against the risk of sickness, loss of the household breadwinner, and old age (CES n.d.).

The earliest pension schemes were designed to address the risk of old-age poverty for industrial workers with low-to-middle incomes. Otto von Bismarck, the chancellor of Germany, was the first to set up a contributory pension scheme in 1889. The scheme included only workers with incomes below a modest threshold, who were perceived to need a safety net. Higher-income workers were assumed to have other resources with which to self-insure against the risk of poverty in old age. Benefits were paid when a person reached the age of 70, but only if he retained no more than one-third of normal working capacity. Benefits were only provided if the individual had made contributions during his working life, and on average they amounted to only 18 percent of the average wage (Verbon 1988, 17).

This model of income provision to the elderly spread widely. As in Germany, the programs focused on protecting a limited part of the labor force, typically the lower-income segment that was considered more vulnerable. Benefits were modest and were provided only at very advanced ages, and only when working capacity was reduced. Benefits were treated as a supplement to other forms of old-age income and were not intended to be the sole income source (Cutler and Johnson 2004).[1]

In the contributory pension programs that copied the blueprint of Bismarck, the pension amount depended on contributions paid by workers and employers. At the beginning, no workers were eligible for benefits, since no worker had a contribution history. Because of this initial program immaturity, reserves accumulated very fast. A new system in its first few years takes in contributions but pays out few pensions, as few retirees are eligible for benefits. In addition, the few retirees who become eligible receive very low pensions, since their contributions were paid for only a few years. Pension expenditures gradually rise as more individuals satisfy eligibility conditions for retirement and as benefit levels increase in recognition of longer contribution histories. Full career pensions are awarded only once those who have contributed throughout their working careers begin to retire. This can take 40 to 50 years from the time the system is set up; during this time, full cohorts of the labor force are paying contributions, but full pensions are not being paid. When the first cohort of individuals who contributed throughout their entire working career begins to retire, the retiree pool will include some of these people, but also many others who had retired earlier with lower pensions. Only when all living retirees have made a full career's worth of contributions is the system considered fully mature. This takes 60 to 70 years from the time the system starts.

Bismarck's model in its pure form could not ensure full poverty protection, and it was later complemented by features that provided minimum income to elderly workers who had contributed for only a short time or whose contributions were based on very low incomes. These took the form of either a minimum pension guarantee that required some minimum years of contributions, or a minimum income support benefit for the elderly that did not require contributions but involved an income test to establish need.

In many cases, the model was also complemented by redistributive features such as maximum limits on pensions, formulas that compressed past earnings, slower benefit accrual rates for workers with long careers, and so on. These features were intended to reduce pension program costs and to favor low- and middle-income workers, who might not have had complete work histories. However, they also tended to complicate benefit formulas and were often counteracted by other design elements that unintentionally redistributed income from poorer workers to higher-income ones.

A simple alternative to the earnings-related pension model was suggested by William Beveridge in the United Kingdom in 1942 and has been adopted by that country along with Denmark, Iceland, Ireland, the Netherlands, and Norway. This model implies provision of the same public pension benefit to all elderly, usually funded from general taxes. Technically, in the United Kingdom and Ireland, contributions are still required and flat-rate pensions are prorated for shorter contribution histories. But these countries also have a noncontributory income-tested benefit for the elderly of a similar amount, which for practical purposes translates into a universal benefit. Since these are all de facto noncontributory schemes, they can be considered mature from the outset, since those above retirement age are immediately eligible for benefits when the scheme begins, regardless of their lack of contribution history. This model does not offer enough protection against significant decline in income for middle- and high-income workers, which has stimulated large private pension asset buildup in five of the six countries. Norway, the only country without significant private pension assets, chose another approach and by 2011 had built up public pension assets of around 122 percent of gross domestic product (GDP) instead, largely from its oil revenues. Among countries that did not follow the flat-benefit approach in their public pension systems, only Finland and Switzerland have built up private pension assets of significant size.

From Limited "Insurance" to Generous "Savings" Schemes

All the European contributory pension systems started with an accumulation of reserves, as described above, but for various reasons these disappeared over time. In the case of Germany, by 1910 reserves were eight times greater than annual benefit payments; two world wars and a major economic contraction in between were the major contributors to the depletion of those reserves in Germany, as in most countries of Europe. As life expectancy increased, benefits were paid for longer periods, also slowing reserve accumulation. However, the biggest reason for the disappearance of the reserves was their very existence, which tempted governments always short of revenues to use the pension reserves to finance other spending.

The existence of reserves also stimulated increased generosity of the pension systems. New beneficiaries were added as the schemes expanded from old-age coverage to include widows and orphans, younger disabled people, and sometimes children of the disabled. Workers who were in midcareer at the time the systems started were often provided full pensions with less than a full career of contributions. Retirement ages began to fall, and the requirement of incapacity for work, which had characterized the earliest programs, disappeared in countries like France, Germany, and Sweden. Programs were also made more generous so that the elderly could live entirely on the benefits provided rather than use them to supplement other income (Diamond 1997).

Even with all the new spending, the revenue surpluses continued as coverage of the labor force expanded. While pension systems initially were limited only to certain groups of workers, systems quickly grew to include most of the employed population. First, the composition of the labor force changed, with more and more workers joining occupations that provided old-age coverage. In addition, the number of covered occupations continued to grow. While the pace of expansion varied across countries, as did the order in which different sectors were covered, the systems grew from covering only industrial workers to include salaried employees, employees in commerce, civil servants, employees in agriculture, the self-employed, farmers, and domestic servants. With each new wave of entrants into the system, the program once again became immature, as new contributions were added but few benefits were paid to the newly covered group. These new contributors expanded the pension pyramid within the demographic pyramid.

Figure 2.1 shows that the coverage rate of the labor force grew as these systems continued to expand throughout Europe. For example, the system in Belgium covered as few as 20 percent of the labor force when it began, but by 1960, about 85 percent of the labor force was covered. A similar pattern holds for each of the countries for which historical data are available.[2]

In addition, the labor force itself grew as the population increased and women entered paid employment in greater numbers. As figure 2.2 shows, the population in each of the European countries grew by at least 50 percent, and in some cases by more than 400 percent, in the course of the twentieth century.[3] Much of this growth occurred in the working-age population, expanding the population pyramid. The entry of women swelled the labor force still further, expanding the pension pyramid even more.

Figure 2.3 demonstrates the tremendous growth in the labor force despite the impact of the two world wars. For contributory pension schemes, the expansion of coverage combined with growth of the

FIGURE 2.1

Increase in the Proportion of the Labor Force with Pension Scheme Coverage in Selected European Economies with Contributory Pension Schemes, 1900–1975

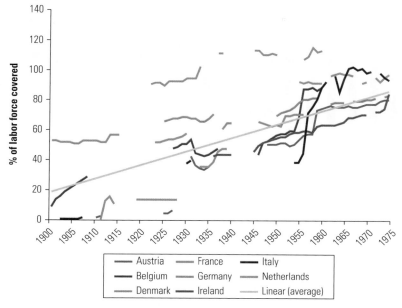

Source: Flora et al. 1983, 466–550.

Note: Coverage rates over 100 percent may reflect the fact that some people were contributing at ages older than 65, while the standard definition of the labor force counts only those between 15 and 64 years of age.

labor force resulted in even stronger growth of contributor numbers, as shown in figure 2.4. For example, in Belgium, active contributors doubled while the labor force only grew by 25 percent. Growth in the labor force also indirectly benefited noncontributory programs, as it helped swell general budget revenues, which in turn made financing of all public programs much easier.

The increased demands on pension reserves of contributory programs induced the shift toward the PAYG financing model by the mid-twentieth century. Contribution revenue differs from other forms of government revenue in that each contribution comes with a liability: that is, the government takes in contributions from workers today in exchange for retirement benefits that government will provide in the future. If the programs were actuarially fair and reserves were invested safely, then the large gap between the contributions of large contributor cohorts and benefits paid to the small beneficiary cohorts while a pension program was immature would lead to

FIGURE 2.2

Population Growth in the Twentieth Century in Selected European Economies

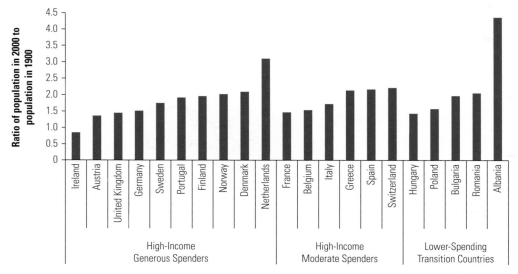

Source: Madison 2010a, 2010b.

the accumulation of large reserves. These reserves would then be available later to pay benefits to the elderly cohorts that had contributed to the buildup of reserves when they were young. But the combination of governments' inability to maintain these reserves during the war and interwar years, fiscal demands outside the pension system, and the continued increase in benefit generosity led almost all governments to abandon the system of maintaining reserves to fully cover future liabilities. Current contribution revenue was spent immediately, with future pensions to be paid out of future contributions. Even the few countries that chose to maintain a reserve accumulated far greater liabilities than the reserve could cover. Initially, given the pension program immaturity, the new financing model easily allowed countries to meet ongoing pension payment needs. However, the contributory pension programs later became precariously dependent on continuing growth in the number of contributors.

The switch to the PAYG financing model increasingly blurred the line between contributory and noncontributory pension schemes. Initially, reserves and surpluses generated within contributory schemes were sometimes used to finance other government programs. A few decades later, many of the "contributory" schemes now finance their deficits from the general budget. Even in countries where the contributory pension scheme budget and the government

FIGURE 2.3

Labor Force Growth in the Twentieth Century in Selected European Economies

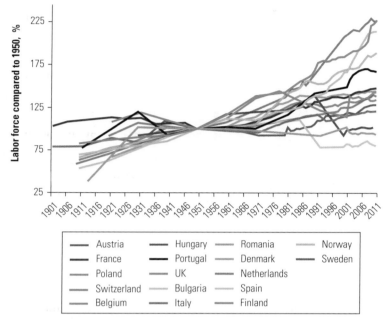

Sources: Flora, Kraus, and Pfenning 1987, 451–606. Data for 1980 and later from ILO LABORSTA (database).
Note: Gaps between data points are filled with straight lines.

budget are clearly separated, the government still implicitly stands behind most of the unfunded promises made by the public pension scheme. Therefore, the distinction between public pension schemes with earnings-related benefits and those with flat benefits often tends to be more striking than the difference between schemes financed in different ways, whether through contributions or general revenue.

Another fundamental shift occurred in the perceived role of pension benefits, which went from providing a limited "insurance" function to acting as a "savings" scheme. The initial dual eligibility criteria of minimum retirement age and incapacity to work meant that the pension program insured against the relatively unlikely contingency of an individual being able to survive to a very old age, but with significantly diminished work capacity. The benefit was low and was only meant to supplement other income, often from part-time or lesser-paid labor. The removal of the second eligibility condition—incapacity to work—and an increase in benefit levels introduced a completely new concept: individuals *should not* work after reaching a certain age, healthy or not, because through their lifetime

FIGURE 2.4

Growth of Active Contributors in Selected European Economies with Contributory Pension Schemes, 1900–2005

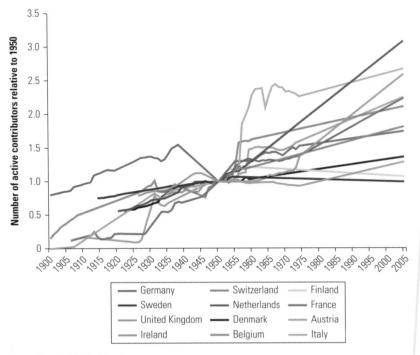

Source: Flora et al. 1983, 466–550.
Note: Gaps between data points are filled with straight lines.

contributions they have "earned" the right to a work-free period of retirement. Thus, pension programs that had initially functioned purely on the insurance principle were transformed into public "savings" schemes, especially in countries with an earnings-related pension benefit design, where people assume they have publicly managed savings accounts that entitle them to pension benefits. In reality, little money was actually accumulated and these contributions were spent as soon as they were received. In contrast, countries with flat-benefit pension programs tended to create additional private pension savings schemes to meet the need for income smoothing during old age.

Moreover, the expectations were formed that living standards of pensioners should rise in line with the living standards of the employed. These expectations were fueled by the postwar boom in contribution revenue that led to the automatic indexation of pension benefits. The interwar and postwar inflationary experiences coupled with rapid wage growth after the war led to political pressure on politicians to increase pensions to keep up with living standards. The prevailing view was that since individual contributions grew with wage growth, providing pension increases linked to wage increases would be financially feasible. Some countries tied pension increases explicitly to growth in wages; others were more cautious, tying the benefit increases to growth in prices; still others used some combination of these approaches. However, in almost all cases, the actual pension increases were even greater than what the respective indexes would have indicated.

Figure 2.5 shows that pension increases exceeded wage growth in the Netherlands and Switzerland; increases were roughly equal to wage growth in France, Germany, the United Kingdom, and Sweden; and pension increases were below wage growth, though above inflation, in Austria (see also International Labour Office 1977; Galasso and Profeta 2004).

Examples of increasing generosity can be seen in the Netherlands and Hungary, where pensions more than doubled as a percentage of average wage in a relatively short period of time (figure 2.6). While some of the overall increase for Hungary can be attributed to system maturation, with new retirees having longer periods of contribution and thus higher benefits, the more discrete jumps are attributable to policy changes. Also, as individuals with less regular contribution history were brought into the pension system, many became eligible for the minimum pension guarantee, which raised their benefit level above what they would have contributed or earned.

FIGURE 2.5

Comparison of Growth in Pensions, Wages, and Prices in Selected European Economies, 1965–1979

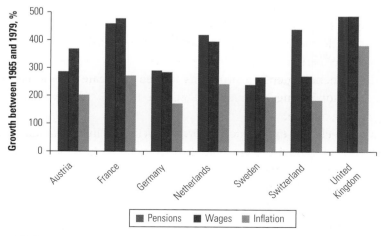

Source: U.S. Senate 1981.

FIGURE 2.6
Growth in Average Pension Compared to Average Wage in the Netherlands and Hungary, 1950–1990

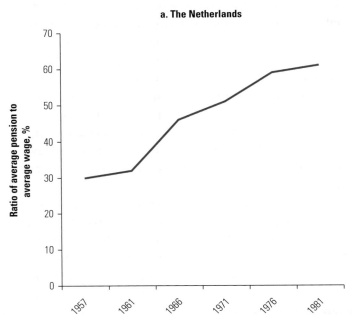

Source: Verbon 1988, 24.

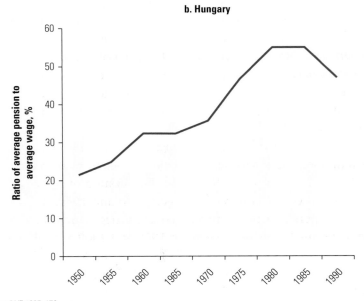

Source: IWE 1995, 179.

However, the most important increase in benefit generosity came through the reduction in retirement ages, similarly prevalent among contributory and noncontributory pension programs. Lower retirement ages have a double impact on a contributory pension program: they reduce the number of contributors and increase the number of beneficiaries. Nonetheless, despite the fiscal implications and despite increasing life expectancy, retirement ages were lowered for several reasons. First, with the abundance of revenue, politicians could easily grant early retirement to some occupations as a political bonus in exchange for votes. Second, decisions were guided by the mistaken view that youth would find jobs more easily if older workers retired early to make room for them. And finally, given seniority-based remuneration schemes that automatically pay higher wages to workers who have been at a given job longer, older workers, who often experience some decline in productivity as they age, were becoming too expensive in light of their decreased productivity.

Even in countries where the statutory retirement ages were not lowered, early retirement options and flexible retirement resulted in a decline in the effective retirement age (figure 2.7). As individuals became wealthier, their taste for leisure increased, encouraging them to choose leisure over additional work. Moreover, as benefit levels increased, people could afford to retire earlier and still enjoy a comfortable lifestyle. And with technological changes, skills of some older workers became obsolete, making continued employment difficult. For example, in Austria and Germany, the percentage of new retirees below the statutory retirement age increased from approximately 5 percent in 1960 to more than 50 percent by 1976. Similarly, in Sweden, early retirement rose from 9 percent of the total in 1967 to 21 percent by 1974. As retirement ages fell, labor force participation (LFP) rates of workers above the retirement age, those aged 65 and older, also fell from 16 percent in 1955 to 8 percent by 1980 in Europe as a whole.

The duration of retirement increased dramatically because effective retirement ages declined while life expectancies increased rapidly. Figure 2.8 shows the changes in the duration of retirement for Belgium, Spain, and Sweden. Between 1970 and 1990, the average retirement period increased in all three countries.[4] Duration of retirement continued to increase between 1990 and 2009 as well, outpacing the rise in the retirement age in Sweden and Belgium. It is also important to note that the probability of contributors reaching retirement age and claiming the benefit also rose due to decreased mortality at younger ages, further increasing the overall benefit costs generated by later-born cohorts (Chomik and Whitehouse 2010).

FIGURE 2.7

Change in Effective Retirement Ages in Selected European Economies, 1970–2010

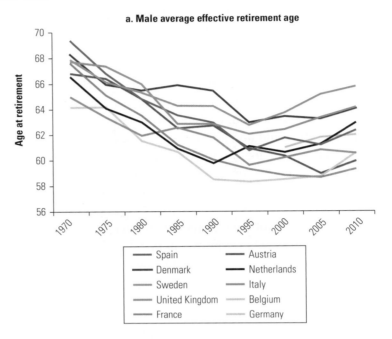

a. Male average effective retirement age

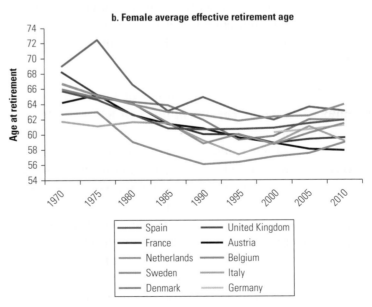

b. Female average effective retirement age

Source: OECD 2013.

FIGURE 2.8

Changes in Retirement Age and Impact on Duration of Retirement in Belgium, Spain, and Sweden, 1970–2009

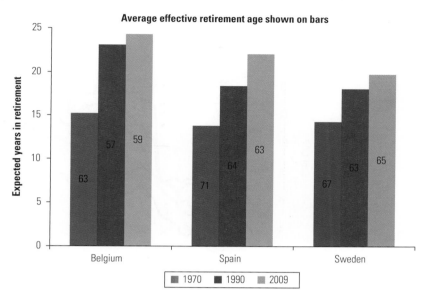

Average effective retirement age shown on bars

Legend: 1970, 1990, 2009

Source: OECD.

Increase in benefit generosity, the aging of societies, and pension program maturation led to an enormous increase in public pension spending relative to GDP from the 1950s to the end of the twentieth century (figure 2.9). The countries with contributory, earnings-related pension schemes tended to exhibit higher spending growth (figure 2.9a), while the flat-benefit schemes showed slower increases (figure 2.9b).

Outcomes of Pension Program Introduction in Western Europe

Pension programs made an enormous contribution to reducing poverty rates among the elderly in the developed countries of Europe (figure 2.10). All components of the pension system added to this result, but flat-benefit contributory and noncontributory programs, as well as minimum pension guarantees and minimum income support for the elderly, were the most important contributors. By now, all pension systems of Western Europe have introduced at least one of these redistributive features. The only exception is Italy, which supports poor elderly through the general social assistance program.

In 1987, the average relative poverty gap between the elderly and the rest of the population was close to zero for the group of countries

FIGURE 2.9
Pension Spending as a Percentage of GDP in Selected European Economies, 1954–2004

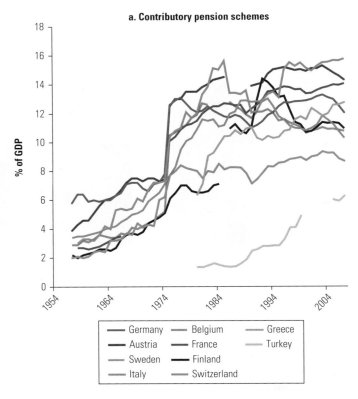

a. Contributory pension schemes
18
16
14
12
10
8
6
4
2
0
% of GDP
1954
1964
1974
1984
1994
2004
Germany
Belgium
Greece
Austria
France
Turkey
Sweden
Finland
Italy
Switzerland
b. Flat-benefit pension schemes
18
16
14
12
10
8
6
4
2
0
% of GDP
1954
1964
1974
1984
1994
2004
Denmark
United Kingdom
Netherlands
Ireland
Norway

Source: Flora et al. 1983, 457.

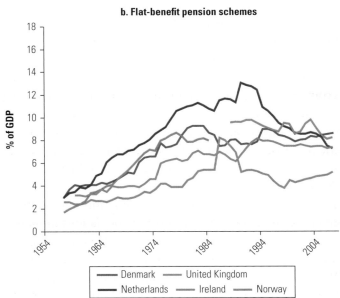

FIGURE 2.10

Gap between Elderly Poverty and Poverty in the General Population, Selected European Economies, 1987 and 2004

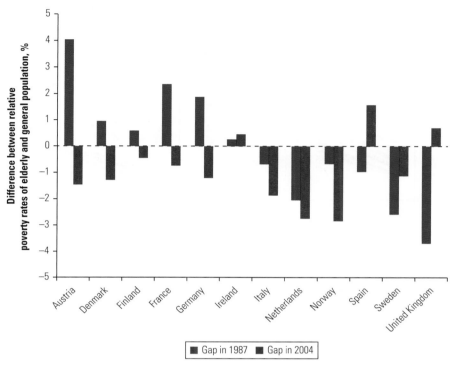

Source: LIS 2013.
Note: Data are for 1987 and 2004 or closest available years.

shown in figure 2.10. By 2004 it even tended to be negative in nine of the 12 countries, although not significantly. This suggests that the pension systems first adopted in Europe in the late nineteenth century fully accomplished the goal of reducing poverty among the elderly. In the beginning, the elderly possessed limited work capacity and little or no safety net, but the pension systems are now providing them with sufficient resources so that their poverty rates are comparable to or even lower than those of the other age cohorts (see also European Commission 2012).

Pension programs also provide a vehicle for significant income replacement for middle- and high-income populations in many countries (figure 2.11). The data shown are based on modeling results from the Organisation for Economic Co-operation and Development (OECD) series *Pensions at a Glance*. Pre-retirement earnings of individuals relative to average wage are shown on the horizontal axis. Expected benefit entitlements as a percentage of economy-wide average wage

FIGURE 2.11

Link between Pre-Retirement Earnings and Benefit Entitlements as Reflected in Pension System Design in Selected European Countries

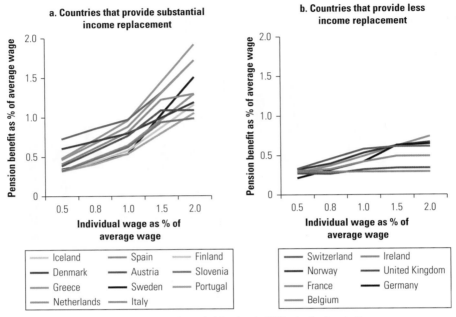

Source: Based on data from the OECD Pension Modeling Team, using methodology from the OECD series *Pensions at a Glance.*

are shown on the vertical axis for workers who begin work at age 20 in year 2010 and work continuously at their pre-retirement relative wage until they reach the retirement age in their country. The steeper the line for a country, the more emphasis it places on income replacement; the flatter the line, the greater the focus on redistribution. Countries for which the line starts higher provide higher benefits for the lowest-income contributors. Since the OECD methodology models future entitlements for those starting work only recently, the results include all the legislation enacted to date.[5]

Different countries chose to provide income replacement to greater or lesser degrees. Some countries, such as the ones in figure 2.11a, provide substantial income replacement for earners with moderately high incomes. Greece, for example, provides benefits almost equal to twice the average wage to those who earned twice the average wage. Other countries, such as the ones in figure 2.11b, provide limited income replacement for high earners. France, which pays 74 percent of average wage to those who earn twice the average wage, is the most generous of this group; some others, like Ireland, pay as little as 29 percent of average wage to similarly high earners (OECD 2011; see also Conde-Ruiz and Profeta 2007).

However, introduction of the PAYG financing mechanism and the accompanying increased benefit generosity also introduced undesirable intergenerational transfers. Cohorts of the elderly that made small contributions were able to enjoy increased benefits over long retirement periods, benefiting greatly from the system. These arrangements could be upheld temporarily because of the rapid increase in the numbers of contributors, rising contribution rates, and small numbers of pensioners due to program immaturity as the pension pyramid expanded. But the longer these unsustainable arrangements continue and the more implicit pension liabilities are built up, the higher will be the financial and social costs of unwinding these arrangements. And the higher the costs, the more abrupt the transition to a fiscally sustainable system will have to be, as the pension pyramid reaches the boundaries of the demographic pyramid or starts to invert. Unfortunately, these benefits in Western Europe have been perceived as realistic, desirable, and sustainable by other countries of the region with weaker demographic and economic fundamentals, leading them to aspire to the same results.

Choices Made by Other Countries of the Region

The collapse of the centrally planned economic systems in Central Europe, the former Soviet Union, and the Balkans in the early 1990s was devastating for government finances. Enormous cuts had to be made in all government programs, including pensions. Pensions were drastically reduced, paid late, and sometimes even paid in kind, although the most extreme measures were avoided in the countries of Central Europe. Pensioner numbers swelled as old-age pension programs were used to absorb huge numbers of older unemployed workers, adding to fiscal strains. In this environment, protection against extreme poverty of the elderly was the main goal, and most pensioners ended up with similarly low incomes, regardless of their contribution history. Yet again, Central European countries suffered a bit less, and some income differentiation in pension levels was preserved in these countries.

Earnings-related benefit design seemed to be the best fit for the Central European and Baltic countries that were rebuilding their pension systems in the late 1990s as their economies started to grow again. At the time, with their liquid savings largely destroyed, most elderly depended largely on public pension benefits that were relatively flat, reflecting both the fiscal constraints and the low differentiation in their past wage levels. This focused the minds of the reformers on reinstituting the income replacement function of the pension systems to mirror the new differentiated wage structure. In addition, it was hoped that a contributions-linked pension benefit design would induce badly needed formalization of the labor market. On the other hand, the region did not have the experience of wide income inequality in recent memory, so the objectives of income redistribution and protection of the most vulnerable were not at the forefront of the agenda (Hirose 2011).

Privately owned individual pension accounts were seen as a desirable option, as people in the region yearned to harness market-based solutions and had developed a deep distrust of governments. The fact that this arrangement would entail high transition costs, when pension contribution revenues redirected to individual accounts had to be replaced by alternative financing sources, was understood but not considered insurmountable. The promise of high growth rates, as the region joined developed Western European countries in the European Union, was expected to bring quick prosperity that would help to pay the costs. Privatization revenue was another financing source commonly assumed to be sufficient in paying much of the transition costs. Finally, borrowing would provide short-term financing before parametric reforms of the current PAYG pension scheme started to yield significant savings. Since there were limited other financial assets for pension funds to invest in, pension funds could easily lend to governments the funds they needed to borrow to finance the transition costs (Holzmann 2009).

It was realized that existing PAYG pension schemes were too big to be replaced altogether and might even be a desirable component of the pension system for diversification purposes. To make these schemes sustainable and attractive to populations, innovations like notional pension accounts and point systems were introduced. Minimum pension provisions remained in most PAYG systems, but they were assumed to be small additions to the main design rather than key components of the system to be relied upon by a large proportion of the population. Similarly, minimum income provisions for the elderly without pension coverage were not considered to be important elements, as at the time of the reform an overwhelming majority of the population had long contribution histories (also see Chlon-Dominczak and Strzelecki 2013).

Pension system designs chosen by the countries in this subregion reflect the plethora of different decisions made, as shown in clusters 3, 4, and 5 of table 2.1. Box 2.1 provides some details on the main features of each pension system.[6]

TABLE 2.1

Pension System Designs and Components in Selected European and Central Asian Economies

Cluster	Country	Universal	PAYG	Mandatory savings
(1) High-Income Generous Spenders	Belgium	—	DB	—
	Cyprus	—	DB	—
	France	—	DB/points	—
	Greece	—	DB	—
	Italy	—	NDC	—
	Luxembourg	—	DB	—
	Malta	—	DB	—
	Slovenia	—	DB	—
	Spain	—	DB	—
	Switzerland	—	DB	X
(2) High-Income Moderate Spenders	Austria	—	DB	—
	Denmark	X	—	X
	Finland	—	DB	X
	Germany	—	Points	—
	Iceland	—	DB	X
	Ireland	X	—	X
	Netherlands	X	—	X
	Norway	—	NDC	—
	Portugal	—	DB	—
	Sweden	—	NDC	X
	United Kingdom	X	DB	X
(3) Lower-Spending Transition Countries	Albania	—	DB	—
	Armenia	—	DB	—
	Belarus	—	DB	—
	Bulgaria	—	DB	X
	Croatia	—	Points	X
	Czech Republic	X	DB	—
	Estonia	X	Points	X
	Georgia	X	—	—
	Hungary	—	DB	—
	Latvia	—	NDC	X
	Lithuania	—	DB	X
	Moldova	—	DB	—
	Poland	—	NDC	X

continued

TABLE 2.1
Continued

Cluster	Country	Universal	PAYG	Mandatory savings
	Romania	—	Points	X
	Russian Federation	—	NDC	X
	Slovak Republic	—	Points	X
(4) High-Spending Transition Countries	Bosnia and Herzegovina (both entities)	—	Points	—
	Macedonia, FYR	—	DB	X
	Montenegro	—	Points	—
	Serbia	—	Points	—
	Ukraine	—	DB	—
	Azerbaijan	—	DB/NDC	—
	Kazakhstan	X	—	X
	Kosovo	X	—	—
(5) Young Countries	Kyrgyz Republic	—	NDC	X
	Tajikistan	—	DB	—
	Turkey	—	DB	—
	Turkmenistan	—	NDC	—
	Uzbekistan	—	DB	—

Note: DB = defined benefit; NDC = notional defined contribution; PAYG = pay-as-you-go; — = does not exist.

Country choices often reflected historical and geographic groupings as well as aspirations. The pension systems of Central Europe and the Baltics tended to have more elaborate multipillar designs than the Western European countries presented in clusters 1 and 2 of table 2.1.

The countries of the former Soviet Union, excluding the Baltics, have been less ambitious in redesigning their pension systems. The collapse of economies in this cluster of countries was deeper and more prolonged. The fall in formal employment and government revenue base was more pronounced, and poverty among the general population, as well as the elderly, became more entrenched. High inflation also eroded the value of the benefits, bringing them down to a more basic level. The region was also less optimistic about the

---

BOX 2.1

World Bank Definitions of Pension Pillars and Characteristics of Different Pension Systems

Zero Pillar

The zero pillar refers to pension benefits provided without a contribution requirement. These are financed from general revenues. One form of a zero pillar is the universal pension noted below; other forms are based on need and can be part of, or separate from, the social assistance system.

Universal Pension

- All residents or citizens above a certain age are provided with a *universal pension*.

- After retirement, benefits are typically increased over time through some type of indexation.

First Pillar

The first pillar refers to pensions where eligibility depends on the person having made contributions during his or her working life. These pensions are largely financed on a pay-as-you-go (PAYG) basis, with contributions from current workers and their employers being used to finance benefits for current pensioners. These systems can accumulate some reserves when they are immature; conversely, contribution revenues can be supplemented with general revenues when a system runs deficits. These systems are primarily run as conventional defined benefit (DB) systems, but they can also include basic pensions, point systems, and notional defined contribution (NDC) systems.

Conventional Defined Benefit System

- Pension benefits are calculated as some percentage of a person's past salary (*accrual rate*) per year of contribution or service.

- The salary base from which the pension is calculated can be the last salary, an average of some years of past salaries, or the average of a person's lifetime salary.

- The salaries used to calculate the salary base are typically revalued or *valorized* by a parameter such as the cumulative growth of average wage between when the salary was earned and the date of retirement.

- Pension increases after retirement are indexed to an observable parameter, typically inflation, but sometimes the rate of average wage growth.

continued

BOX 2.1 *continued*

Basic Pension

- All those who have fulfilled a minimum years-of-service requirement receive a flat benefit, unrelated to their own wages or the value of their contributions.

- Benefit may vary depending on years of service.

- After retirement, benefits are typically indexed to some parameter.

Point System

- The individual is awarded *personal points* for each year he or she contributes. The number of points awarded each year is based on the relationship between the wage on which contributions are made and the average wage and the length of time during the year that the person actually makes contributions.

- At retirement, all the points the person has earned are added up and multiplied by the value of the *general point*, which is typically some percentage of the average wage of the year in which the individual retires.

- This value of the general point, set when the system begins, is typically indexed to average wage growth, making the value of the general point as a percentage of average wage identical to the accrual rate in the traditional DB system. Indexing the general point to parameters other than wage growth is equivalent to setting cohort-specific accrual rates in the traditional system.

- After retirement, the pension follows some indexation rule.

Notional Account System

- Each individual's contributions are recorded as if they were going into a saving account.

- *Notional interest rate* is granted on each individual's account balance, with the notional interest rate tied to measurable indicators, such as average wage growth, growth in the wage bill, or gross domestic product growth.

- At retirement, the account balance is divided by life expectancy at the age of retirement, in the simplest case, or by a factor that takes into account some interest rate and life expectancy.

- As life expectancy grows, the benefit available at a particular retirement age tends to fall as the account balance is divided by a longer life expectancy, thus providing some degree of fiscal balancing.

- After retirement, the pension follows some indexation rule.

continued

BOX 2.1 *continued*

Second Pillar

The second pillar refers to mandated defined contribution systems where individuals put their contributions into savings accounts with financial institutions, typically specialized pension funds. These funds invest the money, with retirement benefits paid out of the proceeds of that investment.

Fully Funded Defined Contribution System

- Contributions are collected, transferred to a pension fund, and invested. There are typically multiple pension funds or asset managers, and the individual chooses one of them to manage his or her retirement savings.

- Some administrative fees are deducted before the remaining funds are invested.

- The person earns an interest rate based on what the invested savings earn.

- At retirement, the individual typically purchases an *annuity* from an annuity provider who guarantees the retiree a pension benefit throughout his or her lifetime for a fee. The benefit may be indexed or not.

- In some cases, payouts can also be taken as *scheduled withdrawals,* where the account balance is divided by life expectancy, with the remainder continuing to generate interest. This process is repeated the following year, with the resulting pension rising or falling depending on realized returns.

Third Pillar

The third pillar is almost identical to the second pillar, but savings are made on a voluntary rather than mandatory basis. The third pillar can be organized as individual savings accounts or, alternatively, as occupational pension schemes, where members of one occupation hold savings accounts with a particular financial institution and contributions are made as part of the benefits package.

Multipillar System

A multipillar pension system contains more than one of the pillars outlined above.

---

future and less motivated to embark on structural reform than Central Europe, where reform fever was augmented by the promise of European Union accession. Therefore, some FSU countries chose to reform their pension systems with much more modest goals in mind, while others opted only to patch up their existing pension systems rather than redesign them. The reformers generally targeted much lower pension levels and continued to be torn between the need for poverty prevention and the desire for income replacement, finding that it was hard to accommodate both within the limited fiscal envelope. The countries that opted for maintaining their one-pillar PAYG model generally struggled to prevent their pension costs from rising unsustainably.

The war-ravaged economies of the Balkan region had a delayed start on the pension reform agenda. They have closely followed the Central European countries in making reforms, with similar aspirations for their redesigned pension systems. However, the conditions for achieving these objectives are more difficult, as labor markets tend to be less buoyant, financial markets are less developed, and pension systems are more burdened with large disability and veteran pension costs. Poverty in this region is also much more prevalent, which tends to sway the pension system objectives toward poverty protection, although there are some high spenders in this group that have focused on income replacement.

Finally, the Young Countries of the region, including Turkey, have generally been preoccupied with other government programs, as their elderly populations are still quite small. In the pension policy area they have tended to fine-tune their existing simple pension system structures. The two exceptions are the Kyrgyz Republic, which has tried to implement an elaborate pension design and pays relatively high pensions, and Kazakhstan, which has introduced a relatively radical reform, having abolished its PAYG system altogether. The rest of the Young Countries of the FSU generally only provide poverty-level benefits to their elderly through PAYG financed programs, as shown in cluster 5 of table 2.1.

Pension system designs chosen in the last two decades in this broad region rested on some important assumptions:

- LFP and formalization in the post-transition economies would return close to the levels observed before the transition.

- Earnings-related benefit design could provide sufficient incentives to workers to participate in the pension system and to voluntarily delay retirement.

- Pension structures, once chosen, would be insulated from political interference.

- Development of the financial markets, financial literacy, efficient portfolios, and growth-producing investments would naturally follow from the introduction of funded individual pension accounts.

- The sharp fall in fertility rates, observed early in the transition, would fully reverse. The strong emigration experienced when the economies first opened would not continue.

In all of these reforms across countries, a convergence on a single pension paradigm did not emerge. The lack of convergence can be traced back to the dual purpose of pension systems, which exist both to prevent poverty in old age and to replace the income individuals earned during their working years. The first objective often requires redistribution from middle and high earners toward low earners, while the second suggests that high earners should keep the benefits of their higher contributions in the form of higher pensions for themselves. These two objectives have conflicting impacts on policy, especially when fiscal space is limited. Different countries place varying weights on the two objectives: countries focused on poverty alleviation are more likely to choose basic pensions and universal pensions, while countries favoring income replacement are more likely to choose options like notional accounts, point systems, and funded defined contribution systems. In the second case, there is a danger that if many people do not contribute for long, earn very low returns on contributions, or contribute on the basis of low wages, most of the elderly will eventually qualify only for the same minimum pension, which results in a burden of accounting and administration without much of the intended contribution-benefit link (see Conde-Ruiz and Profeta 2007).

Countries of Central Europe and the Balkans largely focus on moderate replacement of incomes, as shown by the simulated results of different options in figure 2.12. The exception is the Czech Republic, where there is greater redistribution and only limited income replacement (figure 2.12a). In the Balkans (figure 2.12b), the very high benefits accruing to low earners in Albania are notable, as is the long-run elimination of virtually all income replacement in Serbia.

By contrast, FSU countries with older populations tend to have more limited income replacement. For example, a person who earns half the average wage will get a pension benefit equal to 34 percent of average wage in the case of Ukraine, while a person who earns twice average wage will get a pension equal to 80 percent of average wage. Only the Russian Federation and Armenia achieve moderate-income replacement (figure 2.13a). However, these countries also tend to have more generous benefits for the elderly from lower-income groups. The younger countries of the FSU, as well as Turkey, tend to aim for both high-income replacement and relatively high benefits for low earners (figure 2.13b).

FIGURE 2.12

Link between Pre-Retirement Earnings and Benefit Entitlements as Reflected in Pension System Design in Central Europe and the Balkans

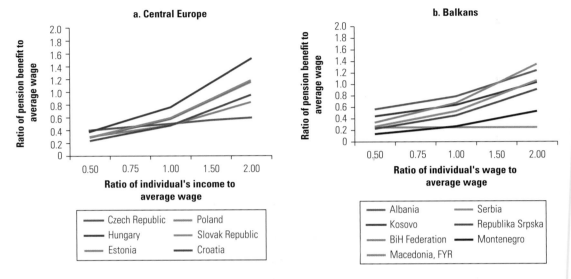

Source: Based on data from the OECD Pension Modeling Team, using methodology from the OECD series *Pensions at a Glance*.
Note: The Federation of Bosnia-Herzegovina (BiH Federation) and Republika Srpska, which together make up the country of Bosnia and Herzegovina, have separate pension systems and are treated as separate data points in the figure.

FIGURE 2.13

Link between Pre-Retirement Earnings and Benefit Entitlements as Reflected in Pension System Design in the Former Soviet Union Countries and Turkey

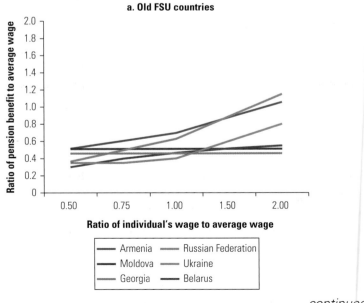

continued

FIGURE 2.13
Continued

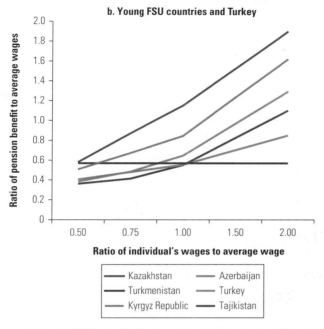

b. Young FSU countries and Turkey

Legend: Kazakhstan, Turkmenistan, Kyrgyz Republic, Azerbaijan, Turkey, Tajikistan

Source: Based on data from the OECD Pension Modeling Team using methodology from the OECD series *Pensions at a Glance.*

This analysis ignores the fact that in some countries many people contribute only sporadically: they are not able to reach the full careers assumed in figures 2.12 and 2.13 because of high unemployment, a large informal economy, long employment gaps among women raising children, lax early retirement rules, and other reasons. In those cases, especially when the minimum pension guarantee is relatively high and the accrual rate in the benefit formula is relatively low, the actual differences in pension levels across income groups are likely to be much smaller than those suggested in the figures.

The Inverting Pyramid: Structural Break in the PAYG Financing Model

The early twentieth century saw a successive expansion of groups covered by the pension system in Western Europe, but this trend has waned. From the beginning, with each new group of entrants, the system became immature again. By the mid-1950s there were few, if any, occupational groups left out of the system. However, the system

FIGURE 2.14

Extension of Coverage and Its Impact on Pension Systems in Europe and Central Asia, 1900s through 2050

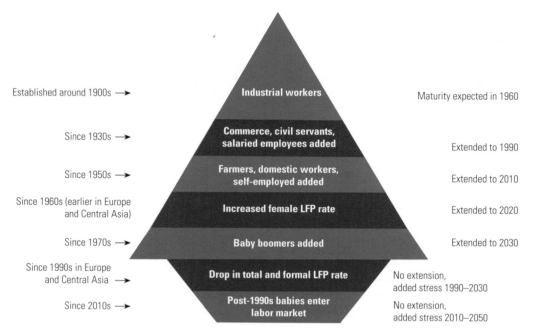

Established around 1900s → **Industrial workers** Maturity expected in 1960

Since 1930s → **Commerce, civil servants, salaried employees added** Extended to 1990

Since 1950s → **Farmers, domestic workers, self-employed added** Extended to 2010

Since 1960s (earlier in Europe and Central Asia) **Increased female LFP rate** Extended to 2020

Since 1970s → **Baby boomers added** Extended to 2030

Since 1990s in Europe and Central Asia → **Drop in total and formal LFP rate** No extension, added stress 1990–2030

Since 2010s → **Post-1990s babies enter labor market** No extension, added stress 2010–2050

found new sources of expansion, first women joining the labor force in greater numbers and then the large baby-boomer cohort.

The top portion of the pyramid depicted in figure 2.14 summarizes the development of the pension system through the mid-1970s. By that time, women's LFP had nearly reached its current levels among young cohorts, and demographic projections were beginning to show the impact of lower fertility on the future working-age population. The first alarms sounded in the more fiscally conservative countries as they started to doubt the ability of the pension scheme to sustain its previous growth in the number of contributors.

Compared to Western Europe, the growth in contributor numbers slowed earlier in transition countries as women's LFP rates equaled men's much earlier. Furthermore, the transition to a market economy in the early 1990s resulted in a sharp drop in LFP rates, particularly in the formal sector. The accompanying acute and sustained drop in fertility rates in these countries coupled with ongoing emigration has advanced by several decades the impact of the system maturation and demographic change (see also Galasso, Gatti, and Profeta 2009).

Governments initially reacted to the slower growth in contributor numbers, current and projected, by raising contribution rates in an attempt to maintain the earlier pace of revenue increases. Figure 2.15 shows how countries attempted to raise revenue by raising contribution rates. The figure also demonstrates that these rates, after rising quite dramatically in some cases, have stabilized since the mid-1990s. Countries soon learned that higher contribution rates did not

FIGURE 2.15

Increasing Pension Contribution Rates in Response to Expanding Expenditures in Selected European Economies, 1940–2012

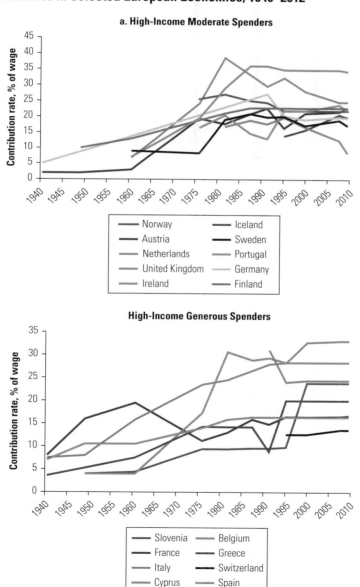

a. High-Income Moderate Spenders

High-Income Generous Spenders

continued

FIGURE 2.15
Continued

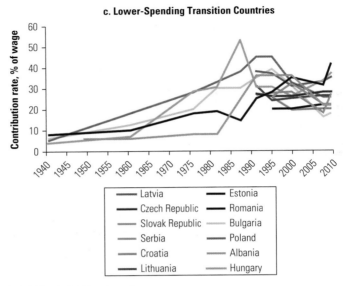

c. Lower-Spending Transition Countries

Source: U.S. Social Security Administration, various years.

necessarily generate higher revenue, as they resulted in a less globally competitive labor market and led to a rapid expansion of the informal sector. While the Northern European countries generally did not suffer from growth in the informal sector, the potential loss of competitiveness in an increasingly global economy halted further increases in the contribution rate.

Having approached the limits of raising additional revenue through coverage expansion and higher contribution rates, countries now face the challenge of an expected decline in the working-age population. As shown in figure 2.16, the working-age population, defined as people 15 to 64 years of age, peaked at around 2010 for most countries in Western Europe (figure 2.16a and b). Central European countries peaked a couple of decades earlier (figure 2.16c).

The cumulative effect of this trend was an important structural change: the rapid growth in working-age population abruptly changed into prolonged decline. Between 1970 and 2010, very few countries had faced a decline in the working-age population. Only three countries in Central Europe—Bulgaria, Latvia, and Hungary—experienced such a decline in this period. But between 2010 and 2050, almost all of the countries not labeled as "young" will face a shrinking working-age population (figure 2.17). The only exceptions are Sweden, the United

FIGURE 2.16

Working-Age Population from 1950 to 2050 Relative to 2013, Selected European and Central Asian Economies

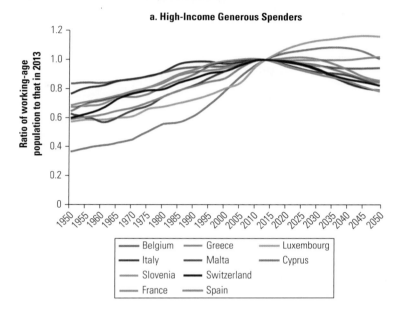

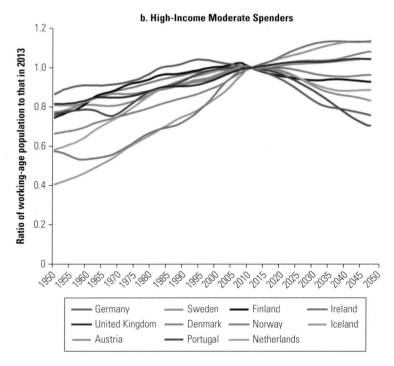

continued

FIGURE 2.16
Continued

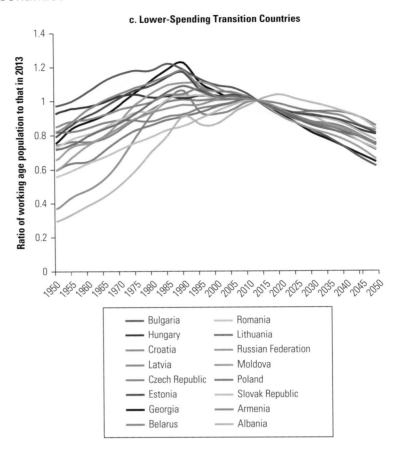

c. Lower-Spending Transition Countries

continued

FIGURE 2.16
Continued

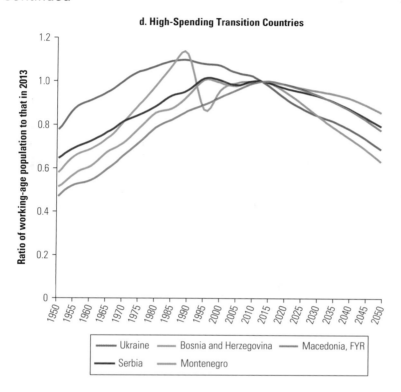

d. High-Spending Transition Countries

Legend: Ukraine — Bosnia and Herzegovina — Macedonia, FYR — Serbia — Montenegro

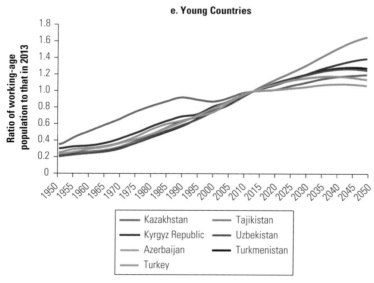

e. Young Countries

Legend: Kazakhstan — Tajikistan — Kyrgyz Republic — Uzbekistan — Azerbaijan — Turkmenistan — Turkey

Source: United Nations population projections (UN 2011).
Note: Working-age population refers to people 15–64 years of age.

FIGURE 2.17

Change in Working-Age Population in Selected European and Central Asian Economies, 1970–2010 and 2010–2050

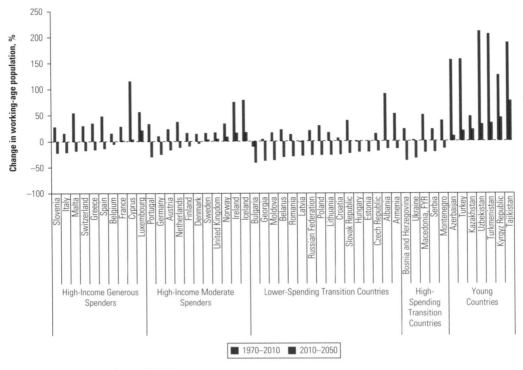

Source: United Nations population projections (UN 2011).

Kingdom, Norway, Ireland, and Iceland, from the High-Income Moderate Spenders group, and France and Cyprus, from the High-Income Generous Spenders group. In some cases, such as Bulgaria, the expected decline in the working-age population is sizable. Even among the Young Countries, while the percentage of elderly is expected to triple, the working-age population is not expected to even double.

The projected decline in the working-age population is partly due to a sharp and sustained decline in fertility that occurred in the transition countries over the last 20 years. Figure 2.18 shows the decrease in the number of children under the age of 5 between 1990 and 2010 in these countries. While the high-income countries experienced minor fluctuations, the other three clusters experienced sharp and fairly sustained fertility reductions.

While many countries are hoping for increased fertility rates, policies intended to encourage this change are rarely successful. Furthermore, changes in fertility have a demographic momentum of their own. Lower numbers of children in one cohort lead to a small

FIGURE 2.18

Number of Children under Age 5 Compared to 1990, Europe and Central Asia

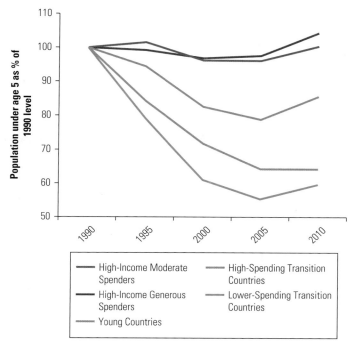

Source: United Nations population projections (UN 2011).

childbearing cohort, which results in lower numbers of children in subsequent cohorts. Figure 2.19 illustrates this fertility trajectory in Poland. It shows that the number of babies born would continue to decline in the future even if fertility rates stay constant at 2011 levels (and to keep the number of children the same as in 2011, the number of children per family would have to increase by 40 percent by 2025). This decline is attributable solely to the reduction in the cohorts of potential parents, which was predetermined by fertility declines 20 years ago.

The other major element leading to the decline in the working-age population is emigration. Figure 2.20 shows the impact of emigration on the working-age population in the 2000s in most countries in the region. The blue diamonds indicate average annual growth rate in the working-age population (aged 15–64) over the last decade. In countries where the blue diamonds are below the zero line, the working-age population is already falling. Note the prevalence of the emigration component in the total growth rate in the countries that recorded the largest declines in working-age population, namely Romania, Lithuania, Latvia, and Bulgaria.

FIGURE 2.19

Births in Poland in 1990–2011 and Projected Future Births through 2026

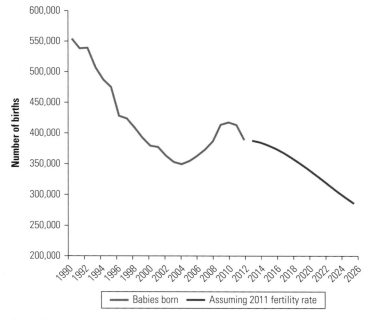

Source: Eurostat Statistics Database.

In the high-income countries, the countries with the largest immigration experienced growth in their working-age population. Those with lower or no net immigration experienced little growth in the working-age population.

For example, between 2000 and 2010 in Greece, the working-age population expanded on average by 1.5 percent per year due to new entrants in the labor force turning 15, but this was negated by the 1.6 percent of the labor force that reached the age of 65 and left. Immigrants aged 15–64 added 0.4 percent to the labor force per year, but 0.2 percent of the working-age population died, resulting in a 0.1 percent net increase in the working-age population.

The working-age population projections shown might be considered optimistic, as they do not take into account the impact of the recent financial crisis. Ireland's growth in this projection is largely due to assuming the large inflow of immigrants in the past 20 years continues. However, since the financial crisis, Ireland has experienced a significant outflow of population, and the degree to which this outflow will reverse in the future is unclear. Because the United Nations population projections forecast immigration based on historical flows, they also do not take into account the increasing

FIGURE 2.20

Decomposition of Average Annual Change in Working-Age Population in Selected European and Central Asian Economies, 2000–2010

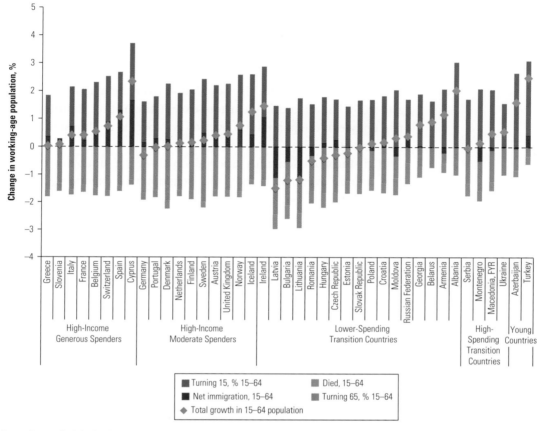

Sources: Eurostat Statistics Database; United Nations population projections (UN 2011).

emigration outflows that Central European, Balkan, FSU, and Young Countries might experience as the higher-income countries start to experience labor shortages and pull in workers from countries that pay lower wages. They also do not take into account the possibility that substantial immigration from outside the region might replace some of this lost labor force, although such immigration would require social and political consensus on the desirability of welcoming and integrating people with different social and ethnic backgrounds (see Bongaarts 2004).

Similarly, projections assume that fertility rates will follow a pre-crisis path. The hardest-hit countries have already experienced a significant decline in fertility during the crisis. This not only will affect the labor market entrants in 2030, but also will lead to a reduction in the size of the childbearing cohort; this in turn will reduce the number of labor market entrants in 2050, compared to what has been projected.

Finally, while life expectancies have been increasing until now, continued increases can be expected to burden the pension system much more significantly in the future, as they will apply to much larger cohorts of elderly with wide pension coverage. Figure 2.21 shows the percentage of the population over the age of 65 in 2010 and 2050. In all country clusters except the Young Countries, the percentage of the population over 65 is expected to almost double in the next 40 years.

High-Income Generous Spenders will see a doubling of their populations over 65. France and Belgium will experience slightly lower increases, but almost a quarter of their populations will be elderly by 2050. Among the High-Income Moderate Spenders, the United Kingdom, Sweden, Denmark, and Finland elderly populations

FIGURE 2.21

Percentage of Elderly in the Population in Selected European and Central Asian Economies, 2010 and 2050

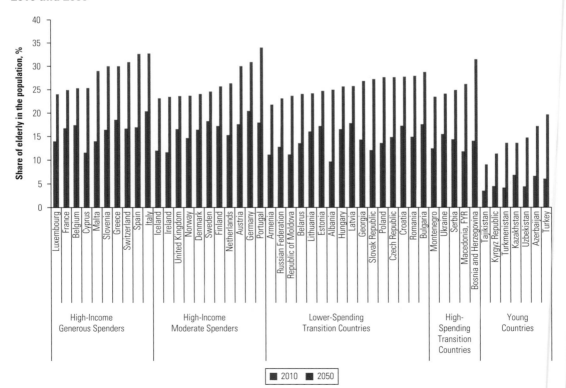

Source: United Nations population projections (UN 2011).

will expand a bit less than in the other countries, but on average in 2050 more than one person in four will be over age 65 in these countries. Countries like Austria and Germany will exceed this average, with closer to one of every three people being elderly; the proportion in Portugal will be even higher.

In the transition countries, both low-spending and high-spending, the percentage of elderly in the population will double. On average, these countries are projected to have one elderly for every 3.5 people, but Bosnia and Herzegovina expects to have one elderly for every three people. Even countries currently considered younger in this region, like Albania, should expect to have elderly account for one of every four people. The surprising result comes in the Young Countries. While these countries often do not worry about aging, they will see a tripling of the percentage of elderly in their populations in the 40-year period and will have one elderly for every seven people. Turkey will be a bit older, with one of every five people being elderly. For these younger countries as a whole, this is a significant change from the present demographics, where on average only one in 20 people is elderly.

Slower working-age population growth translates into fewer contributors, and this, combined with growing numbers of elderly, leads to large deficits in the pension system. Another way of thinking about this is to consider how many elderly each working-age person needs to support, often called the old-age dependency ratio. Figure 2.22 shows the striking growth in the old-age dependency ratio from 1970 to 2010 and from 2010 to 2050. By 2050, on average, each working-age person will have to support more than three times as many elderly as in 1970, and the rate of change in 2010–50 will be greater than it was in 1970–2010. Projections for a stylized Central European country show that the resulting deficits might be as high as 7 percent of GDP by 2050 if contribution rates, benefit levels, and effective retirement ages remain unchanged (figure 2.23).

Policy Conclusions

Pension systems in Western Europe have successfully achieved social goals of reducing poverty among the elderly and providing a mechanism to replace wage income in old age. The systems became a cornerstone of society and expanded coverage toward all elderly. With the concept of the pension system firmly in place, pensions came to be understood as an earned right, and pensioners' incomes were expected to rise with the living standards of workers.

FIGURE 2.22

Old-Age Dependency Ratios in Selected European and Central Asian Economies, 1970, 2010, and 2050

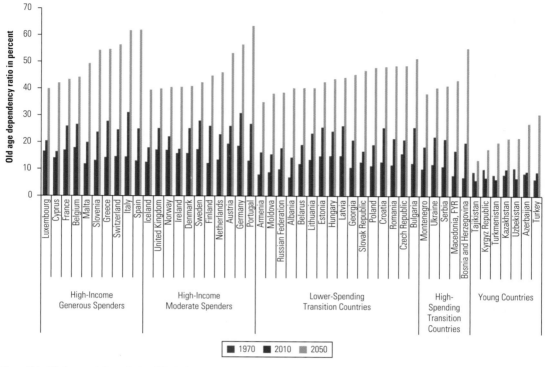

Source: United Nations population projections (UN 2011).

FIGURE 2.23

Projected Pension Deficits in an Average Central European Economy, 2007–2077

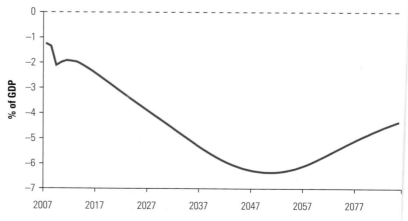

Source: Projections generated using World Bank's Pension Reform Options Software Toolkit (PROST).

However, introduction of the PAYG financing mechanism, and the increased benefit generosity associated with it, has resulted in high and growing pension costs and undesirable intergenerational transfers, especially in earnings-related benefit schemes. Cohorts of the elderly that made small contributions but were able to enjoy increased benefits over long retirement periods benefited greatly from the system. However, these arrangements could only be upheld because of the rapid increase in the numbers of contributors, increasingly higher contribution rates, and small numbers of pensioners due to program immaturity—the expansion of the pension pyramid within the expanding demographic pyramid.

Other countries of Europe and Central Asia aspire to reach the same social goals already achieved in Western Europe, despite the associated high costs. They have introduced a plethora of pension system designs, hoping to further improve on the model of income provision to the elderly developed in Western Europe.

Pension system designs chosen in the last two decades in this broad region rested on some important assumptions. First of all, it was widely assumed that LFP and formalization in the post-transition economies could be expected to return close to the levels observed before the transition. It was believed that earnings-related benefit design could provide sufficient incentives to workers to participate in the pension system and to voluntarily delay retirement. Moreover, it was expected that the pension structures, once chosen, would be insulated from political interference. Development of the financial markets, financial literacy, efficient portfolios, and growth-producing investments would naturally follow the introduction of funded individual pension accounts. Finally, the sharp fall in fertility rates, observed early in the transition, was expected to fully reverse, and a protracted period of strong emigration was not expected.

Some of the assumptions made at the time of the reform were quite optimistic and were bound to disappoint, but the unpredicted turn for the worse in demographic developments had the largest impact on the pension systems in the transition countries. Sharp and prolonged decline in fertility coupled with large emigration waves in some countries has added to the already challenging problems of population aging and program maturation, leading to the inverting of the demographic pyramid.

The importance of the structural break in the PAYG financing model of pension programs prevalent throughout the region cannot be emphasized enough. By an unfortunate coincidence, many pension systems in the region are reaching full maturity just as the size of younger cohorts is starting to decline. Many pension systems will have to adjust to the structural shift from an environment of continued contributor growth to an environment of prolonged contraction in contributor numbers. The longer these changes are postponed, the more implicit pension liabilities are built up, the higher will be the financial and social costs to current and future cohorts of workers of unwinding these arrangements, and the more abrupt this transition will have to be.

The next chapters review implementation challenges faced by the countries of the region when introducing their chosen pension system designs. For successful implementation, the parameters of different pension system components had to be set in a fiscally and socially sustainable manner, transition from the old to the new system had to be handled smoothly and without disruptive fiscal implications, new institutions had to be set up, and the population had to be persuaded to accept the reforms and participate in the new pension system structures. Accompanying reforms of capital and labor markets were also necessary. Finally, the system had to be made robust to economic shocks, which was soon to be tested by an economic boom in the middle of the 2000s and the subsequent financial crisis. Negative demographic developments made some of these tasks even harder to accomplish.

Notes

1. Much of the historical description comes from Verbon (1988) for Germany and the Netherlands. While each country has its individual story of how social security developed, similar patterns can be seen in the other European countries. See, for example, Boldrin, Jimenez-Martin, and Peracchi (1997) for a discussion of Spanish social security; Hohman (1940) and Palme and Svensson (1999) on Swedish social security; Queisser (1996) on German social security; Tomka (2002) for a discussion of social security in Hungary; and Cutler and Johnson (2004), Gruber and Wise (1999), and U.S. Social Security Administration (n.d.) for international comparisons.
2. These same patterns of limited initial systems with gradually expanding coverage can be seen throughout the Central European, Balkan, and FSU countries. The increases in coverage were especially great in the former Soviet Union, as the entire working-age population, men and women, joined the contributing labor force. Data constraints preclude providing time series for these countries, but historical sources suggest that the progression was similar to what can be seen in Western Europe.
3. Population comparisons are only valid for a limited number of countries, given the changes in boundaries over the twentieth century.

4. Looking forward, the duration of retirement for those who in 1970 reached age 63 in Belgium, 71 in Spain, and 67 in Sweden is even greater, so the figure underestimates the impact of retirement age decline on retirement duration for retirees with the same characteristics.

5. OECD assumptions for the modeling include real earnings growth of 2 percent per year in all countries, inflation of 2.5 percent per year in all countries, and real return on funded, defined contribution rates of 3.5 percent per year. A more detailed description of the methodology used may be found in OECD (2011).

6. Details on pension system design can be found in the European Commission's Mutual Information System on Social Protection (MISSOC 2012); in studies by Holzmann and Guven (2009), Holzmann and Hinz (2005), Pallares-Miralles, Romero, and Whitehouse (2012), and Börsch-Supan (2012); as well as in the OECD *Pensions at a Glance* series (various years) and the U.S. Social Security Administration's *Social Security Programs throughout the World* (various years).

References

Boldrin, Michele, Sergi Jimenez-Martin, and Franco Peracchi. 1997. "Social Security and Retirement in Spain." NBER Working Paper 6136, National Bureau of Economic Research, Cambridge, MA.

Bongaarts, John. 2004. "Population Ageing and the Rising Cost of Public Pensions." *Population and Development Review* 30 (1): 1–23.

Börsch-Supan, Axel H. 2012. "Entitlement Reforms in Europe: Policy Mixes in the Current Pension Reform Process." NBER Working Paper 18009, National Bureau of Economic Research, Cambridge, MA.

CES (Committee on Economic Security). n.d. "Old Age Security Abroad." Available on the U.S. Social Security Administration website, http://www.ssa.gov/history/reports/ces/cesbookc9.html.

Chlon-Dominczak, Agnieszka and Pawel Strzelecki. 2013. "The Minimum Pension as an Instrument of Poverty Protection in the Defined Contribution Pension System—An Example of Poland." *Journal of Pension Economics and Finance* 12 (3): 326–50.

Chomik, Rafal, and Edward R. Whitehouse. 2010. "Trends in Pension Eligibility Ages and Life Expectancy, 1950–2050." OECD Social, Employment, and Migration Working Paper 105, Organisation for Economic Co-operation and Development, Paris.

Conde-Ruiz, J. Ignacio, and Paola Profeta. 2007. "The Redistributive Design of Social Security Systems." *Economic Journal* 117 (520): 686–712.

Cutler, David M., and Richard Johnson. 2004. "The Birth and Growth of the Social Insurance State: Explaining Old Age and Medical Insurance across Countries." *Public Choice* 120 (1–2): 87–121.

Diamond, Peter A. 1997. "Insulation of Pensions from Political Risk." In *The Economics of Pensions: Principals, Policies, and International Experience*, edited by Salvador Valdés-Prieto, 33–58. New York: Cambridge University Press.

European Commission. 2012. *Pension Adequacy in the European Union 2010–2050*. Brussels: European Commission, Directorate-General for Employment, Social Affairs and Inclusion, Social Protection Committee.

Eurostat Statistics Database. European Commission, Brussels. http://epp.eurostat.ec.europa.eu/portal/page/portal/statistics/search_database.

Flora, Peter, Jens Alber, Richard Eichenberg, Jürgen Kohl, Franz Kraus, and Winfried Pfenning. 1983. *State, Economy, and Society in Western Europe 1815–1975: A Data Handbook in Two Volumes*. Vol. 1 of *The Growth of Mass Democracies and Welfare States*. Frankfurt, Germany: Campus Verlag; London, U.K.: Macmillan; Chicago, IL: St. James Press.

Flora, Peter, Franz Kraus, and Winfried Pfenning. 1987. *State, Economy, and Society in Western Europe 1815–1975: A Data Handbook in Two Volumes*. Vol. 2 of *The Growth of Industrial Societies and Capitalist Economies*. Frankfurt, Germany: Campus Verlag; London, U.K.: Macmillan; Chicago, IL: St. James Press.

Galasso, Vincenzo, Roberta Gatti, and Paola Profeta. 2009. "Investing for the Old Age: Pensions, Children and Savings." *International Tax and Public Finance* 16 (4): 538–59.

Galasso, Vincenzo, and Paola Profeta. 2004. "Lessons for an Ageing Society: The Political Sustainability of Social Security Systems." *Economic Policy* 19 (38): 63–115.

Gruber, Jonathan, and David A. Wise, eds. 1999. *Social Security and Retirement around the World*. Chicago, IL: University of Chicago Press.

Hirose, Kenichi, ed. 2011. *Pension Reform in Central and Eastern Europe: In Times of Crisis, Austerity and Beyond*. Budapest: International Labour Organization.

Hohman, Helen Fisher. 1940. "Social Democracy in Sweden." *Social Security Bulletin* 3 (2).

Holzmann, Robert. 2009. *Aging Population, Pension Funds, and Financial Markets: Regional Perspectives and Global Challenges for Central, Eastern, and Southern Europe*. Washington, DC: World Bank.

Holzmann, Robert, and Ufuk Guven. 2009. *Adequacy of Retirement Income after Pension Reforms in Central, Eastern, and Southern Europe: Eight Country Studies*. Washington, DC: World Bank.

Holzmann, Robert, and Richard P. Hinz. 2005. *Old-Age Income Support in the 21st Century: An International Perspective on Pension Systems and Reform*. Washington, DC: World Bank.

ILO (International Labour Organization), Department of Statistics. LABORSTA (database). http://laborsta.ilo.org/.

International Labour Office. 1977. *Pensions and Inflation*. Geneva, Switzerland: International Labour Office.

IWE (Institute for World Economics of the Hungarian Academy of Sciences). 1995. *Human Resources and Social Stability during Transition in Hungary*. San Francisco, CA: International Center for Economic Growth.

LIS (Cross-National Data Center in Luxembourg). 2013. "Inequality and Poverty Key Figures," (accessed March 15, 2013), http://www.lisdatacenter.org/data-access/key-figures/inequality-and-poverty/.

Madison, Angus. 2010a. "Revision of Population Estimates: Explanatory Background Note on Historical Statistics (2010)." University of Groningen, Sweden. http://www.ggdc.net/maddison/Maddison.htm.

———. 2010b. "Statistics on World Population, GDP and per Capita GDP, 1–2008 AD." University of Groningen, Sweden. http://www.ggdc.net /maddison/Maddison.htm.

MISSOC (European Commission, Mutual Information System on Social Protection). 2012. *Comparative Tables on Social Protection*. http://ec.europa .eu/social/main.jsp?catId=815&langId=en.

OECD (Organisation for Economic Co-operation and Development). 2002. *OECD Economic Outlook*, no. 72 (December). Paris: OECD.

———. 2011. *Pensions at a Glance 2011: Retirement-Income Systems in OECD and G20 Countries*. Paris: OECD.

———. 2013. "Ageing and Employment Policies: Statistics on Average Effective Age of Retirement." http://www.oecd.org/insurance/public -pensions/ageingandemploymentpolicies-statisticsonaverageeffective ageofretirement.htm.

Pallares-Miralles, Montserrat, Carolina Romero, and Edward Whitehouse. 2012. "International Patterns of Pension Provision II: A Worldwide Overview of Facts and Figures." Social Protection Discussion Paper 70319, World Bank, Washington, DC.

Palme, Marten, and Ingemar Svensson. 1999. "Social Security, Occupational Pensions, and Retirement in Sweden." In edited by Jonathan Gruber and David A. Wise, 355–402.

Queisser, Monika. 1996. "Pensions in Germany." Policy Research Working Paper 1664, World Bank, Washington, DC.

Tomka, Bela. 2002. *Social Security in Hungary in a Long-Run and Comparative Perspective: Expenditures, Social Rights, and Organization, 1918–1990*. Berlin: Osteuropa-Inst.

UN (United Nations). 2011. *World Population Prospects: The 2010 Revision*. New York: United Nations, Department of Economic and Social Affairs, Population Division. CD-ROM.

U.S. Senate. 1981. "Social Security in Europe: The Impact of an Aging Population." Information paper prepared for use by the Special Committee on Aging, U.S. Senate, Washington, DC.

U.S. Social Security Administration. n.d. "Social Security History." http:// www.ssa.gov/history/pre1935table2.html.

———. Various years. *Social Security Programs throughout the World*. http:// www.ssa.gov/policy/docs/progdesc/ssptw/.

Verbon, Harrie. 1988. "The History of Transfer Payments for the Old." Chapter 2 in *The Evolution of Public Pension Schemes*. Berlin: Springer-Verlag.

CHAPTER 3

Have the Pension Reforms to Date Been Enough?

Introduction

While the choice of pension system design reflects some clear societal preferences, it does not necessarily ensure fiscal and social sustainability, as is sometimes believed. Instead, the design addresses philosophical beliefs about the main goals of the pension system and the need for income redistribution. It reflects the definition of fairness as understood by the society and the level of trust in the government, markets, the political process, and an individual's ability to choose. The design also attempts to ensure against demographic, political, and market risks most feared by the society and offers a tool for some risk diversification.

Ensuring the sustainability of a given design entails restructuring unsustainable liabilities, choosing the right program parameters, and implementing competent regulation and administration. All this must be done while avoiding impediments to economic growth and to the efficient functioning of capital and labor markets. At the same time, social sustainability of the chosen design requires a tireless educational campaign, open discussion of inherent trade-offs in pension policy, honest intergenerational dialogue, and public acceptance of necessary sacrifices. The planning of these reforms in the context of transition is further complicated by the volatility of the economies, with underlying conditions—economic growth, growth in the formal labor force, trends in remuneration, willingness of workers to contribute to the pension system, and willingness of bond markets to help finance transition costs—particularly difficult to predict.

The goal of ensuring long-term fiscal sustainability, always elusive, was far out of reach at the time of pension system reform in Europe and Central Asia. Accrued implicit pension liabilities were large, and demographic projections seemed discouraging, even before they turned for the worse in some transition countries. The introduction of a private pension system component required finding a new source of financing, as some of the pension contributions were now redirected to individual savings accounts in many countries of the region. Attempts to increase long-term fiscal sustainability included immediate restructuring of some of the accrued pension liabilities, gradual reduction of future pension promises, and changes in contribution rates.

The political uproar surrounding pension reforms often limits the ability of policy makers to try for a politically sustainable solution immediately. Instead it typically leads to a series of smaller reforms, all moving in the same direction. Complications arise when there is a change of government and the forward momentum for further reforms either stalls or reverses. So the reformers opted to go as far as they could toward fiscal sustainability, assuming that once the public had accepted the initial changes, further reforms could be enacted. But these reformist governments often were voted out at the next election, replaced by populist governments that backtracked on reforms. After reformers were voted back in, they had to restart the reforms, but from a point that was further back than where they had left off, making it difficult to make progress. This cycle of reformist/populist governments continues to this day.

A further challenge to sustainability was lack of understanding or acceptance of system trade-offs. The public seemed favorable toward the goals and main design features of the new pension systems, which focused on an income replacement function. However, time and again, political pressure to increase the minimum pension amount revealed that the public was not ready to make trade-offs between income replacement and minimum income provision, but instead demanded both kinds of protection. Cooperation from workers and employers was also needed in raising contribution revenue and increasing retirement ages, but public pension programs could not afford to offer big financial incentives to motivate such behavior. Finally, expectations for pension levels were high, in part because of what was being delivered by pension systems in Western Europe, but also because of a narrow gap between wage levels and the high cost of minimal living standards. Negative demographic developments were also eroding trust of the younger generation in the new pension system. Consequently, public enthusiasm for participation in public pension programs was not high, and contributor coverage did not expand as much as initially expected. In some countries participation in the pension system was simply unaffordable for low-paid workers.

This chapter describes the parametric changes to date and evaluates the gains in fiscal and social sustainability of public pension programs in Europe and Central Asia. It starts by discussing the scale of the restructuring challenge and then describes the parametric reforms of public pension programs, including attempts to implement these reforms through self-adjusting mechanisms. The chapter assesses reform achievements to date, measuring gains in fiscal and social sustainability of pension systems by the shortening of the average benefit receipt period, lower benefit generosity, reduction in current and projected pension spending, coverage rates, benefit adequacy, and observed frequency in the changes of system design. The discussion then touches upon the cycle of reform, observing that initial reforms born from worries about fiscal sustainability were partially reversed in some countries during subsequent boom years and as a consequence of the financial crisis. The chapter concludes with policy implications moving forward.

The Need for Parametric Reforms

For most European governments, the estimates of future pension obligations exceed explicit government liabilities. Müller, Raffelhüschen, and Weddige (2009) provide some estimates of the implicit pension liabilities of a selected group of European countries. As shown in figure 3.1, the amount of implicit pension liabilities is significantly higher than explicit liabilities, except in the United Kingdom. While these figures are highly sensitive to the discount rate (and to other assumptions as well), other reports (e.g., Mink 2005) also suggest that implicit pension debt levels are very high in most countries of the region.

High implicit liabilities become unaffordable when contributor numbers start to shrink. The average implicit pension liabilities shown in figure 3.1 are on the order of 200 percent of gross domestic product (GDP). Given that these liabilities have risen from zero in about 100 years, this amounts to an average increase in liabilities of about 2 percent of GDP per year, which is the outcome of making increasingly generous promises to an increasingly large number of

FIGURE 3.1

Implicit Pension Liabilities and Explicit Debt as a Percentage of GDP in Selected European Economies, 2006 and 2011

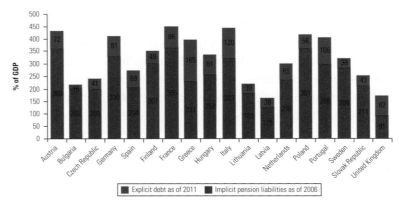

Source: Müller, Raffelhüschen, and Weddige 2009.

contributors, often in return for increasingly large contributions. This pattern could continue as long as even more contributors were joining pension programs each year, allowing governments to "refinance" the liabilities coming due by "borrowing" from numerous new contributors. However, when the number of new "lenders" starts to shrink, implicit liabilities due can no longer be fully refinanced: they have to be paid from other sources or made explicit by borrowing in capital markets. At the time of structural pension reforms, governments realized that however difficult the payment of pensions was currently, future pension deficits would be even higher. Thus, the need to lower implicit pension liabilities as soon as possible was well understood.

Restructuring already accrued liabilities, which normally affect current pensioners and older workers, can reduce implicit liabilities. This can involve a retroactive reduction in the accrual rate, redefinition of insured income, a rapid increase in retirement age without actuarially fair compensation, elimination of early retirement options, levying of a new tax on pension benefits, and less generous benefit indexation. All of these have been tried by different countries under various circumstances, and in some cases they have been challenged in court. However, more often than not, significant restructuring of accrued liabilities did not happen in this group of countries, and the pension rights of older populations were largely grandfathered, exacerbating issues of intergenerational inequity.

Most governments, instead, have opted for the slower accrual of new liabilities introduced through gradual parametric reforms or through a reduced degree of income insurance going forward. As a result, lower contributions are combined with lower benefits; this was

increases the average duration of retirement and thus the value and cost of retirement benefits. Still, most countries allow it in some circumstances. Early retirement, usually with full pension, might be offered to certain special occupations like military personnel, policemen, and miners. The list can also include a host of other categories like opera singers in Austria, ballerinas in Serbia, and bullfighters in Spain. While employers in these professions are often required to make higher contributions to help finance full benefits for their workers, these are not sufficient to cover the costs of the early retirement; this leaves early retirement programs to be subsidized by workers in other industries, introducing some interoccupational inequities. Alternatively, some countries allow all individuals the option to retire early, but with some type of reduction in pension. Meanwhile, a few countries allow anyone to retire earlier than the normal retirement age with a full pension, but they put limits on the number of years a person can retire early or on the earliest eligible age for retirement to avoid allowing people to make choices that will leave them in poverty in advanced old age (Zaidi and Whitehouse 2009; Chomik and Whitehouse 2010).

Country policies regarding early retirement vary considerably, but the overall trend is toward reduction of this practice. Some countries, like Ireland, do not allow early retirement except for special occupations, while others, like Greece, allow retirement up to 10 years before the normal retirement age. Benefit reductions for early retirement also differ across countries, with countries like Spain reducing benefits as much as 7 percent per year for early retirement, and others, like Belgium and Luxembourg, not reducing early retirement pensions at all. Reforming countries have been moving toward reducing the number of occupations eligible for early retirement and restricting the type of work within the occupation that is eligible for early retirement, such as by providing these benefits only to underground miners and not to other workers connected with the mining industry. Poland, for example, successfully limited the number of people eligible for early retirement from 1.53 million to 860,000 in a 2009 reform (see annex 3A). Countries have also been raising the benefit reductions for early retirement to discourage the practice (OECD 2011).

Another common benefit eligibility condition that is often revised pertains to the minimum number of contribution years. As pension system designs have changed, the number of working years required to collect a pension has risen in some countries and fallen in others. To improve fiscal sustainability, countries have been increasing the minimum number of working years required. However, policy makers also worry that tighter eligibility conditions will leave some people, who have sporadic contribution histories, without a pension and will discourage others, who do not foresee having long careers, from contributing altogether. This has often led to retirement options: full pension with increasingly high number of contribution years required, or partial pension with fewer required years, lower benefits, and possibly a higher minimum retirement age. Given these complicated changes that tighten eligibility for one group while relaxing it for another, quantifying overall impact on sustainability and coverage is difficult.

The region has been struggling in setting eligibility conditions for disability benefits. The number of disability beneficiaries depends heavily on the definition of disability as well as on the disability certification process, policies on requalification, and rehabilitation efforts, all of which introduce an element of subjectivity. The minimum eligibility age for old-age pension also affects disability benefits, as the probability of becoming disabled before reaching a now-higher retirement age increases. The high retirement age of 67 in Iceland and Norway could be a significant contributor to the high proportion of disability spending in those countries, as shown in figure 3.4, although in Iceland relatively low old-age benefit spending is probably a more important factor. Broadening the definition of disability to include mental illness and substance abuse also tends to increase the number of beneficiaries substantially. Finally, wars also leave their mark on disability programs, as shown by the example of Croatia in figure 3.4.

During downturns, disability applications and the number of newly certified beneficiaries tend to rise, as the unemployed turn to disability benefits to replace wage income. Suggesting some degree of flexibility in how criteria are applied. Some of the increases could derive from downturn-related mental stress, but in many countries the increases are too large to be explained in this manner. In many transition countries, the disruptions caused by the move from centrally planned to market economies led to large jumps in the number of disability beneficiaries. Even though rules and certification procedures have been tightened subsequently, people who qualified under earlier, more lenient rules are still on the disability rolls, and countries have found removing them to be difficult and in some cases unconstitutional. As a result, many of the transition countries are spending a sizable but declining budget on disability benefits, as newly eligible cohorts of disabled are typically smaller than previous ones. Disability spending has again started to increase due to the financial crisis that began in 2008 and continues in some countries. This could be another contributor to high disability spending in Iceland in 2010.

FIGURE 3.4

Proportion of Pension Spending on Old Age, Disability, and Survivors in Selected European and Central Asian Economies, 2010

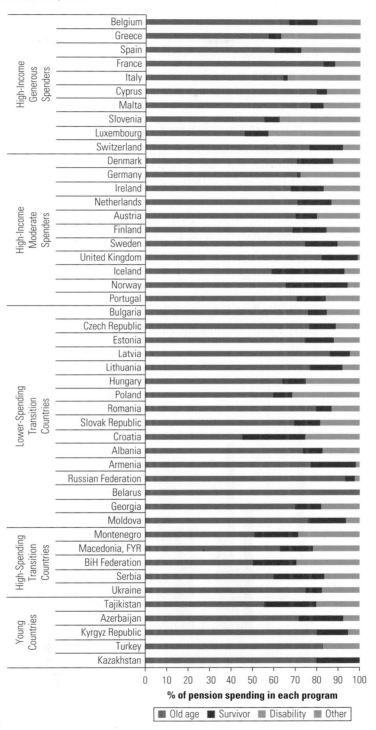

Source: Eurostat Statistics Database.

Note: Data are for 2010 or latest year available. The Federation of Bosnia-Herzegovina (BiH Federation) and Republika Srpska, which together make up the country of Bosnia and Herzegovina, have separate pension systems and are treated as separate data points in the figure.

Transition countries have adopted more survivor benefit eligibility tests than countries in Western Europe, as shown in figure 3.5. These tests include age restrictions, remarriage restrictions, and restrictions based on employment status, where surviving spouses who can work are not eligible for benefits. The exceptions to the pattern are means testing and marriage vesting, which are more prevalent in Western Europe.

However, eligibility tests are not the only determinants of survivor pension program costs. Survivor benefit spending tends to be higher in countries with low women's labor force participation in the past or with large wage differentials between genders. Most countries provide individuals with only one pension benefit, either their own pension or the survivor pension from their deceased spouse, and most women survivors tend to choose the survivor pension over their own

FIGURE 3.5

Eligibility Restrictions for Survivor Benefits in Pension Systems of Europe and Central Asia, 2012–2013

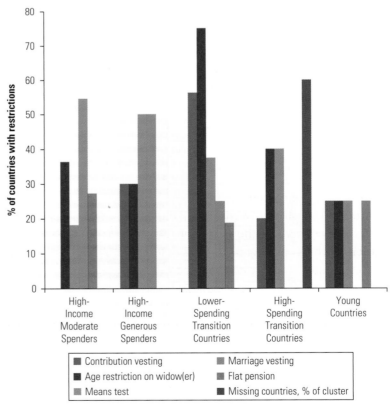

Sources: MISSOC Comparative Tables on Social Protection; U.S. Social Security Administration 2012.

pension in those countries. For example, Sweden has high female labor participation rates and generous maternity benefits, which include pension credits for the years spent raising children. Consequently, Sweden spends very little on survivor benefits compared to, for example, Italy or Spain, where labor force participation by women is not nearly as high. Transition countries currently also benefit from higher female labor force participation rates in the past, which tend to reduce the reliance on survivor benefits. These countries may find that survivor payments increase in the future, following the drop in women's participation in the formal sector labor force after transition.

While all of these eligibility conditions pertaining to old age, disability, and survivors determine the numbers of people who collect benefits, the number of beneficiaries is only one component of pension spending. The other component is the level of benefits and the growth of those benefits.

Changes in Benefit Levels

Countries have also tried to enact changes in benefit parameters that would reduce pension levels in relation to wages, thereby reducing pension spending. On the benefit rates themselves, it is difficult to identify a trend, given the substantive changes in the way pensions are provided in these countries. However, two components of the benefit levels can be readily quantified: the number of years in the averaging period and the indexation of benefits post-retirement. The averaging period, as mentioned earlier, is the number of years included in the average wage on which the pension benefits are calculated. The indexation of benefits determines how benefits are increased during the retirement years from the initial benefit provided on the day of retirement.

The trend is clearly toward lengthening the averaging period for wages that constitute the base on which pensions are paid. Lengthening the averaging period has at least five positive outcomes: (a) it better links the contributions paid by the individual with the benefits received, making the benefit levels fairer within a cohort; (b) it limits the fraud associated with extremely high wage increases being granted in the last year before retirement to benefit an individual's retirement, but with large costs to the system; (c) it limits the fraud involved in underreporting earnings and contributions in the years prior to those included in the averaging period; (d) it avoids rewarding high earners who often see large wage increases toward the end of their career compared to lower earners who receive much lower wage increases throughout their career; and (e) it lowers benefit levels, since including low wages earned in the early part of one's career (and on which commensurately lower contributions have been paid) brings down the average wage used to calculate the benefit level.

Of the High-Income Generous Spender countries, only France, Greece, and Slovenia use averaging periods shorter than full career. France has raised the averaging period from best 10 to best 25 years of earnings, and Slovenia from last 10 years of earnings to any consecutive 24 years of earnings. The gradual increase in the averaging period in Slovenia will be complete by 2018; in 2013 it stands at any consecutive 19 years of earnings. Greece maintains a 5-year average. Among the High-Income Moderate Spender countries, only Norway and Austria use a wage base other than full career for earnings-related benefits: Norway uses 20 years, while Austria is increasing the averaging period from best 20 years of earnings to best 40 years. Most transition countries have legislated a move to full-career average wages, with some still in flux due to the unavailability of old wage records. The Czech Republic uses a 30-year career average, while Lithuania uses a 25-year average. Most of the Young Countries use full-career averages, with the exception of Uzbekistan.

Rules governing benefit indexation are one of the greatest influences on fiscal sustainability of pension programs in the short to medium term, since benefit indexation is the only parameter that affects spending on the already retired. The other parameters all affect the rights of not-yet-retired workers, so the impact tends to be delayed. When pension spending is deemed already unsustainably high, policy makers need to address not only future generations but the current elderly as well. In their reassessment of the financial sustainability of pension programs in the 1970s and 1980s, most countries in Western Europe began moving to inflation indexation of benefits, in contrast to the earlier trend, when immaturity of pension programs stimulated a move toward benefit indexation that followed wage growth. The prevailing view in Western Europe in recent decades has been that the elderly can afford to be protected only against inflation risk, to ensure that their absolute, rather than relative, living standards do not fall.

Most of the transition countries have legislated at least partial moves toward inflation indexation, with Albania, Bulgaria, Hungary, Kosovo, Latvia, and Serbia having legislated 100 percent inflation indexation, along with the Young Countries of Azerbaijan, the

Kyrgyz Republic, and Uzbekistan. However, inflation indexation has been difficult to achieve for a couple of reasons. First, successful reformers experienced rapid wage growth prior to the financial crisis as their economies made up for the declines of the 1990s. Pensioners whose benefits increased only with inflation fell significantly behind other cohorts, leading to political dissatisfaction. Second, the earlier retirement ages prevalent in many of these countries resulted in long periods of retirement. The discrepancy between the wage growth experienced by the working-age population and the inflation increases received by the elderly became more noticeable over the long retirement periods. In Russia, for example, where the pre-crisis wage growth was 20 percent each year after inflation, inflation indexation of the basic benefit helped drive the overall pension levels to 26 percent of average wage by 2008. In response to this experience, Hungary and Serbia have legislated inflation indexation with the caveat that if real GDP growth rises above a certain level, some of that growth will be shared with pensioners.

The combination of eligibility conditions and benefit levels determines pension spending. Countries have also implemented changes on the revenue side, such as changes in contribution rates.

Changes in Contribution Rates

In terms of contributions, countries appear to be converging toward an average contribution rate of about 24 percent. Countries that had higher contribution rates are reducing them, while countries that had lower rates are increasing them. Figure 3.6 shows the average contribution rates by cluster, omitting countries where the main public system is not based on contributions. In High-Income Generous Spender countries, where rates are highest, France and Italy increased rates, while Slovenia, Greece, and Cyprus reduced them. Among the High-Income Moderate Spender countries, where contribution rates are near average, a number of countries raised rates. Initially, many of the transition countries responded to the drop in contribution revenue due to labor restructuring by raising contribution rates. After experiencing a significant rise in informal labor markets, defined as employment where workers do not make contributions, many have tried to induce workers to participate by reducing contribution rates.

A fourth type of parametric change, which tries to link benefits with contribution revenue, is the introduction of self-adjusting mechanisms in the pay-as-you-go design.

FIGURE 3.6

Average Pension Contribution Rates in Europe and Central Asia, 2013

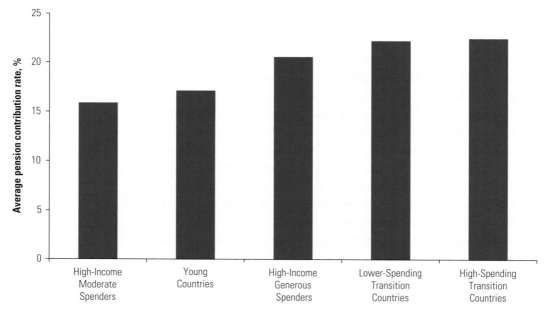

Source: World Bank HDNSP Pensions Database.
Note: Applies to first and second pillars.

Introduction of Self-Adjusting Pay-as-You-Go Designs

Recent innovations in the pay-as-you-go program design have been developed to create a self-adjusting pension program, influencing both benefit eligibility conditions and benefit levels.[1] Pension policy has long-term effects, but politicians usually have short-term horizons. They tend to raise benefits when revenues grow, yet refrain from taking action when benefits and generosity need to be cut in response to life expectancy changes or demographic and economic developments outside the pension system. Therefore, policy makers have long searched for a means to automatically trigger adjustments that politicians are reluctant to make. For example, when life expectancy increases, the system could automatically reduce benefits or raise retirement ages without politicians having to make the difficult choices.

The simplest of the self-adjusting mechanisms are the pension indexation rules. These tie future pension increases to average wage growth, as in Ireland; to inflation, as in Serbia; to some combination of the two, as in Switzerland; to GDP growth, as in Turkey; or even to the growth in contribution revenue per pensioner, as in Russia. However, these rules were often ignored even when legislated, and politicians could always change the effective level of pensions by other means, like instituting an end-of-year bonus payment or adding pension supplements to different categories of pensioners. As chapter 2 showed, although legislated increases were limited to inflation, pension increases in many countries of Western Europe historically exceeded wage growth.

The valorization rules governing revaluation of past wages used in benefit calculation have also been linked to economic and even demographic parameters (the revaluation rate could be thought of as interest paid on past contributions). Conventional defined benefit formulas commonly use wage growth as a revaluation rate, as do point systems. Tying the revaluation rate to wage bill growth, as has been done in Latvia and Poland, and contribution revenue per pensioner, as in Russia, introduces a demographic component to the calculation in addition to a purely economic component. A complication of this approach, as commonly applied in these countries, is that economic and demographic parameters are calculated annually and locked into the eventual benefit calculation formula sometimes observed decades before benefits are actually paid. In the interim, the economic and demographic situation may change significantly and may require different adjustments than those that were locked in based on observed variables in the past.

More recently, changes in life expectancy have started to be automatically incorporated in setting benefit eligibility conditions or calculating benefit levels. In Denmark and Italy, the minimum retirement age is adjusted to reflect the increase in life expectancy, an approach also currently proposed in Germany. In Italy, Latvia, Poland, and Sweden, this is accomplished through the notional accounts scheme by adjusting benefit levels to life expectancy. Notional accounts combine this approach with automatic revaluing of past contributions, as discussed above, giving individuals the option of choosing either a lower benefit level or a higher retirement age. While it was hoped that this would result in a significant increase in the effective retirement age, most workers tended to retire at the first available opportunity, opting for the lower pension amount. The approach, however, may have helped explain inherent trade-offs between benefit levels and retirement ages to the public and may have softened the opposition to subsequent statutory retirement age increases in Italy, Latvia, and Poland (Holzmann and Palmer 2006).

However, some dangers are involved in overreliance on automatic stabilizers. First, automatic adjustments can be introduced into an overly generous program. For example, linking retirement ages to changes in life expectancy makes great sense. However, if policy makers create the link at a time when the expected duration of retirement is 25 years, the link is not going to make the pension system sustainable in the long run, and policy makers will have lost the tool of a discretionary future increase in the retirement age that might help make the system more sustainable. Even if the initial parameters seem balanced, unpredictable events inevitably happen at some point, as policy makers cannot accurately predict all future events when drafting the initial legislation. Once the system is out of balance, pension programs with high degrees of interconnections between parameters become impossible to fix within the existing framework in a reasonable time horizon. Governments then make ad hoc changes that undermine the legitimacy and underlying rationale of the self-adjusting mechanisms. Examples of these issues can be found in the recent experiences of Latvia, Russia, and Serbia, among many others.

The more stable and predictable the economy, the greater the likelihood that automatic stabilizers will perform successfully. However, the volatility and unpredictability in the transition countries has led to some concerns. For example, an unforeseen permanent drop in the number of contributors, which might be due to an emigration wave, could increase today's pension scheme deficit. In a traditional system this could be addressed by raising the contribution rate. However, in the notional accounts system, an increase in the contribution rate automatically raises future pension benefits, making the deficit smaller in the short run but increasing long-run pension liabilities. Alternatively, the number of contributors might rise in a period of economic boom, especially if the retirement age is increased at the same time, which further fuels the growth in contributor numbers, the wage bill, and the notional interest rate. This in turn raises future benefits. However, at the same time, the long-term trend for contributor numbers might be declining, and the boom-time adjustment of benefits upward is counterproductive with respect to long-term fiscal sustainability.

The volatility experienced by transition economies through automatic stabilizers is transferred to benefit levels and might lead to wildly different outcomes for adjacent cohorts. When individuals with similar work histories born days apart receive vastly different pensions, the fairness of the system is questioned and there is political pressure on governments to remove the differences. This invariably means increasing the lower benefit to the level of the higher one in an ad hoc manner, undermining long-run fiscal sustainability.

Given all the reforms of the last 15 years, it is useful to see what impact, if any, these reforms have already had on controlling pension spending and changing retirement outcomes for individuals. While many of the reforms are being implemented only gradually, some impact should already be visible. Measuring the pace of reforms also matters: the countries that are able to achieve some results in increasing fiscal sustainability and adjusting social expectations in the first years and decades of the reform process are able to spread the needed adjustments among more age cohorts and can avoid treating different cohorts unequally. The next sections analyze the impact reforms have had on pension spending and retirement behavior.

Effects of the Reforms on Fiscal Sustainability and Policy Space for More Reforms

As discussed in the previous sections, countries have been choosing different pension system designs and undertaking all kinds of parametric reforms. They have tightened benefit eligibility conditions, changed benefit parameters, raised and then lowered contribution rates, and introduced incentives to contribute and retire later, all in an attempt to address the projected pension deficits, increase coverage, and provide adequate pension levels in the future. Countries have made different choices, with some being more aggressive on retirement age changes while others have relied more heavily on reducing benefits.

Ultimately, all these reform efforts can be measured with a few important statistics. Gains in fiscal program sustainability can be measured by the shortening of the average benefit receipt period, lowered benefit generosity, and past and projected changes in total pension spending. Social sustainability of reform is measured in current and projected benefit adequacy and observed frequency in the changes to system design. Gains in pension system coverage are important for both goals, as higher coverage signals public confidence in the pension system and also helps make the system fiscally sustainable in the short and medium run.

Effective retirement ages, the ages at which people actually retire, rose as a consequence of the reforms, but the average duration of retirement remained constant over the 2001–09 period in the three clusters included in figure 3.7. Increases in retirement age are shown by the blue bars, which are positive for most countries where data were available. However, the duration of retirement, essentially life expectancy at the effective retirement age, shown by the red bars, did not fall in tandem with the rise in retirement age. In a static environment, if effective retirement ages rise, the duration of retirement falls

FIGURE 3.7

Change in Effective Retirement Age Compared to Change in Life Expectancy, Selected European Economies, 2001–2009

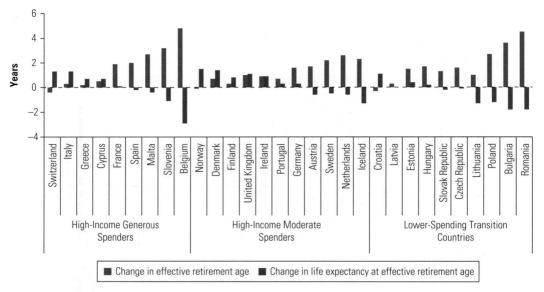

Source: Eurostat Statistics Database.

a bit less because those who die at ages between the old and the new retirement age are no longer included in the new average. In addition, during the period that retirement ages were rising, life expectancies continued to rise as well, resulting in an even smaller fall in the duration of retirement. Note the substantial increases in effective retirement age in countries like Slovenia, Belgium, Sweden, the Netherlands, Iceland, Poland, Bulgaria, and Romania. However, in each case, the duration of retirement fell much less than the retirement age increase, indicating that life expectancy probably increased substantially during the period, counteracting the impact of the retirement age increase.

Effective retirement ages remain quite low in most countries and could be increased further, as signaled by the relatively high duration of retirement (figure 3.8). Figure 2.8 in chapter 2 shows that the duration of retirement stood on average at about 15 years in Western European countries in 1970, which implies life expectancies for women higher than 15 years and life expectancies for men lower than 15 years. The duration of retirement today is considerably higher in most countries. In all countries except Kazakhstan, Lithuania, Latvia, Albania, and Russia, duration of retirement for men is above 15 years. Lithuania is the only country where duration of retirement for women is below 20 years.

FIGURE 3.8

Duration of Retirement in Selected European and Central Asian Economies, 2009

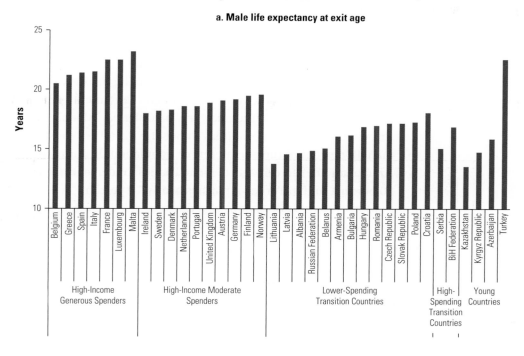

a. Male life expectancy at exit age

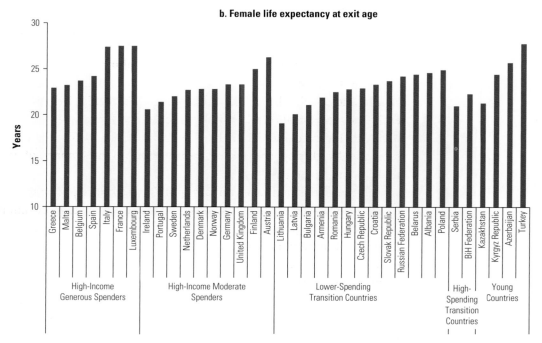

b. Female life expectancy at exit age

Source: Eurostat Statistics Database.

Note: The Federation of Bosnia-Herzegovina (BiH Federation) and Republika Srpska, which together make up the country of Bosnia and Herzegovina, have separate pension systems and are treated as separate data points in the figure.

Another way to assess the remaining policy space for increasing effective retirement ages is to look at the percentage of old-age beneficiaries who are younger than 65, which not so long ago was an internationally accepted standard for a reasonable retirement age. Figure 3.9 provides these data for countries where detailed data are available, showing that a sizable proportion of old-age beneficiaries are still younger than 65. The percentages are higher for women than for men because in these countries women's retirement ages are typically lower. Only in Lithuania, Latvia, Bulgaria, Albania, Georgia, Armenia, and Serbia do retirees under the age of 65 constitute less than 40 percent of the overall retiree population. In Kazakhstan and Azerbaijan the percentage of beneficiaries under age 65 is above 50 percent, and in Turkey it reaches nearly 70 percent.

Many reforms also sought to reduce the relative value of the pension benefit package, which is still high in some countries if measured

FIGURE 3.9

Percentage of Old-Age Pension Beneficiaries below Age 65 in Selected European and Central Asian Economies

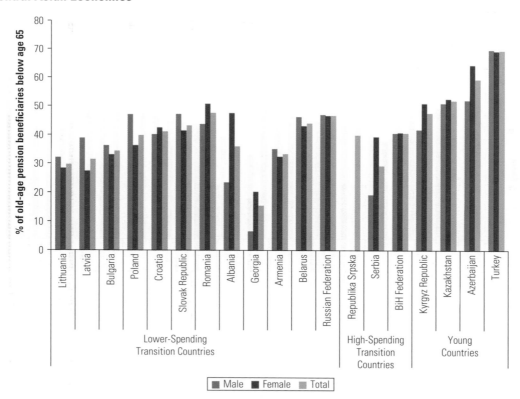

Source: Country-provided data, latest available year.

by pension spending per elderly. Pension spending per elderly person (aged 65 or older) as a percentage of GDP per capita provides one measure of the relative benefit level, or benefit generosity. As discussed in the previous sections, many countries also increase generosity of the overall benefit package by allowing people to retire early or obtain disability benefits fairly easily. If a country allows many early retirements, its pension spending per elderly person will be high. Similarly, pension spending per elderly will also be high if spending is just on the elderly and the benefit levels are high.

Figure 3.10 shows that in many countries, pension spending per elderly person is still high relative to GDP per capita. In the Netherlands, Austria, France, Poland, Serbia, and Tajikistan, pension spending per elderly person exceeds 80 percent of GDP per capita. In Montenegro, Ukraine, Turkey, and the Kyrgyz Republic, it exceeds 100 percent of GDP per capita.

Pension spending per pensioner is lower and again reflects the presence of many relatively young beneficiaries. This measure, compared to GDP per person in the country, isolates the generosity of the benefit level from the generosity of the overall benefit package

FIGURE 3.10

Pension Spending per Elderly Person Compared to GDP per Capita, Selected European and Central Asian Economies, 2009

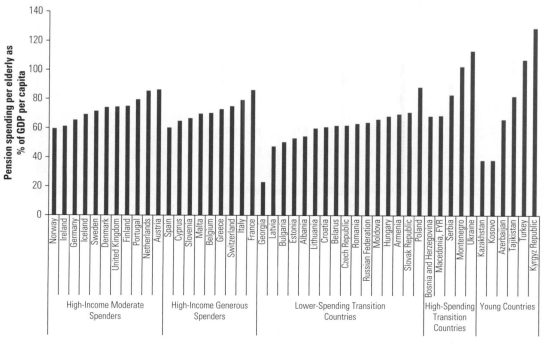

Sources: Eurostat Statistics Database; country-provided data.

FIGURE 3.11

Pension Spending per Beneficiary Compared to GDP per Capita, Selected European and Central Asian Economies, 2009

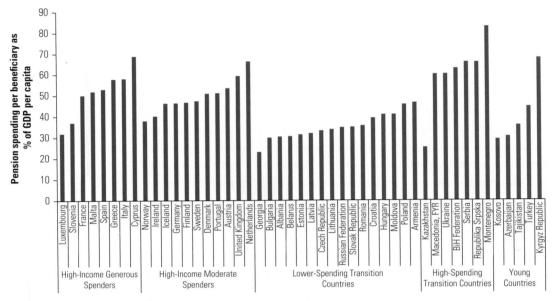

Sources: Eurostat Statistics Database; country-provided data.
Note: The Federation of Bosnia-Herzegovina (BiH Federation) and Republika Srpska, which together make up the country of Bosnia and Herzegovina, have separate pension systems and are treated as separate data points in the figure.

(figure 3.11). The average pension spending per beneficiary for the countries shown is 46 percent of GDP per capita. In Cyprus, the Netherlands, the former Yugoslav Republic of Macedonia, Ukraine, both Bosnian entities, Serbia, Montenegro, and the Kyrgyz Republic, the corresponding figure is at least 60 percent. Austria, France, Poland, Ukraine, Tajikistan, and Turkey are high on the graph in figure 3.10 but not on this one, suggesting that each of these countries has many younger beneficiaries, but the benefits themselves are not necessarily very high. Cyprus, FYR Macedonia, and both Bosnian entities appear high in figure 3.11 but not in the preceding one, suggesting that these countries have relatively high benefit levels rather than an excessive number of young beneficiaries.

Pension spending per elderly person did not fall relative to GDP per capita on average over the period between 2001 and 2009, as shown in figure 3.12. The reforms, by increasing retirement ages, tightening disability rules, increasing the averaging period, strengthening links between contributions and benefits, and reducing the generosity of indexation post-retirement, were expected to cause significant decreases in this statistic.

FIGURE 3.12

Growth in Pension Spending per Elderly Person Compared to Growth in GDP per Capita, Selected European and Central Asian Economies, 2001–2009

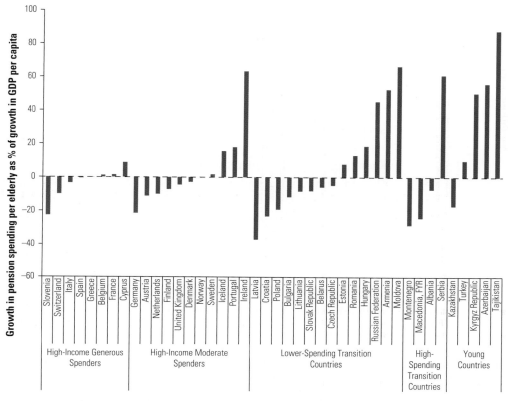

Sources: Eurostat Statistics Database; country-provided data.

The majority of High-Income Generous Spenders experienced no change in spending, but relative pension spending declined in Slovenia, Switzerland, and Italy and increased significantly in crisis-affected Cyprus. Among High-Income Moderate Spenders, pension spending fell, for the most part, relative to GDP per capita, but there were steep increases in Iceland, Portugal, and Ireland, where the financial crisis sharply reduced GDP but not pension spending. Among Lower-Spending Transition Countries, spending declined in eight of 14 countries, with significant reductions in Latvia, Croatia, and Poland. The sizable decline in Latvia is especially surprising, given the large post-crisis decline in GDP, and reflects the strong pre-crisis GDP growth and restrained pension spending. However, Estonia, Romania, Hungary, Russia, Armenia, and Moldova instead experienced sizeable increases. In the High-Spending Transition Countries, while relative pension spending declined in most countries, Serbia shows a hefty increase in spending. In the Young Countries, with the exception of Kazakhstan, there were sizable increases rather than decreases. While the objective of many of these reforms was to restrain the growth in spending, this objective was only achieved in some of the High-Income Moderate Spenders, some of the Lower-Spending Transition Countries, and a few of the High-Spending Transition Countries.

In general, countries moved their spending levels toward a norm. Countries with high benefit levels in 2001 decreased their pension spending, while countries with low benefit levels tended to increase spending between 2001 and 2009, as shown in figure 3.13. For example, Iceland and Ireland, which had below-average pension spending, moved to increase it, and high spenders like Latvia and Poland moved to decrease their pension spending. However, there are many outliers. Serbia and Turkey, which were both already relatively high spenders, increased spending dramatically. Ukraine, which was one of the highest spenders initially, did not reduce spending. On the other hand, Kazakhstan, which was one of the lower spenders, reduced spending even further.

Most reforms fully compensated longer careers with higher pension benefits, a policy that has limited the long-term effect on overall

FIGURE 3.13

Change in Pension Spending in 2009 Relative to Spending Levels in 2001, Selected European and Central Asian Economies

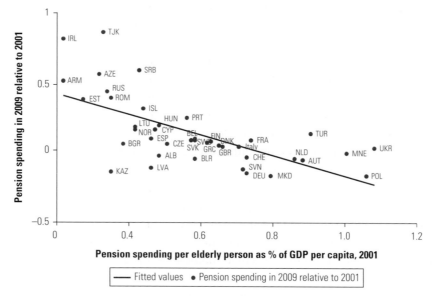

Sources: Eurostat Statistics Database; World Bank World Development Indicators (database); country provided-data.
Note: $R^2 = 0.4237$. Elderly is defined as aged 65 and above.

pension spending. This partially explains the absence of a downward trend in the average generosity of the benefit package and the apparent convergence of pension spending between countries. Policy makers recognized that the impending demographic crisis would require much higher retirement ages and less benefit generosity. However, the mismatch between the short-term horizons of politicians and the long-term nature of the changing demographics reduced the willingness of politicians to endure the political pain of simultaneously enacting cuts and establishing harsher benefit eligibility conditions. Therefore, many countries took a politically easier route by increasing retirement ages under the existing linear accrual rate schedule, fully compensating longer careers with higher pension benefits.

The cuts in benefit generosity that were enacted, often under the automatic adjustment rules, were often offset by subsequent ad hoc pension increases. Trying to avoid explicit public and legislative debate about the needed benefit cuts, policy makers opted to legislate rules that would take the discretion out of pension policy and automatically reduce benefits in a gradual manner, but they chose not to clearly explain the implications of the rules they were passing to the public.[2] As a result, when the automatic measures began to cut expenditures as expected, the population at large objected, and politicians reverted to ad hoc measures. This effect can be seen throughout the region, in countries like Hungary, Latvia, Russia, Serbia, and Ukraine. For example, as noted previously, the indexation reforms did not fully hold, and pensions were frequently increased by more than what was prescribed by the automatic adjustment rules. In addition, countries added supplements, bonuses, and end-of-year bonus pensions in response to political pressures, all of which counteracted the move toward inflation indexation and the objective of reduced pension spending.

Some countries were fairly successful in enacting disability reform, while others were not.[3] Since older workers are more likely than younger workers to develop disabilities, as the work force ages, the number of disabled is expected to increase. Moreover, rising retirement ages in the old-age programs tended to increase the number of applications for disability pensions, as people eager to retire, but prohibited under the new legislation from doing so through the old-age programs, tried to become eligible through disability programs. The financial crisis also put pressure on disability programs, as individuals who faced unemployment tried to become eligible. As a result, while there were some attempts at disability reform, the overall impact was not always strong enough to counteract the pressure to expand the number of beneficiaries (also see Lafortune, Balestat, and the Disability Study Expert Group Members 2007).

FIGURE 3.14

Growth in Number of Disability Beneficiaries in Bulgaria, 2000–2011

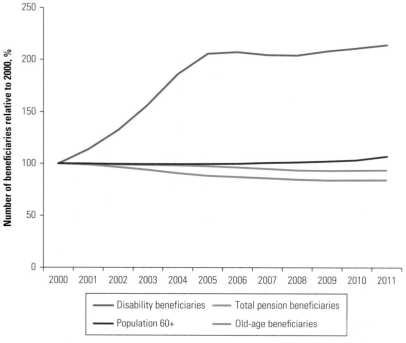

Source: NSSI 2013.

Bulgaria is an example of a country where the increase in disability beneficiaries coincided with a gradual introduction of tighter eligibility conditions in the old-age program (figure 3.14). As a result, disability spending as a percentage of GDP more than doubled between 2001 and 2011. While disability inflow rates have stabilized since 2006, they have not decreased back to their original levels despite attempts at reform (NSSI 2013).

The Netherlands and Poland were successful at reducing the number of disability beneficiaries from extremely high levels (figure 3.15). Elements of their reforms included (a) redefinition of eligibility with stricter examination criteria, (b) reexamination and recertification of those who might recover from disability, (c) emphasis on rehabilitation and retraining, and (d) reemployment of the partially disabled. The Netherlands uses experience ratings for employers with riskier employees; these employers are charged higher premiums to encourage better workplace safety. Dutch employers are also responsible for reintegration of the disabled (OECD 2007; De Jong 2008; van Sonsbeek and Gradus 2012).

FIGURE 3.15

Decline in Number of Disability Beneficiaries in Poland, 2000–2010

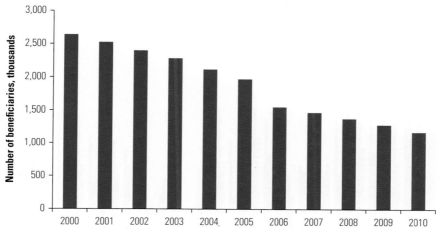

Source: ZUS 2012.

While the transition countries clearly undertook what were perceived as substantial and painful reforms, these actions have not yet resulted in meaningful adjustments to the generosity of benefit packages or the duration of benefit receipt in preparation for the upcoming demographic crisis. Retirement age changes to date have in most cases only kept pace with life expectancy changes, leaving the duration of retirement unchanged. Furthermore, as enacted, increases in retirement ages normally imply higher benefits, limiting the fiscal impact of these reforms. Benefit reductions often are reversed as soon as the impact of the changes begins to be felt by the population, and benefit levels remain high by historic standards in many of the countries. Some of the reforms are still unfolding and their full impact will be felt in future years, as countries frequently grandfathered the currently retired or soon to be retired cohorts, leaving their more generous benefits in place. However, this only means that future generations will have to endure greater reforms (see also European Commission 2012a, 2012b).

For most countries, already legislated future adjustments are not expected to bring the average pension system to fiscal sustainability either. A comparison of pension spending as a share of GDP in 2010 with projected pension spending in 2060 provides a sobering outlook (figure 3.16). Very few countries can expect to see declines in pension spending over this period, despite the reforms legislated to date. Those projected to experience a decline include Italy, Denmark, Croatia, Latvia, Armenia, Poland, Estonia, Russia, Serbia, Bosnia and

FIGURE 3.16

Current and Projected Pension Spending as a Percentage of GDP in Selected European and Central Asian Economies, 2010 and 2060

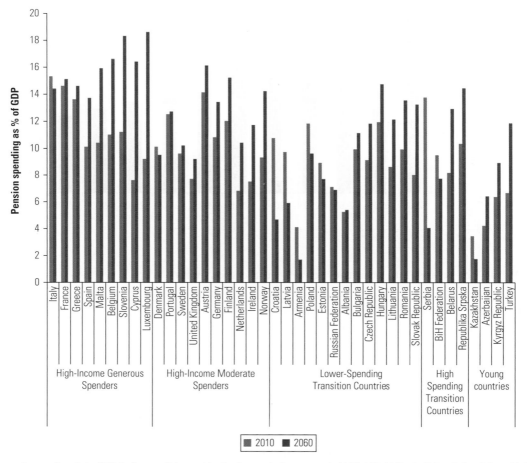

Sources: European Commission 2012c for European Union countries; for others, projections generated with World Bank's Pension Reform Options Software Toolkit (PROST).
Note: The Federation of Bosnia and Herzegovina (BiH Federation) and Republika Srpska, which together make up the country of Bosnia and Herzegovina, have separate pension systems and are treated as separate data points in the figure.

Herzegovina (BiH Federation), and Kazakhstan. Given that pensions are financed by taxes on wages and that the number of wage earners is projected to stop growing or even shrink, most governments will have to find alternative sources of revenue, find ways to increase the labor force, or undertake further pension reforms.

For some countries with a projected decline in pension spending, the credibility of this decline is questionable. When one compares the current and projected pension levels relative to average wage, as shown in figure 3.17 for Poland and Serbia, pensions fall dramatically in the future. In Poland, pension benefits are expected to fall from 51 percent of average wage today to 26 percent in the future, without

FIGURE 3.17

Decline in Projected Pension Benefit as a Percentage of Average Wage in Poland and Serbia, 2007–2072

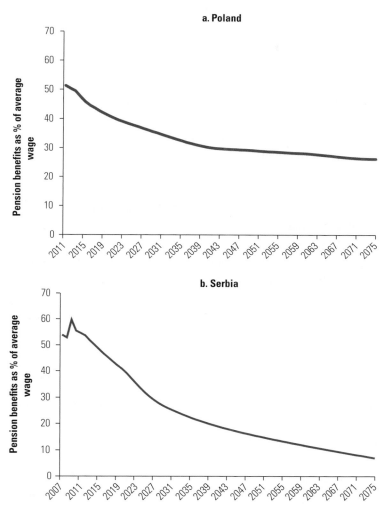

Source: PROST projections using country-provided data.

taking into account the new changes announced in August 2013. In Serbia, the projected decline is even greater, from 52 percent today to as little as 7 percent. It is not clear whether such huge declines are politically sustainable. In general, if politicians revert to ad hoc benefit increases, as they have done in the past, the projected decline in pension spending may be a mirage. It is also not clear whether such low benefit levels will provide enough incentives for the working-age population to continue contributing. If the working-age population further withdraws from contributing to the scheme, fiscal sustainability issues could arise even if pension levels are in fact very low.

It is also unclear whether projected low benefit levels in countries like Poland and Serbia can be considered adequate even under the most stringent definitions. After all, the stated goal of the Polish and Serbian pension systems, presented here as examples, is not only to protect against poverty, but also to provide a reasonable level of income replacement. Therefore, the improvements in fiscal sustainability, coming at the expense of adequacy, might not be socially sustainable. Moreover, if benefits provided by the pension system are inadequate, the rationale for having a pension system at all can be questioned.

This leads to the overall question of whether pension benefits are adequate even today. Do pensions provide enough income to keep the elderly out of poverty?

Impact of Benefit Adequacy on Social Sustainability of Pension Reforms

Living alone is typically costlier than living in larger households, so understanding pensioner living arrangements is important when discussing the importance of pension income. In the transition countries, only a little over half the elderly, defined as individuals aged 65 or older, live with nonelderly people (figure 3.18). This makes pension income even more important for the elderly in this region than in many other parts of the world.

The percentage of elderly living with nonelderly varies, from a low of 40 percent in Central Europe to a high of 69 percent in the Young Countries. The percentage of elderly living with nonelderly is higher among the very old, defined as individuals aged 80 or older, with almost two-thirds of the very old living in larger households. Among the very old, the greatest increase in living with nonelderly comes in Central Europe, where the percentage jumps to 56 percent. In 11 of the 22 countries shown in the figure, elderly men are more likely than elderly women to live in larger households, while in the other countries the ratios are about the same. In the Young Countries and the Balkans, almost 15 percent of elderly live alone and almost 22 percent of the very old live alone. In the FSU countries and in Central Europe, the percentages are much higher, with almost 30 percent of the elderly living alone and as many as a third of the very old living alone. As expected, elderly women are more likely to live alone than elderly men, given that they tend to outlive their spouses. More than 45 percent of elderly women live alone in the urban areas of the Kyrgyz Republic, Moldova, and Poland, while 56 percent of rural elderly women live alone in Belarus.

FIGURE 3.18

Living Arrangements of Elderly in Selected European and Central Asian Economies, by Gender and Rural/Urban Residence

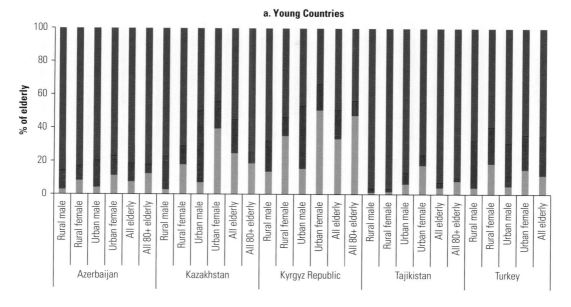

a. Young Countries

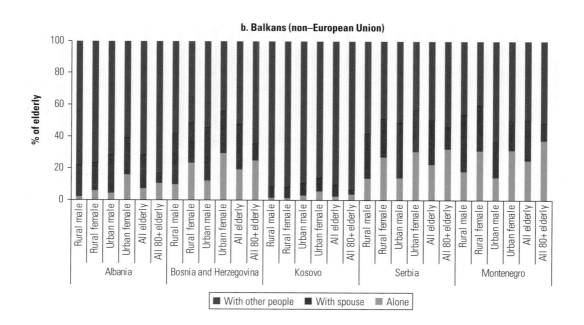

b. Balkans (non–European Union)

■ With other people ■ With spouse ■ Alone

continued

FIGURE 3.18

Continued

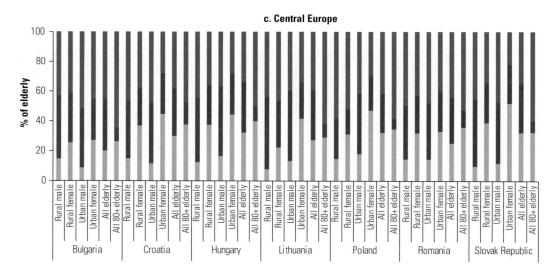

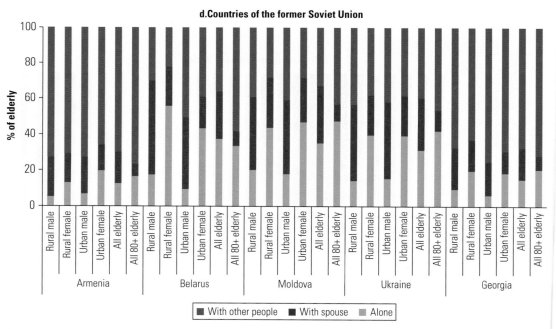

Source: Household survey data, latest available year.

FIGURE 3.19

Percentage of Households, with and without Pensioners, in Poverty in Selected European and Central Asian Economies, 2009

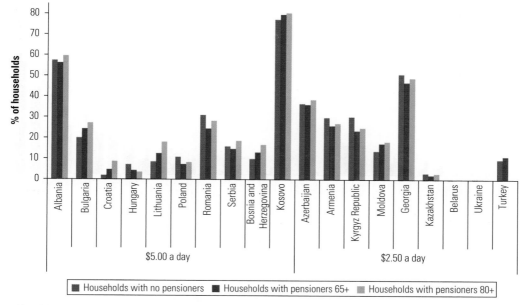

Source: Household survey data.

On average, pensioners are not poorer than the working-age population in transition countries. Figure 3.19 compares poverty rates of pensioner and nonpensioner households using the World Bank standard poverty rates: households living on less than $5.00 per day for Central Europe and the Balkans and less than $2.50 per day for the FSU countries and Young Countries. Among the 19 countries for which data were available, in only six—Bulgaria, Croatia, Lithuania, Bosnia and Herzegovina, Kosovo, and Moldova—are households with pensioners perceptibly more likely to be poor than households without pensioners, based on a measure of income. And in Hungary, Poland, Romania, Armenia, the Kyrgyz Republic, and Georgia, they are less likely to be poor than households without pensioners. While we would expect similarity across pensioner and nonpensioner households in countries where most pensioners live with others, in Georgia and Armenia it appears that pensioners are bringing enough regular income into the household to pull the entire household out of poverty.

Similar results are apparent from Eurostat data for the European Union member states, as shown in figure 3.20. Among the high-income countries, only in Slovenia is the rate of severe material deprivation higher among the elderly than among the working-age

FIGURE 3.20

Rate of Severe Material Deprivation among Different Age Cohorts in European Union Member States, 2011

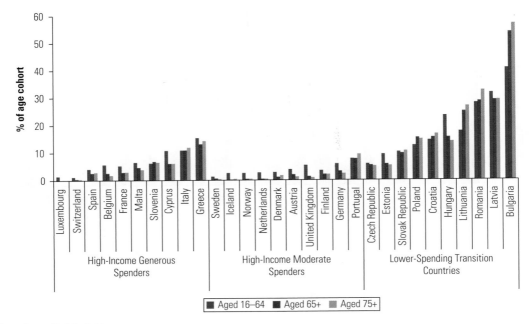

population.[4] Among the Lower-Spending Transition Countries, from suffer pensioners greater material deprivation in Bulgaria, Croatia, Lithuania, Romania, and Poland (Eurostat poverty measures, which refer to relative poverty, differ from the absolute poverty measures shown in figure 3.19). Both sets of evidence suggest that in most countries, the elderly are not poorer than the working-age population.

Poverty declined by a similar degree for both pensioner and nonpensioner households between 2001 and 2010 in countries where data are available, with the exception of Croatia, where poverty increased for pensioner households, and Bosnia and Herzegovina and Georgia, where poverty increased among households with very old pensioners (figure 3.21). In Romania, Serbia, Armenia, and the Kyrgyz Republic, the poverty status of pensioners improved more than that of nonpensioner households. In Hungary, Lithuania, Poland, Kosovo, Bosnia and Herzegovina, Moldova, and Turkey, pensioner households were less poor in 2010 than in 2001 but showed less improvement than nonpensioner households.

Consumption by households with and without pensioners is also similar (figure 3.22). Consumption in some sense can be a better measure of a pensioner's well-being than income, since many

FIGURE 3.21

Reduction in Poverty across All Households with and without Pensioners, Selected European and Central Asian Economies, 2001–2010

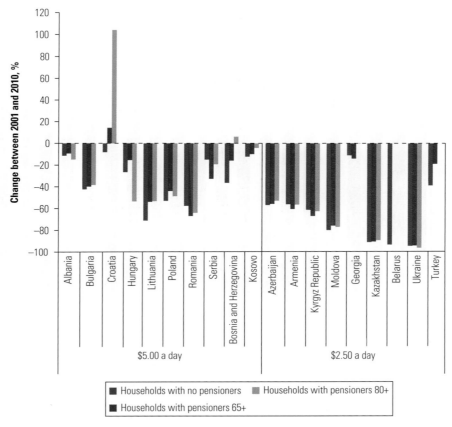

Source: Household survey data.

countries provide pensioners with various discounts on fuel, electricity, transportation, bread, entertainment, medicines, and other goods. These in-kind payments and discounts help increase the pensioner's consumption but might not be reflected in income. Furthermore, a pensioner's income is often taxed less than wage income, increasing the difference in disposable income and consumption even further. In most countries, households with pensioners have per capita consumption above 100 percent of the per capita consumption of nonpensioner households. Consumption by households with pensioners is below consumption by households without pensioners in Lithuania, Croatia, Moldova, Bosnia and Herzegovina, and Azerbaijan. These are some of the same countries for which pensioner households had higher income poverty rates than nonpensioner households. In all other countries, households with

FIGURE 3.22

Comparison of per Capita Consumption by Households with and without Pensioners, Selected European and Central Asian Economies

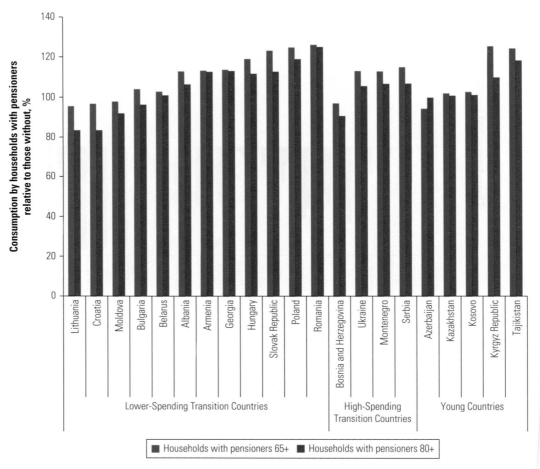

Source: Household survey data, latest available year.

pensioners have higher consumption per capita than households without pensioners.

A more direct way to evaluate the adequacy of pensions in their ability to replace income is to compute gross replacement rates, defined as the average pension benefit divided by average wage. This is essentially a measure of what proportion of wage income is replaced by pension benefits on average. The data in figure 3.23 show a wide variance in replacement rates across countries. Some countries provide pensions that replace a fairly substantial portion of today's average wage, which is typically higher than the average wage earned by the person during his or her working career and higher than the wages on which the person made contributions.

FIGURE 3.23

Average Pension Benefit Relative to Average Wage, Selected European and Central Asian Economies, 2009

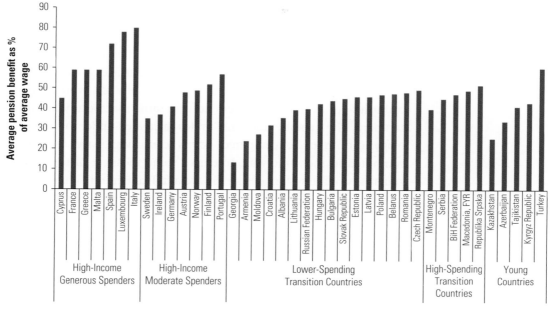

Source: Country-provided data.

Note: The Federation of Bosnia-Herzegovina (BiH Federation) and Republika Srpska, which together make up the country of Bosnia and Herzegovina, have separate pension systems and are treated as separate data points in the figure.

Other countries, like Georgia, are providing pensions that cover a relatively small proportion of today's average wage. Given that most countries tax wages more than they tax pensions, and require social security contributions[5] on wages but not on pensions, replacement rates as a proportion of net wages are often much higher, sometimes exceeding 100 percent.

All of this evidence suggests that pensioners in most transition countries are doing as well as nonpensioners, if not better. This is not to claim that all individual pensioners are doing well, as there are unquestionably some who suffer from material deprivation in all of these countries. However, where benefit increases are being considered, a selective targeted approach seems to be more appropriate than a blanket increase in pensions for all. In some countries, benefits might also be adjusted downward without making pensioners worse off than the working-age population and children.

While the discussion above provides a snapshot of where pensioners are today, considering future pension levels is even more important, especially given various reforms that are still unfolding in the region. The APEX methodology used by the Organisation for Economic

Co-operation and Development can provide some insight into the generosity of pension system designs, taking into account all of the reforms that have been legislated and are being implemented gradually. While the projected replacement rates are not applicable to any one person or even to groups of people in a specific country, they show the results for a hypothetical individual who starts work at age 20 in the year 2010, earning the average wage of that country. That person is further assumed to work continuously until retirement age, always earning the average wage of the current year, and all such workers in all countries are assumed to experience the same macroeconomic environment. The hypothetical benefit rates calculated under this methodology can then be compared across countries, since they were computed in the same way, to derive some measure of the relative generosity of the system design toward a full-career individual.

Figure 3.24 shows the benefit that an average earner would receive relative to the prevailing average wage. Pension systems across countries will provide very different outcomes for pensioners, under common assumptions. Typically, pension schemes are expected to provide benefits equal to 40 to 50 percent of wages for full-career earners. The benefits currently provided are considerably

FIGURE 3.24

Hypothetical Wage Replacement Rates for Individuals Earning the Average Wage and Beginning Work in 2010 in the Pension Systems of Selected European and Central Asian Economies

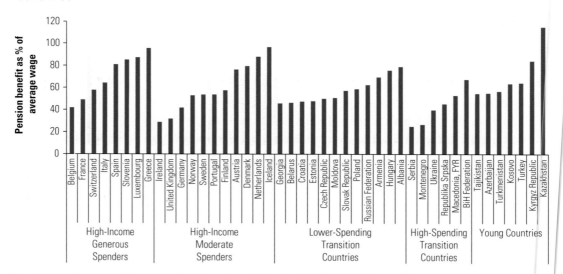

Source: Based on data from the OECD Pension Modeling Team, using methodology from the OECD series *Pensions at a Glance.*

Note: The Federation of Bosnia-Herzegovina (BiH Federation) and Republika Srpska, which together make up the country of Bosnia and Herzegovina, have separate pension systems and are treated as separate data points in the figure.

higher than that for a significantly shorter average career except in the FSU countries, where they fall within that range. The High-Income Generous Spender countries have hypothetical future benefits averaging 70 percent, while the High-Income Moderate Spender countries have hypothetical future benefits averaging 60 percent. However, within these two groups, Spain, Slovenia, Luxembourg, Greece, Austria, Denmark, the Netherlands, and Iceland are well above those averages. The Lower-Spending and High-Spending Transition Countries, which have been active reformers, have lower average replacement rates, at 58 percent and 43 percent respectively, although the average for the High-Spending Transition Countries is brought down by future lower—but unlikely—benefits in both Serbia and Montenegro. The Young Countries average a very high 72 percent, but this is largely due to the extremely high benefits in Kazakhstan, which skew the average upward.

Replacement rates for individuals earning half the average wage illustrate how well protected a low-income person might be under

FIGURE 3.25

Hypothetical Wage Replacement Rates for Individuals Earning Half the Average Wage and Beginning Work in 2010 in the Pension Systems of Selected European and Central Asian Economies

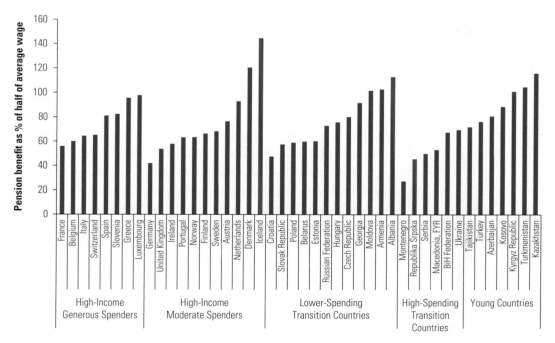

Source: Based on data from the OECD Pension Modeling Team, using methodology from the OECD series *Pensions at a Glance.*
Note: The Federation of Bosnia-Herzegovina (BiH Federation) and Republika Srpska, which together make up the country of Bosnia and Herzegovina, have separate pension systems and are treated as separate data points in the figure.

these various pension systems (figure 3.25). The ordering of countries in this case changes only slightly. Average replacement for individuals earning half the average wage comes in at 76 percent for
High-Income Generous Spenders, 77 percent for High-Income
Moderate Spenders, 77 percent for Lower-Spending Transition
Countries, 52 percent for High-Spending Transition Countries, and
92 percent for the Young Countries. These values suggest that all of
the regions tend to protect lower-income elderly with work histories,
providing higher replacement rates for them than for the average
earner. It is also worth noting that in Denmark, Iceland, Moldova,
Armenia, Albania, the Kyrgyz Republic, Turkmenistan, and
Kazakhstan, a person earning half the average wage and continuously contributing throughout his career would have higher income
once he retires compared to the income he earns while working.
While this might appear to be an indicator of excessive old-age insurance, in reality many lower-income contributors do not have full
careers and will likely retire with lower pensions than those suggested by the figure.

While these replacement rates seem reasonable and sometimes
even high, they should be regarded as the maximum that individuals can expect to receive. Most people do not begin work at age 20
and work continuously until reaching retirement age. They also do
not begin work at the average wage, but typically begin at some
lower wage and receive wage increases as their experience increases.
Therefore, someone who retires at the average wage might receive
the replacement rates shown, but as a percentage of a lower career-
long average wage and not the pre-retirement wage, which tends to
be higher. Also, the replacement rates shown here reflect what pensioners will receive in their first year of retirement. With the trend
toward inflation indexation, the average pension that an individual
receives during his retirement period could be considerably lower.
However, this analysis suggests that some countries with higher
replacement rates might have room to adjust benefits further as the
demographic crisis nears, while others will have to make adjustments elsewhere.

The increase in informal employment in the transition countries
in the last 20 years means that in the future many people will not
have accumulated a sufficient formal sector contribution history to
qualify for a pension. In contrast, today most elderly have substantial
past work histories and are collecting benefits on that basis.
Figure 3.26 shows the percentage of elderly who are currently collecting regular pension benefits and the percentage of elderly who
can expect to collect benefits in the future. Projections here are based

FIGURE 3.26

Percentage of Elderly Receiving Social Insurance Benefits in Selected European and Central Asian Economies, 2010 and 2050

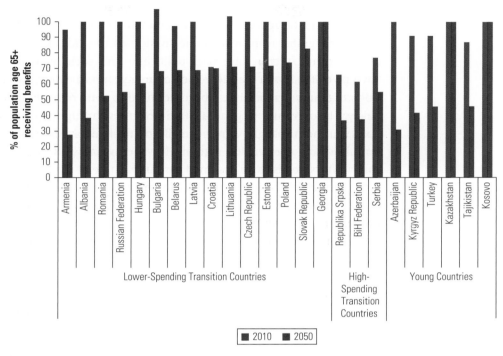

Source: Country-provided data.

Note: The Federation of Bosnia-Herzegovina (BiH Federation) and Republika Srpska, which together make up the country of Bosnia and Herzegovina, have separate pension systems and are treated as separate data points in the figure.

on the percentage of the population currently in prime working years, defined as those aged 35–39, who contribute to the social security system today.

Of the 24 countries where detailed age-specific data were available, only in Croatia, both entities of Bosnia and Herzegovina, and Serbia is the percentage of elderly currently collecting benefits less than 80 percent. One explanation for the lower coverage rates in the former Yugoslavia is the relatively common occurrence of single-earner families, even in the pre-1990 period. As a result, older women who never worked in the formal sector and whose spouses are still alive are not yet collecting pensions. In the future, based on current labor force participation and contribution records, only about 60 percent of the elderly in the Central Europe subregion will be eligible for pensions; elsewhere in transition countries, the number falls to 50 percent or less. The three countries with universal pensions, Georgia, Kazakhstan, Kosovo, and will continue to pay benefits to 100 percent of the elderly population.

Governments need to start thinking about how they will address the needs of the 40–50 percent of elderly who will have no pension rights in the future. The solution for each country will depend on its own circumstances, but the issue of future elderly without pension rights cannot be ignored. First, whether or not governments have explicit programs to provide some support to the elderly who were not in formal sector jobs, it is politically and socially difficult to have no provision in place for such a large group of elderly. Second, from an equity perspective, it becomes hard to deny rights to individuals who contribute to general state revenues through value-added taxes, but not through payroll contributions, if general revenue ends up subsidizing the pension system. However, what is offered to noncontributors needs to be designed carefully. Some of the contributors today are already only contributing for enough years and on the basis of the lowest wage required to become eligible for a minimum pension. Benefits provided to those who do not contribute reduce the incentive to contribute and might result in a reduction in the number of contributors. Offering a universal pension to all removes this distortion, but this is a more expensive approach than providing it only to those who do not have alternative means. Alternatively, benefits could be offered to noncontributors at higher ages, which might provide incentives to individuals to contribute so that they might retire earlier.

The sections above discuss policy makers' intentions in undertaking reform. The outcome of the reforms also rests heavily on general economic developments in the countries and in the region as a whole.

Influence of Economic and Political Cycles on Pension Reforms

Transition countries started their pension reform process vigorously. Countries in Central Europe chose their bold new pension designs in the late 1990s and early 2000s. The countries of the FSU that chose to radically change their pension system designs did so around the same time, while Balkan countries reformed a bit later, in the mid-2000s. At the time of setting their new pension system designs in place, some countries, like Hungary, also restructured their existing pension liabilities. In the Hungarian case, for workers choosing to switch to the new pension design, liabilities accrued to date were reduced by 25 percent. The majority of the reformers set retirement ages on a gradually increasing path, often narrowing the gap between male and female eligibility requirements. Formulas governing the conventional pay-as-you-go scheme component were often revised, lengthening past wage-averaging periods, tightening the link between benefits and contributions, and linking benefit indexation to inflation or some mixture of inflation and wage growth. Given assumptions at the time about high long-term GDP growth and coverage expansion, these systems were generally expected to return to fiscal sustainability in the medium term, or at least to significantly narrow pension deficits in that time frame.

During the economic boom years of the mid-2000s, the pace of reforms slowed. Echo boomers—the children of baby boomers—were joining the labor market in great numbers. This was coupled with increased formalization of the labor market fueled by the high rate of economic growth. The numbers of contributors grew. Wages also rose rapidly, and a greater proportion of wages was declared. The economic boom was felt most strongly in countries of Central Europe that were also boosted by early entry to the EU or the promise of imminent entry. Fueled by credit expansion, countries like Russia also grew rapidly, benefiting from buoyant commodity markets. All these developments led to contribution revenue growth that exceeded even the most optimistic projections in these countries. As in so many instances described in chapter 2, the rise in the pay-as-you-go and general budget revenues led to increased generosity of benefits. Retirement ages continued to increase, but tight benefit indexation rules were undermined and different benefit supplements were added.

Some original public pension scheme parameters proved socially and politically unsustainable in the high-growth environment, especially those governing benefit indexation. Real wage growth reached double digits in some countries, and pensioners were feeling left behind. Some revision of benefit indexation rules was therefore in order. However, instead of carefully discussing the options and ensuring long-term sustainability of proposed changes, for example by trading elimination of early retirement for a higher indexation rate, politicians and pension scheme administrators tended to raise pensions as much as current revenue would allow. Luckily, some of the new revenue was redirected to individual savings accounts in countries that had instituted them, which may have prevented pensions from being raised to even more unsustainable levels.

Countries also strayed from their chosen reform path in other ways. The high-growth environment offered a perfect opportunity to pay down some of the transition costs with swelling pension scheme and general budget revenues and increasingly high-priced public asset sales. Many countries were instead tempted by low borrowing costs and built up public debt rapidly. Accruing a small reserve fund against economic shocks was part of almost every original pension reform plan, but this rarely occurred on a significant scale during the boom years. Policy makers started to forget that the observed increase in contributor numbers could only be a temporary phenomenon, as demographic projections were increasingly pessimistic due to the steadily low fertility rate and strong emigration outflows.

The pace of rapid change that these economies faced as they transitioned from centrally planned economies to market economies was also politically unsettling, particularly in new democracies with relatively new political parties. It was not uncommon to find people voting for a government that promised to restore the old system or status quo following a period of vigorous reforms. As a result, the series of public pension reforms and enabling reforms in labor markets and financial markets envisaged by the original reformers, and expected to eventually lead to financial sustainability, never happened. In some cases, the reforms not only did not move forward but actually moved in the opposite direction.

The financial crisis caught public pension schemes unprepared. Like the economic boom, the crisis was felt most strongly in Central European economies, which among the transition countries had developed deeper financial markets and stronger trade links with Western Europe. Contributor numbers dropped and revenue quickly declined, but pension spending stayed at the same level, as it was impossible to change the number of pensioners who had already been granted pensions and difficult to reduce their benefits. In fact, the inflow of new pensioners increased, as many older workers chose an early retirement option or, with rising unemployment, attempted to qualify for a disability pension. Many countries stopped indexing benefits and some even attempted to cut pension payments. End-of-year bonus payments for pensioners in countries like Bulgaria and Hungary were no longer paid. Pensions of working pensioners were curtailed. All these measures tended to be of an ad hoc nature, presented unpredicted negative surprises for pensioners, eroded public trust in the system, and led to reduced incentives to contribute. However, even these relatively drastic measures were not able to bring pension spending to the level of sharply reduced revenues. General state budgets were also stretched to the limit and could not offer much help.

Unable to ensure financial sustainability of the pension system, policy makers were forced to revise the design. In response to fiscal pressures, some countries decided to temporarily or permanently reduce contribution flows to the individual pension savings accounts (discussed in more detail in chapter 4). With their hands tied by constitutional and political constraints, politicians turned to the resources accumulating in the second-pillar pension funds to bail out the first-pillar (or public) pension system. While in some cases suboptimal pension design did require revisions—as in Kazakhstan, where a flat pension component was introduced to protect the poorest population—more frequently these forced changes were not part of a productive pension policy and masked the lack of real reform. A reasonable fiscal policy cushion should have been created soon after the chosen pension system design was in place and maintained so that the system could withstand economic downturns. Similarly, open public dialogue about long-term trends in the pension system could have helped to ensure broad public support for the chosen design and fiscally sustainable scheme parameters, discouraging drastic policy changes.

While immediate responses to the onset of the financial crisis tended toward ad hoc reform measures, the subsequent reaction to the economic downturn was slightly more strategic. As the financial crisis started to enlarge into an economic crisis in Western and Central Europe, the FSU countries, Balkan countries, and Turkey started to find themselves under fiscal stress from spillover effects. This forced policy makers to return to a reform agenda, and many countries legislated further rises in retirement ages and reaffirmed their commitment to more stringent benefit indexation rules. Others, including several Balkan countries, found that advancing the reform agenda further became difficult, especially given extremely high unemployment rates. In some cases, as in Greece and Italy, the reforms had to be extremely painful, marked by substantial cuts in pensions and sharp overnight increases in retirement ages, pushing the limits of social acceptance. It remains to be seen whether these reforms, forced on the population by the financial crisis without much public debate, can hold once economic growth returns.

As of 2013, five of the 14 countries that originally instituted private pension savings accounts have reduced contribution flows into these accounts, but of these five, only Estonia has reaffirmed its commitment to fully return to the previous pension system design. The remaining four feel they are still unable to recommit to the transition costs required. The private pension savings accounts were meant to reduce the public pension expenditures when the countries start to age. These countries now need alternative strategies to reduce future pension liabilities and ensure that social goals of their pension systems can still be met in the long term. More details on these reversals can be found in the next chapter.

Policy Conclusions

The countries of Europe and Central Asia have undertaken an active reform agenda, but with limited impact, particularly in light of the demographics they are facing. Retirement ages have risen, but these adjustments have been more or less matched by increases in life expectancy. Pension spending has not fallen for the region overall, nor have benefits become less generous. The reforms also have not been very equitable: the majority of countries did not restructure pension liabilities accrued to date, but instead grandfathered old pension promises for most current pensioners and older workers, while young cohorts in some countries face harsh benefit declines. The self-adjusting mechanisms, adopted by many countries in order to slowly decrease benefit package generosity, have been undermined in many cases by ad hoc pension increases whenever pensions seem to fall below expectations of the public, however unrealistic these expectations may be.

During the years of the economic boom, countries relaxed their reform efforts. They did not take advantage of the high-growth environment to pay transition costs and strengthen government and pension program balance sheets, which was especially needed in the countries that had elected to introduce private pension savings accounts. Rather, policy makers started to act as if the choice of pension system design could solve long-term fiscal sustainability problems by itself, without the hard work of continued parametric reforms.

When the financial crisis hit, they were forced to make revisions to their chosen pension system designs. As a consequence of the crisis, contributor numbers dropped, contribution revenue declined sharply, and new pensioner inflows increased. Despite some hurried actions to curb spending, large pension program deficits could not be closed, and a few of the countries that had adopted individual pension saving accounts decided to redirect some or all of the contribution flows from them to the cash-strapped pay-as-you-go schemes, on a temporary or permanent basis. These countries have improved their short-run fiscal circumstances but have worsened their long-term pension liabilities, putting them farther from achieving fiscal sustainability of their pension systems together with adequacy of benefits. They will now need to make deeper reforms in their public pension systems than they would otherwise have had to make. Policy makers in these countries must now think of alternative strategies for reducing future pension liabilities and ensuring that the social goals of their pension systems can be met in the long term—and they will need to build the political consensus to do so.

Looking forward, the reforms legislated to date do not appear to have been sufficient to curb the projected growth of pension spending. This suggests that more reforms may be necessary unless new financing sources are found or the number of contributors increases substantially. Historically, reforms that did not provide adequate benefits, as defined by social consensus of the time, were not politically sustainable, as they were subject to ad hoc revisions. Social sustainability of the needed reforms will continue to require tireless educational campaigns, open discussion of inherent trade-offs in pension policy, and public acceptance of the sacrifices required. It remains to be seen whether social expectations of what is considered adequate pension provision can shift before the demographic crisis takes hold with full force and drives a much more dramatic revaluation of expectations.

While pensioners as a whole do not appear to be poorer than other cohorts today, countries have set up very different benefit levels for the years ahead. While some countries may have space for further benefit adjustment, others have only limited room to maneuver without sacrificing benefit adequacy, even under the most stringent definitions. In these cases, availability of retirement savings to supplement low publicly provided benefits will be particularly important. Finally, transition countries need to address the issue of old-age support for those who are not part of the formal labor market and who will begin to retire in substantial numbers in the next 20 years.

Annex 3A The Polish Experience with Curbing Early Retirement

When Poland began its economic transition, the country inherited a typical pension system with widespread early retirement privileges. The list of occupations eligible for early retirement covered more than 300 jobs and 1,000 types of workplaces. Separate laws gave early retirement rights to miners, railway workers, teachers, members of army, police, border guards, professional firefighters, prison guards, judges, and prosecutors. Women with long careers could retire at age 55 if they had worked for 30 years or more. The average actual retirement age at the beginning of the 1990s was around 56 for women and

58–59 for men, even though the legislated retirement ages were 60 for women and 65 for men. Early retirement was also possible through pre-retirement benefits and allowances granted to workers who lost their jobs due to restructuring or bankruptcy of their employer.

Given the long list of occupations with early pension rights, a new approach was proposed in 1999. Under the reform, which covered people born after 1948, early retirement was to be significantly limited by introducing new "bridging pensions." Instead of revising the existing list of occupations eligible for early retirement, the reform defined two broad categories of work that confer the right to bridging pensions. These are (a) work in special conditions, and (b) work of a special nature. The first refers to work conditions that cannot be changed and that may harm the health of workers who work in such conditions until retirement age (for example, work underwater or underground). The second refers to jobs where the worker (for example, a pilot) is directly responsible for the safety and lives of other people. The definitions and lists were developed with the participation of occupational health specialists. Anyone who had worked in the occupations listed before 1999 is eligible to retire up to 5 years early with a bridging pension. Once the person reaches legal retirement age, the bridging pension is discontinued and a regular old-age pension begins. The reform did not change the legal retirement age, which remained at 60 years for women and 65 years for men.

Initially the plan was to introduce bridging pensions in 2007. However, because of political disagreements, parliamentary elections held in 2005 and 2007, and protests by miners in 2005 (which also resulted in miners regaining the previous defined-benefit early retirement scheme), the bridging pensions law was finally adopted only in 2008 and came into force in 2009.

The reform was launched at a time of economic slowdown in Poland. Despite the unfavorable labor market situation, the number of people receiving early retirement payments dropped from 1.53 million in 2008 to 860,000 in 2012. At the same time, the employment rate of people aged 55–64 increased from 31.6 percent to 38.7 percent (figure 3A.1). The average age at retirement also increased, particularly for women (by 3.7 years between 2008 and 2012), and the number of newly granted old-age pensions decreased. Unfortunately, the number of retiring men increased after the Constitutional Court ruled that men born between 1944 and 1948 could retire at age 60 if they had worked for more than 35 years (figure 3A.2a). This reduced the overall positive impact of the reform. The reform is expected to have more impact on men's pensions from 2013 onward.

FIGURE 3A.1

Early Retirement Rate and Employment Rate of Older Workers in Poland, 1997–2012

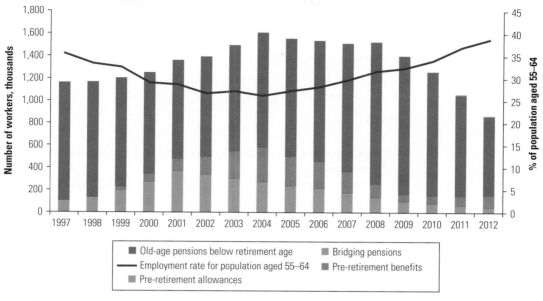

Sources: ZUS (Social Insurance Institution); Eurostat Statistics Database (employment rate).

FIGURE 3A.2

New Old-Age Pensioners and Average Actual Retirement Age for Men and Women in Poland, 1999–2011

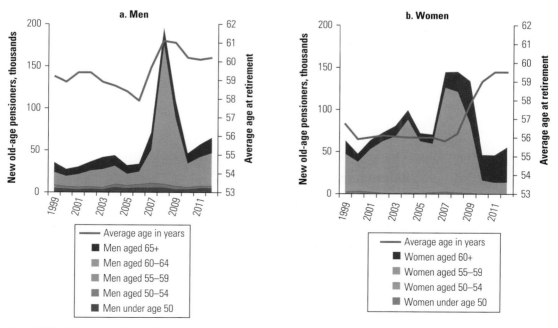

Sources: ZUS (Social Insurance Institution), with data disaggregation by the Institute for Structural Research in Warsaw.

Curbing early retirement eventually led to changes in the official retirement age. In 2012 the government enacted a further increase in the legal retirement age by 3 months each calendar year, aimed at equalizing the legal retirement age at 67 for both men and women. This means that men will retire at age 67 from 2020 and women from 2040.

Notes

1. The discussion of self-adjusting mechanisms draws heavily on Zviniene (forthcoming).
2. Political scientists Guardiancich and Weaver (2012) refer to these as stealth reforms.
3. This section draws heavily from Abels (forthcoming).
4. "Severe material deprivation" is defined by Eurostat as the inability to afford at least four of the following items: (a) pay rent, mortgage, or utility bills; (b) keep the home adequately warm; (c) face unexpected expenses; (d) eat meat or proteins regularly; (e) go on holiday; (f) a television set; (g) a washing machine; (h) a car; (i) a telephone. While this definition is significantly different from the absolute poverty measures used by the World Bank, the point that pensioners are not usually more poor than nonpensioners remains valid.
5. "Social security contributions" refers to the broad set of payroll taxes that finance pensions, unemployment insurance, health insurance, sickness and maternity benefits, as well as worker injury benefits. The exact mix of benefits varies from country to country. Pension contributions, a subset of social security contributions, affect pension system revenues and the rights that individuals hold in the pension system. But in the discussion here, when comparing income when one receives a pension to income when one receives a wage, the correct approach is to compare pension income on which no contributions are paid to wage income from which all relevant contributions have been subtracted.

References

Abels, Miglena. Forthcoming. "Experience with Disability Program Reforms in Central and Eastern Europe." World Bank, Washington, DC.

Chomik, Rafal, and Edward R. Whitehouse. 2010. "Trends in Pension Eligibility Ages and Life Expectancy, 1950–2050." OECD Social, Employment, and Migration Working Paper 105, Organisation for Economic Co-operation and Development, Paris.

De Jong, Philip R. 2008. "Recent Changes in Dutch Disability Policy." APE (Public Economics), The Hague, the Netherlands.

European Commission. 2012a. *The 2012 Ageing Report: Economic and Budgetary Projections for the 27 EU Member States (2010–2060).* Brussels: European Commission, Directorate-General for Economic and Financial Affairs.

———. 2012b. "An Agenda for Adequate, Safe and Sustainable Pensions." White Paper, European Commission, Brussels.

———. 2012c. *Pension Adequacy in the European Union 2010–2050.* Brussels: European Commission, Directorate-General for Employment, Social Affairs and Inclusion, Social Protection Committee.

Eurostat Statistics Database. European Commission, Brussels. http://epp .eurostat.ec.europa.eu/portal/page/portal/statistics/search_database.

Guardiancich, Igor, and R. Kent Weaver. 2012. "The Political Economy of Pension Reform." Presentation at "Reforming Pension Systems in Europe and Central Asia: A Joint European Commission–World Bank Conference," Brussels, June 25–26.

Hirose, Kenichi, ed. 2011. *Pension Reform in Central and Eastern Europe: In Times of Crisis, Austerity and Beyond.* Budapest: International Labour Organization.

Holzmann, Robert, and Edward Palmer, eds. 2006. *Pension Reform: Issues and Prospects for Non-Financial Defined Contribution (NDC) Schemes.* Washington, DC: World Bank.

Lafortune, Gaétan, Gaëlle Balestat, and the Disability Study Expert Group Members. 2007. "Trends in Severe Disability among Elderly People: Assessing the Evidence in 12 OECD Countries and the Future Implications." OECD Health Working Paper 26, Organisation for Economic Co-operation and Development, Paris.

Mink, Reimund. 2005. "General Government Pension Obligations in Europe." *IFC Bulletin* 28 (1): 199–209. http://www.bis.org/ifc/publ/ifcb28y.pdf.

MISSOC (European Commission, Mutual Information System on Social Protection). *Comparative Tables on Social Protection.* http://ec.europa.eu /social/main.jsp?catId=815&langId=en.

Müller, Christoph, Bernd Raffelhüschen, and Olaf Weddige. 2009. *Pension Obligations of Government Employer Pension Schemes and Social Security Pension Schemes Established in EU Countries.* Freiburg, Germany: Research Center for Generational Contracts, Freiburg University.

NSSI (National Social Security Institute of Bulgaria). 2013. *Statistical Yearbook on Pensions 2012.* Sofia: NSSI.

OECD (Organisation for Economic Co-operation and Development). 2007. "Sickness and Disability Schemes in the Netherlands." Background Paper for OECD Disability Review, OECD, Paris.

———. 2011. *Pensions at a Glance 2011: Retirement-Income Systems in OECD and G20 Countries.* Paris: OECD.

U.S. Social Security Administration. Various years. *Social Security Programs throughout the World.* http://www.ssa.gov/policy/docs/progdesc/ssptw/.

Van Sonsbeek, Jan-Maarten, and Raymund Gradus. 2012. "Estimating the Effects of Recent Disability Reforms in the Netherlands." *Oxford Economic Papers.* doi:10.1093/oep/gps043.

Whitehouse, Edward R., Anna D'Addio, Rafal Chomik, and Andrew Reilly. 2009. "Two Decades of Pension Reform: What Has Been Achieved and What Remains to be Done?" *Geneva Papers on Risk & Insurance—Issues & Practice* 34: 515–35.

World Bank. HDNSP Pensions Database. Human Development Network Social Protection, World Bank, Washington, DC.

———. World Development Indicators (database). http://data.worldbank .org/data-catalog/world-development-indicators.

Zaidi, Asghar, and Edward R. Whitehouse. 2009. "Should Pension Systems Recognise 'Hazardous and Arduous Work'?" OECD Social, Employment, and Migration Working Paper 91, Organisation for Economic Co-operation and Development, Paris.

ZUS (Social Insurance Institution). 2012. *Social Insurance in Poland.* Warsaw: ZUS.

Zviniene, Asta. Forthcoming. "In Search of the Ideal Self-Adjusting PAYG System." World Bank, Washington, DC.

CHAPTER 4

The Role of Savings in the Provision of Retirement Income

Introduction

Because of the inverting pyramid, as explained in chapter 3, most European countries will need to adjust pension benefits in order for the schemes to remain fiscally sustainable. In the context of uncertainty about the expected value of public pensions, retirement savings can play an important role in ensuring that individuals do not suffer severe contractions in their consumption pattern after retirement. This chapter analyzes the different mechanisms for incentivizing savings, including public reserve funds as well as voluntary and mandatory savings for retirement.

Consumption smoothing and poverty reduction are the main objectives of any pension system, but the role of savings is stronger in the first. While consumption smoothing can be accomplished through contributory systems, it might be more efficient to finance poverty reduction through government general revenues. Retirement savings are an efficient way to support and preserve purchasing power after retirement. Consumption smoothing implies not only intragenerational smoothing (contributors are able to preserve consumption levels after retirement), but also intergenerational smoothing (retirees of different generations but similar characteristics should receive similar interest rates on their contributions).

Considering the need to diversify the sources of retirement income, it is essential to ensure that savings are properly invested. In the context of multipillar pension schemes, with an important part of the expected retirement income to come from the pay-as-you-go (PAYG) system, it is essential to ensure that the assets of the funded component have low correlation with the repayment capacity of the government.[1] Investments in the domestic and international corporate sector are necessary to reduce the pension risk and support consumption smoothing in the population.

Savings not only provide a diversified source of income for individuals; they also have a positive effect on the growth rate of the economy. As savings have a dynamic effect on increasing growth of gross domestic product (GDP), the impact of savings should be analyzed from an intertemporal perspective. Both the capacity to deliver future income and the effect on economic growth need to be taken into consideration at the time of evaluating the importance of funded pension schemes for the countries.

The effects of pension reforms on savings and investment are not evident because of the involvement of multiple agents. The seminal work of Feldstein and Horioka (1980) helped build consensus on the positive correlation between national savings and the rate of domestic investment. Subsequent studies, including those by Calderón and Schmidt-Hebbel (2003) and Corbo and Schmidt-Hebbel (2003), confirm these findings for a broader number of countries. The effect of the introduction of mandatory funded schemes on national savings needs to be analyzed separately. It depends on four factors[2]:

- *The change in the government's overall saving or surplus stemming from the transitional pension deficit caused by the reform and the fiscal response to that deficit, as reflected in the nonpension deficit.* The government financing of the transitional deficit is one of the most delicate points in the implementation of pension reform, as governments have the capacity to offset the increases in households' savings with greater public sector deficits. As stated by Corsetti and Schmidt-Hebbel (1997), careful consideration should be given to the distortionary nature of the taxes that may need to be raised to finance the transitional deficit (in the case of a tax-financed reform) or to pay the government debt interests (in the case of a debt-financed reform).

- *The response of private saving to the change in total government saving.* This discussion is intrinsically related to the existence of Ricardian equivalence, which supports the view that the private sector responds to a change in public saving by adjusting its saving level by the same amount, but with the opposite sign. Under reasonable assumptions, including credit constraints, finite planning horizons, and different discount rates, the private sector does not fully offset the changes in public savings.

- *The new mandatory pension saving by households in the pension funds.* This is the gross effect of the increases in contribution rates.

- *The response by households in terms of voluntary saving.* Households may adjust their voluntary savings in response to the increases in mandatory pension saving.

While all four factors are important in explaining the overall behavior of savings, it is unlikely that countries will increase their savings ratios if governments follow debt-financing strategies. The evidence in the region suggests that gross national savings have remained relatively stable since the introduction of mandatory funded schemes (figure 4.1). The fact that these reforms have not had a significant impact on national savings rates in countries that reformed their pension systems is a reflection of the partial or total

FIGURE 4.1

Gross National Savings Rates as a Percentage of GDP in Selected European Economies, 2000–2012

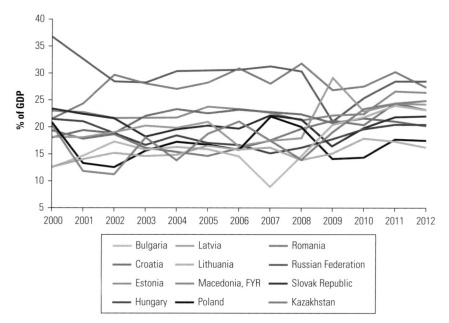

Source: IMF World Economic Outlook Database.

debt financing of the transitional deficit in the years that followed the reform.

Pension reforms are unlikely to have an impact on capital market development unless governments implement proactive public policies to develop the capital market. While the introduction of funded schemes creates an investable pool of assets, capital markets are unlikely to develop unless other enabling conditions are in place or developed simultaneously. More sophisticated capital markets can also help increase total factor productivity, which affects the potential GDP growth of the countries.[3] Even in countries as dynamic as Poland in listing small and medium-sized enterprises in the stock market, the volumes are unlikely to cope with the growth in assets of the pension funds. In this regard, participation of the pension funds in the privatization of assets owned by the state provides the basis for the supply of equity instruments. In the fixed income market, the creation of a government yield curve through issuance of government bonds provides the basis for pricing private sector instruments. The development of the capital market remains a challenge in smaller economies.

Modalities of Retirement Savings

While retirement savings may come from public or private sources, the motivation of public and private savings tends to be different. Public savings are typically designed to build reserves to sustain social security systems, but private savings are created as an additional source of retirement income for pensioners.

The strategy for managing pension fund assets needs to be related to the structure of liabilities of the fund. While the investment strategy of the reserve funds is conditioned on the expected availability of government resources for paying pensions, the investment strategy of private pension funds should be linked to the expected retirement age of the contributors. These different objectives should create different approaches to managing investment risk. In addition, the investment strategy of private savings should be conditioned on the expectation of retirement income derived from social security.[4]

Public Pension Reserve Funds

Public pension reserve funds are common in countries that want to support the sustainability of their social security systems. While in most cases these funds are created to help finance public pension

TABLE 4.1
Pension Reserve Funds in Selected European Economies, 2011

Economy	Fund or institution	Assets	
		US$, billions	% of GDP
Sweden	National Pension Funds (AP1–AP4 and AP6)	124.7	25.3
Spain	Social Security Reserve Fund	85.3	6.2
France[a]	AGIRC-ARRCO	71.7	2.7
France	Pension Reserve Fund (FRR)	40.7	1.6
Ireland	National Pensions Reserve Fund	17.4	8.4
Belgium	Zilverfonds	23.8	5.0
Norway	Government Pension Fund Norway	23.0	5.1
Portugal	Social Security Financial Stabilization Fund	11.5	5.2
Poland	Demographic Reserve Fund	3.7	0.8
Sovereign wealth funds with a pension focus[b]			
Norway	Government Pension Fund Global	553.8	121.7
Russian Federation	National Wealth Fund	87.2	5.1

Source: Country-provided data.
a. Figure is for year 2010.
b. Mandates of these funds go beyond the financing of pension expenditures.

schemes, they can also be used for making pension payments. In addition, the funding of public pension reserve funds may come from contributions, privatizations, or external sources of funds, such as oil revenues in the case of Norway.

Pension reserve funds are relatively small compared to the implicit pension debt of European countries. As shown in table 4.1, nine countries in Europe have public reserve funds and manage assets for amounts that are relatively low, especially when compared to the implicit pension debt obligations of these countries (figure 2.1).[5] For example, while France has implicit pension liabilities that amount to approximately 365 percent of GDP, the amount of assets accumulated in the pension reserve fund accounts for only 1.6 percent of GDP. The relatively small size of these funds compared to the government's implicit commitments creates doubts about their future effectiveness in paying the social security debt in these countries. Without a sizable and permanent source of funding, pension reserve funds will be insufficient to cope with the pension liabilities.

Asset allocation of public reserve funds varies by country. While the public reserve funds of Ireland, Sweden, and Norway have an asset allocation of more than 50 percent to equities, funds in Spain and Belgium are 100 percent invested in bonds (figure 4.2). Policy makers in the first group of countries have targeted a long-term

FIGURE 4.2

Public Pension Reserve Funds in Selected European Economies: Asset Allocation as a Percentage of Total Assets, 2011

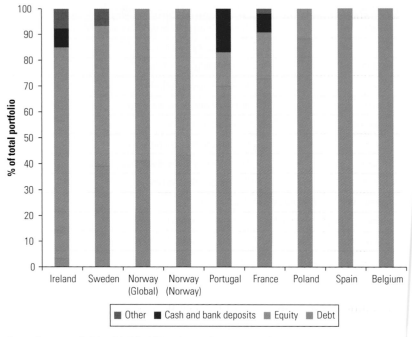

Sources: Country-provided data; World Bank Private Pensions (internal database).

strategy by diversifying assets based internationally. The funds in Portugal, France, and Poland have equity allocations of less than 20 percent of the total portfolio. As expected, performance of pension return guarantees in the past 3 years has been relatively low, but it is not different than performance of private pension schemes (table 4.2).

Public pension reserve funds in Europe have proven not to be immune to the financial crisis. The funds of France, Ireland, and Spain diverted their investment strategies to stabilize the domestic markets. In 2010, the French Pension Reserve Fund reduced foreign equity participation from 81 percent to 45 percent of the overall equity exposure, and foreign bond exposure from 68 percent to 19 percent of the overall bond exposure. In Ireland, the National Pensions Reserve Fund was required to participate in the rescue of the failed Irish banks, and a quarter of the fund assets were invested in Irish banks. Consequently, Irish public pension reserves dropped from $32.3 billion to $17.4 billion between 2010 and 2011. Currently, the majority of the Irish pension reserve fund assets are direct investments in equities of the Irish banking system.

FIGURE 4.6

Voluntary and Mandatory Pension Savings in Hungary, 2002–2012

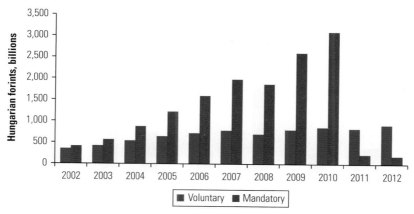

Source: Central Bank of Hungary.

Corporate structure and tax incentives are important drivers of voluntary pension systems. As a part of the compensation package, some state-owned companies (for example in Russia) offer pension benefits to their employees that are more generous than those offered by private sector companies. These agreements are typically supported by unions and respond to the corporate culture of the country. Also, in countries with a high proportion of workers in the formal sector and strong enforcement by the tax collection authority, voluntary pension plans have greater opportunity to grow.

The voluntary pension systems in the Netherlands and the United States provide good examples of the importance of the corporate structure and the presence of a strong tax collection authority in a highly formal labor market, respectively. As shown in figure 4.7, almost 90 percent of the labor force in the Netherlands is covered under these voluntary schemes, and this is considered part of the social contract between employers and employees. Given the support of the unions and corporations, voluntary pension schemes based on corporate plans typically have more consistency than those based purely on tax incentives. These schemes can hardly be replicated in countries with different corporate cultures.

In the case of the United States, the 401(k) plans are based on tax incentives and matching contributions from employers. For an economy with low levels of unionization, 401(k) plans offer a tax relief opportunity to employers and employees that makes these plans attractive. The success of the 401(k) plans in attracting contributors is based on the premise of a tax authority with

FIGURE 4.7
Coverage of Funded Pension Schemes in Selected Economies, 2010

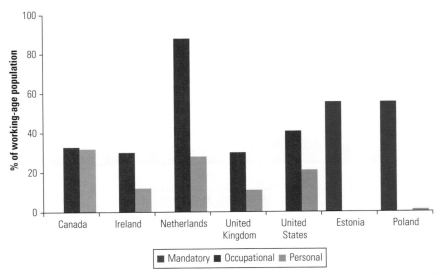

Sources: OECD 2012; Price and Rudolph 2013.

enforcement capacity, the tax benefits for employers in matching employees' contributions, a well-defined default option for new entrants (automatic enrollment), and a labor market with high participation in the formal sector. A similar type of system has insignificant effects in Ukraine, as the economy has a high proportion of workers in the informal sector and the government faces sizable challenges in the area of tax collection.

With progressive income tax structures, voluntary pension schemes tend to favor higher-income individuals. Tax-induced voluntary savings are mainly used by people who face higher income tax rates. This segment of the population has a higher level of substitution between pure voluntary savings and tax-induced retirement savings. In addition, individual savings plans are typically expensive to manage, as they require expensive platforms for distribution of products and sales. In countries with mandatory funded schemes, such as Estonia and Poland, only a small percentage of individuals participate in individual voluntary pension schemes (figure 4.7).[9] One important caveat is that the tax incentives and initial conditions are not necessarily comparable across countries. While tax incentives in the Czech Republic are relatively generous, they are minimal in Poland. As explained below, default options can play a role in motivating people to participate in the system.

Even in the best of cases, coverage of voluntary systems will be low. As shown in figure 4.7, with the exception of the Netherlands, the coverage level of voluntary pension schemes in developed economies such as Canada, the United Kingdom, and the United States is lower than 40 percent of the labor force. These levels of coverage will be insufficient to ensure consumption smoothing for the middle class in these countries. The expectations for coverage of voluntary pension systems are likely to be even lower in developing economies.

Public policy plays an important role in ensuring that voluntary pension portfolios are invested in line with an expected replacement rate. Most of the countries have liberal policies in terms of the portfolio allocation of voluntary savings, accepting the rationale that "It's my money and I can do whatever I want." While this argument is valid to an extent, these savings are incentivized with public money through tax breaks, and therefore the eligibility criteria for voluntary pension plans could be narrowed to plans that are effectively designed to complement the expected replacement rate. Without trying to be prescriptive, one can argue that public policy should play a more important role in guiding portfolio decisions in voluntary schemes. This becomes especially important in countries that will not be able to offer adequate replacement rates with public pension systems and defined contribution systems.

While the literature suggests that financial literacy may help increase savings (not necessarily retirement savings), financial literacy has a more limited effect on individuals' choices of portfolio allocation. In countries with relatively well developed capital markets, pension fund managers might offer many combinations of portfolios, and individuals decide how to invest their money. In the absence of proper financial education, contributors do not necessarily choose pension portfolios that are aligned to their long-term objectives. The low level of financial literacy is an important impediment to building portfolios that are consistent with an expected replacement rate in the future.

The likelihood that improvements in financial literacy will result in proper asset allocation in the near future is minimal. It will take at least two or three decades before such programs have an effect on decisions of savers, especially with respect to the importance of retirement savings and the effect of asset allocation decisions on future retirement income. Assuming that people start saving for retirement early in their life, it is unlikely that individuals with average skills will provide an elaborated response to the question of what portfolio, at each point in a person's life, is most likely to optimize the expected value of his or her pension at the expected retirement age.

This calculation typically requires a college degree in finance or economics or solid training in the financial markets.

The limitations of voluntary systems for achieving coverage and for committing individuals to contribute regularly provide an advantage to mandatory or quasi-mandatory systems. Consumption smoothing can only be achieved with a significant participation of workers, which voluntary schemes in most of the countries unfortunately cannot provide. Madrian (2013) suggests that matching contributions increase savings plan participation and contributions, but the impact is less significant than that of nonfinancial approaches, including automatic enrollment, simplification, planning aids, reminders, and other commitment devices. Mandatory or quasi-mandatory funded schemes for all segments of the population can be more effective in achieving coverage and contribution rates conducive to adequate replacement rates.

Mandatory funded schemes increase the probability of achieving a certain replacement rate for a broader group of future retirees. The main advantages of mandatory funded schemes are the possibility of reaching similar coverage of the social security system and ensuring a consistent contribution rate over an individual's working life.

Quasi-mandatory schemes offer an attractive way to address the weaknesses of voluntary schemes, namely coverage and contribution rate. While mandatory funded schemes are still a legitimate option, quasi-mandatory schemes can achieve similar outcomes by persuading workers to contribute, using both financial and nonfinancial incentives. Foremost among these is automatic enrollment, or auto-enrollment: workers are notified at the time of eligibility that they will be enrolled in the plan at a specified savings rate and asset allocation unless they actively elect not to participate or change the default selections.[10] Quasi-mandatory schemes are based on behavioral incentives that respond to the limited rationality of individuals. In a world with perfect rationality, individuals would make their choices without respect to the way options are presented. However, evidence suggests that given limited rationality, outcomes may vary when options are presented differently.[11] For example, the participation in voluntary savings when the default option is not to save (opt-in schemes) is much lower than when the default option is to save (opt-out schemes).

The extent to which quasi-mandatory systems are at all voluntary is an open question. Auto-enrollment schemes are based on the concept of "libertarian paternalism," which is elegantly presented by Thaler and Sunstein (2008). These authors argue that policy decisions need to take into account the limited rationality of individuals, and consequently default options can play an important role by providing a noncoercive "nudge" toward the desired behavior. Proper default options and proper communication strategies are essential for the success of these plans. However, if the communication strategy strongly promotes the benefits of the default option, it is not evident that the decisions made by individuals will be well informed and voluntary.

Madrian (2013) suggests that opt-out automatic enrollment is the most effective method for increasing participation in defined contribution schemes. The evidence on employer-sponsored savings plans in the United States shows that participation rates are substantially higher when enrollment is the default option.[12] In addition, the impact of automatic enrollment is greatest for young and low-income groups. The evidence on individual pension plans in the Slovak Republic supports these findings, and in the past 7 years the Slovak government has changed the default option four times as a means of incentivizing or disincentivizing participation in funded schemes.[13]

The main difference between the outcomes of the mandatory funded scheme and the opt-out auto-enrollment system has to do with the effect on retirement savings of the most vulnerable sectors of the population: younger and low-income workers. While the expected participation rate with auto-enrollment is much higher than participation in a purely voluntary (opt-in) scheme, it might still be lower than the coverage that results from a mandatory system. As it gives a way out to individuals with financial constraints and a preference for present consumption, auto-enrollment may still induce young and low-income workers to step out of the system. However, proper implementation might mitigate the incentives for opting out. Benartzi and Thaler (2013) suggest including four features in any comprehensive plan to facilitate adequate saving for retirement: availability, automatic enrollment, automatic investment, and automatic escalation.[14]

Given the fiscal cost of funded schemes, government budget considerations are biased criteria for selecting voluntary, auto-enrollment, or mandatory funded schemes. Since they are unable to cover a sizable part of the population, tax-incentivized, individual voluntary opt-in systems create lower fiscal costs than the other two options, but they tend to skew the allocation of fiscal resources toward segments of the population with higher income. Individual voluntary pension schemes actually tend to be more expensive for contributors than mandatory funded schemes because of market imperfections and high distribution costs. Although fees charged by mandatory schemes are high in some countries, fees charged by individual voluntary schemes tend to be even higher, creating an additional disincentive for participating in individual voluntary pension schemes.

Countries with advanced central collection and record-keeping platforms may consider extending these platforms to voluntary pension schemes. Taking advantage of their developed information technology systems, centralized account management system, and extensive distribution channels, social security agencies may consider making their low-cost infrastructure available to low-cost asset managers that can offer voluntary retirement savings. While these asset managers would need to be properly supervised, social security agencies may impose tight requirements in terms of fees. For example, besides the proper regulation from the relevant authority, the social security agency might be willing to collect and manage the accounts of a set of voluntary pension funds managed by independent fund managers. This could encourage the development of a low-cost asset management industry that could foster the development of the voluntary pension fund system.

Some innovative formulas for incentivizing retirement savings can be considered. In the Estonian case, people born before 1983 had the option of contributing to the mandatory funded scheme, but such an option implied an additional contribution by workers. This was called the 2+2+2, which meant a contribution rate of 2 percent of the wage from the employer, 2 percent from the employee, and 2 percent from the state. This simple construction makes it possible to achieve a more reasonable replacement rate (due to the higher contribution rate) at a more moderate fiscal cost during the transition.

Incentivizing savings should be attractive to many of the countries in the region that have decreased the relative size of the mandatory funded pillar and have had difficulty returning these schemes to pre-2010 levels because of expected fiscal constraints. As discussed above, the use of default option is essential to ensure success of the program: participation by individuals is expected to be completely different if they are given the option of making or not making an additional contribution. In addition, the more transparency the government provides on the expected replacement rates for individuals, the more likely it is that people will participate in the program. For example, according to the World Bank (2012), Poland's workers will see their replacement rates reduced by 20 percentage points in the next three to four decades. Consequently, the more the current generations internalize their relative decrease in retirement income compared to the current generation of retirees, the more the current contributors will be willing to participate in voluntary schemes.

Nondiscrimination tests can be powerful in ensuring participation of high- and low-income workers in voluntary pension programs. Personal voluntary programs are typically perceived as a tax incentive used only by high-income people, and consequently some governments are reluctant to expand these programs. Downsizing the tax benefits of personal voluntary plans and expanding the benefits of collective plans—subject to a nondiscrimination test—increases the likelihood of broad participation by lower-income workers in these retirement plans.

Nondiscrimination tests ensure that the contributions of non-highly compensated workers in a company amount to at least a minimum proportion of the contributions of the highly compensated workers. The test works from the perspective of incentives: highly compensated employees have an interest in obtaining tax benefits for their savings, but the regulation may require the plan to pass a nondiscrimination test as a condition for providing such benefits. Motivated by their own interests, highly compensated workers would work with company management and with nonhighly compensated workers and labor organizations (including unions) to ensure that a critical mass of nonhighly compensated workers participate in these retirement savings plans. Strategies for promoting voluntary contributions at the level of the company may include educational campaigns and matching fund contributions by the employers. It is essential for the success of these plans that highly compensated contributors do not receive the same tax benefits through voluntary contributions to personal plans. In the case of the United States, the collective plans (which include a nondiscrimination test) have an annual contribution limit of $17,500, while Individual Retirement Accounts (which resemble voluntary personal pension plans) have a limit of only $5,500.

Other Forms of Retirement Savings

For many people, the equity in their houses is considered a form of retirement savings. Homeowners can continue living in their houses after retirement, and this alternative to making rental payments is considered a form of income. However, the notion that housing prices are always stable or rising needs to be dismissed. Housing, like any other asset, is subject to changes in value: housing prices are affected by idiosyncratic factors (neighborhood, city, schools, etc.) and macroeconomic factors, including interest rates. While housing should be considered as an additional source of retirement savings, people need to complement these savings with other financial assets that can provide a more stable source of future retirement income.

In reverse mortgages, homeowners receive payments from an agency for the rest of their lives and transfer the property to the agency when they die. While this is a promising idea, allowing elderly people to maximize the equity in their houses, the transaction costs are relatively high, which makes this market difficult to develop in emerging economies. First of all, the housing market is not well standardized, and therefore there are large margins for setting the price of a house. Second, given an average retiree life expectancy of 20 years or more, the value of the house can change dramatically during that period of time. Third, once the price of the house has been set, the incentives for home maintenance decrease. Fourth, reverse mortgages are unlikely to be profitable in social housing or for the homes of middle- to lower-income retirees. This tends to bias reverse mortgage programs toward high-end earners, who arguably need them less than other retirees.

The Payout Phase of Funded Pension Schemes

A liberal approach with no restrictions on payout options is not consistent with a mandatory pension pillar that is predicated on the inability of workers to make adequate provision for their retirement needs. Some restrictions on lump-sum withdrawals are therefore advisable.[15]

Pensioners face several risks that often pull in opposite directions. For example, purchasing life annuities protects against longevity risk but eliminates the possibility of bequests. Meanwhile, investing in long-term assets addresses the investment risk but exposes holders to liquidity risks. Policy makers should target an adequate level of annuitization but should be wary of causing excessive annuitization.

A pragmatic approach is to adopt an integrated threshold replacement rate from the compulsory public and private pillars and mandate some form of annuitization in the funded pillar up to the level that reaches the integrated threshold rate. An integrated threshold of between 50 percent and 70 percent of the average real earnings (i.e., adjusted for inflation) over the last 10 years of employment is eminently sensible. Under this approach, unrestricted lump-sum withdrawals are not permitted, but once the threshold replacement rate is attained, any excess balances can be withdrawn.

All retirement products have their advantages, but they also suffer from shortcomings. Fixed nominal annuities do not protect against inflation. Fixed real annuities require access to long-duration inflation-indexed securities issued by both the public and private sectors; otherwise, they are overly expensive. Variable annuities are exposed to investment risk and require a very high level of transparency and integrity on the part of providers. Deferred annuities are difficult to price. Phased withdrawals and term annuities do not protect against longevity risk. Self-annuitization requires considerable financial expertise and is very difficult to manage in advanced old age.

Mandating a single retirement product for all retirees is not the answer, either. A single product avoids market fragmentation and self-selection and has the advantage of simplicity. However, it is not optimal because it disregards the significant shortcomings of all types of retirement products and forces all retiring workers to use the same product despite potentially large differences in risk preferences, longevity, and economic circumstances.

The optimal solution is often a constrained choice from a specified menu of retirement products, given varying circumstances within a country. Taking into account the merits and drawbacks of different types of retirement products and the varying preferences and circumstances of retiring workers, policy makers should allow constrained choice from a specified menu of retirement products to be offered. This would vary across countries, but in principle it should favor a combination of payout options, covering different products at a particular point in time as well as different payout options over time.

The introduction of government guarantee schemes covering all types of retirement products merits serious consideration. The government guarantees should cover benefit payments and could emulate the practice evolving in deposit insurance schemes, including upper limits on the amounts insured and a reasonable amount of coinsurance by pensioners in order to minimize the possible loss of market discipline at the point of purchase. The potential cost of government guarantees should be estimated, and such estimates should be used to determine risk-based premiums for annuity providers.

The Experience with Funded Pension Schemes

With different idiosyncratic features, pension reform in the region has generally followed a multipillar approach.[16] This includes a strong earnings-related PAYG component (public pension systems); mandatory or quasi-mandatory funded schemes (mandatory funded systems) of different sizes; and tax-induced voluntary pension schemes. Between 1998 and 2011, 12 countries in Europe and

Central Asia introduced multipillar pension reforms.[17] The Czech Republic introduced a mandatory funded scheme in 2013, and Armenia is planning to implement a mandatory funded scheme in 2014. Table 4.3 summarizes some key elements of the reformed pension systems in the region before the financial crisis.

During the pre-crisis period, many European and Central Asian countries increased the generosity of their PAYG benefits without proposing sustainable sources of financing. Many countries saw strong economic performance and temporary surpluses in the social security systems and used them to increase the generosity of pension benefits above the initial reform package. Most of these reforms were not complemented by austere fiscal reforms conducive to increases in savings and investments.

Performance of pension systems was mixed, but most of the countries managed to offer positive real returns. As shown in figure 4.8, in the pre-crisis period returns in Latvia and Russia were negative in real terms and below those in other countries. Returns were positive in the rest of the countries, including Poland, with an average return before the crisis of more than 10 percent in real terms. The 2008 financial crisis imposed major temporary losses on most of the pension funds, but most recovered part of the loss the following year (table 4.4). By measuring performance as the value added of pension funds over basic benchmarks (Sharpe ratios), Walker and Iglesias (2010) and Rudolph and Rocha (2007) provide evidence that pension funds in Estonia, Hungary, and Poland exceeded some basic benchmarks in terms of efficiency.

Moving forward, pension funds in the region face important challenges in the area of asset allocation. As shown in figure 4.9, government securities and bank deposits are still a sizable part of the portfolios of the pension funds. On average, they represent approximately two-thirds of the pension portfolios in a selected group of countries in the region that conducted pension reform (figure 4.10). Most countries need to move toward better diversification of assets in order to effectively diversify the future pension risk of individuals.

In countries with multiple types of systems, pension risk is diversified when asset portfolios of pension funds are invested in instruments with low correlation to the source of repayment for the public pension system. Diversification of pension portfolios into equities, corporate bonds, mortgage bonds, and international securities is essential to ensure that the repayment capacity of the state does not affect pensions of unfunded and funded systems. International diversification allows diversification of the sovereign risk, which allows contributors to hedge against country-specific idiosyncratic risks.

TABLE 4.3

Structure of Pension Systems, Selected European and Central Asian Economies, 2008

Country	Public scheme type	Public pension (PAYG) reform	Mandatory pillar contributions	Enactment date	Who participates
Bulgaria	Defined benefit	Retirement age: 60/55 → 63/60	2% ↗5%	2002	Mandatory for workers <42
		Benefits: 55% highest 3 years → full career 1%			
Croatia	Points	Retirement age: 65/60	5%	2002	Mandatory for workers <40, voluntary for 40–50
		Benefits: 0.825% full career			
Estonia	Defined benefit	Retirement age: 60/55 → 63/63	6%	2002	Mandatory only for new entrants
		Benefits: 55% best 5 years +1% → flat component + earnings-related points			
Hungary	Defined benefit	Retirement age: 60/55 → 62/62	6% ↗8%	1998	Mandatory only for new entrants
		Benefits: 33% for first 10 years + 2.5% → 1.65% full career			
Kazakhstan	Defined benefit	Retirement age: 63/58	10%	1998	Mandatory for all
		Benefits: 60% of monthly average of best consecutive 3 years			
Kosovo	Universal flat for all >65	Retirement age: 65/65	10%	2002	Mandatory for all working habitual residents <55
		Benefits: defined annually by value of minimum consumption basket			
Latvia	Notional accounts	Retirement age: 60/55 → 62/62	2% ↗8%	2001	Mandatory for new and young workers <30, voluntary for 30–50
		Benefits: 55% highest 5 years +1% → full career based on notional accumulation			
Lithuania	Defined benefit	Retirement age: 60/55 → 62.5/60	2.5% ↗5.5%	2004	Voluntary for current and new workers
		Benefits: 55% highest 5 years plus 1% → earnings-related and unrelated components			
Macedonia, FYR	Defined benefit	Retirement age: 64/62	7.42%	2006	Mandatory for new entrants
		Benefits: defined by minimum wage ratio and total years of participation			
Poland	Notional accounts	Retirement age: 65/60 (many exemptions) → 65/60 (fewer exemptions)	7.3%	1999	Mandatory for new and young workers <30, voluntary for 30–50
		Benefits: flat +1.3% → full career notional accumulation			

continued

TABLE 4.3
Continued

Country	Public scheme type	Public pension (PAYG) reform	Mandatory pillar contributions	Enactment date	Who participates
Romania	Defined benefit	Retirement age: 62/57 → 65/60	2% ↗ 3%	2008	Mandatory for <35, voluntary for 36–45
		Benefits: 75% first 30–20 years + 1% → full career points based			
Russian Federation	Notional accounts	Retirement age: 60/55	3% ↗ 6%	2002	Mandatory only for those born after 1966
		Benefits: defined by individual lifetime accumulations			
Slovak Republic	Points	Retirement age: 60/53–57 → 62/62	9%	2005	Mandatory only for those born after 1983
		Benefits: 2% first 25 years, 1% thereafter → 1.19% full career			

Sources: Based on data provided by pension fund supervision agencies of the respective countries. See also Kasek, Laursen, and Skrok 2008; Schwarz 2011; OECD 2012.
Note: By 2008, with the exception of the former Yugoslav Republic of Macedonia, all countries had voluntary pension schemes.

FIGURE 4.8

Annual Real Returns of Mandatory Funded Pension Schemes in Selected European and Central Asian Economies, 2002–2012

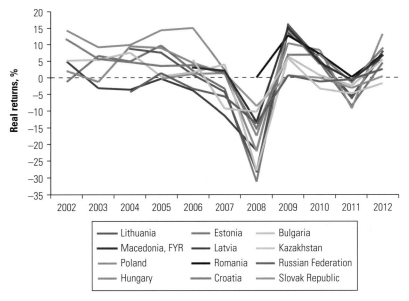

Source: World Bank Private Pensions (internal database).
Note: Returns for the Russian Federation refer to performance of the "enhanced" portfolio of Vnesheconombank (VEB), which in 2012 represented over 70 percent of mandatory pillar assets.

TABLE 4.4

Annual Real Returns of Mandatory Funded Pension Schemes, Selected European Economies, 2002–2012

Annual real rate of return		
Country	Since inception or 2002–2007	Since inception or 2002–2012
Bulgaria	4.0	0.5
Croatia	5.0	3.2
Estonia	3.1	0.1
Hungary	4.2	n.a.
Latvia	−2.0	−1.3
Lithuania	3.2	0.8
Macedonia, FYR	2.6	2.4
Poland	10.8	6.4
Romania	n.a.	5.1
Russian Federation	−3.1	−2.7
Slovak Republic	0.8	−1.2
Average annual rate of return		
Country	Since inception or 2002–2007	Since inception or 2002–2012
Bulgaria	4.0	0.5
Croatia	5.0	3.2
Estonia	3.1	0.1
Hungary	4.2	n.a.
Latvia	−2.0	−1.3
Lithuania	3.2	0.8
Macedonia, FYR	2.6	2.4
Poland	10.8	6.4
Romania	n.a.	5.1
Russian Federation	−3.1	−2.7
Slovak Republic	0.8	−1.2

Source: World Bank Private Pensions (internal database).
Note: Figures exclude fees charged by pension fund management companies. Returns for Russia refer to performance of the "enhanced" portfolio of Vnesheconombank (VEB). n.a. = not applicable.

International portfolio diversification becomes necessary in most countries that reform their pension systems, as pension funds tend to outgrow the size of the domestic capital market. By keeping the pension funds captive inside the country, regulation might increase the risk for pension funds, as the domestic asset prices could be artificially inflated. While Poland's pension funds have all equities

FIGURE 4.9

Government Securities and Bank Deposits in Second-Pillar Portfolios of Pension Funds, Selected European and Central Asian Economies, 2012

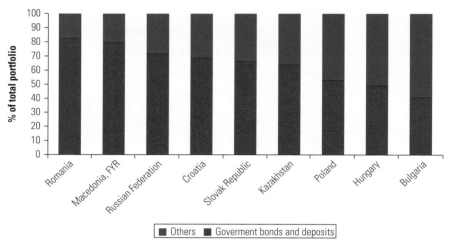

Source: World Bank Private Pensions (internal database).

FIGURE 4.10

Asset Allocation of Mandatory Funded Pension Systems in Selected European and Central Asian Economies, 2012

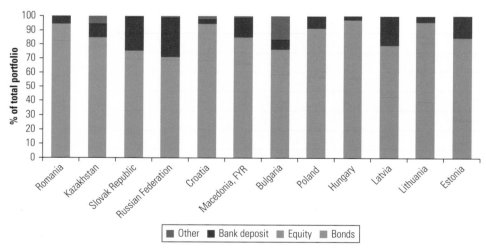

Source: World Bank Private Pensions (internal database).

invested in the domestic market, pension funds in Lithuania and Estonia have the large majority of equities invested abroad.

Individuals are more likely to optimize the expected value of the replacement rate when portfolios are invested in life-cycle strategies. Life-cycle strategies require a higher proportion of equity when contributors are young and a larger proportion of long-term

FIGURE 4.11

Fees Charged by Pension Fund Management Companies in Mandatory Funded Systems, Selected European and Central Asian Countries, 2006 and 2011

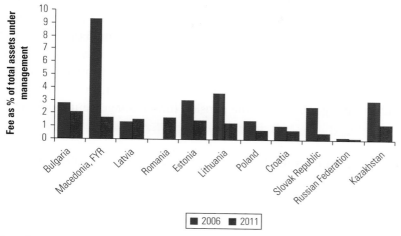

Source: World Bank Private Pensions (internal database).

Note: Data on the Russian Federation refer to the management fee structure of Vnesheconombank (VEB), the largest second-pillar asset manager in Russia (more than 70 percent of total assets in 2011). Russian nongovernment pension funds charged much higher fees, close to 1 percent of total assets in 2011.

inflation-linked bonds when contributors are closer to retirement age. The movement from one asset allocation to another should be automatic along the lifecycle of contributors. While most countries in the region offer at least three portfolios, the mechanisms for allocating individuals among them are relatively underdeveloped, and most countries do not allow automatic movements from riskier to conservative portfolios.

While high fees have captured most of the headlines regarding mandatory funded systems in Europe, these fees have been decreasing in the past few years. As shown in figure 4.11, fees as a percentage of the assets under management have dropped in most countries (with the exception of Latvia). An increase in asset volume explains the fee reduction. In the remarkable case of Poland, fees have dropped by half in 5 years, and pension fund management companies continue performing active asset management of the pension portfolios. In the Slovak Republic, the reduction in fees has come at a high cost to contributors. Pension fund management companies in that country were forced to reduce their fees to 0.5 percent of the assets under management (equivalent to one-fifth of the levels in 2006) and to provide short-term guarantees on the value of the contributions. Under these circumstances, Slovak pension fund management companies lost interest in managing pension portfolios adequately and moved portfolios into short-term government securities and bank deposits.

Despite the relative success of some countries in reducing the fees charged by pension fund management companies, the efforts should continue to ensure reasonable rates of return on the pension funds. As interest rates are expected to be low in the medium term, and returns consequently will become more modest, it is essential that the funded schemes in place be able to operate at low cost. As discussed below, further reduction in fees may require changing the industrial organization of the pension fund management industry.

Lessons from Experiences with Funded Pension Schemes

Mandatory funded pension components have been reduced in some countries. Despite the initial intentions to build long-lasting pension reforms, in the aftermath of the financial crisis some European and Central Asian countries have taken measures to temporarily or permanently reduce the relative size of the mandatory funded component. Table 4.5 illustrates the main adjustments in the relative role of funded schemes in the region, which vary from full nationalization of the mandatory funded schemes, as in Hungary, to transitory reduction in contributions of the mandatory funded scheme as an instrument for accessing the euro area, as in Estonia.

This section explains the main drivers of recent downsizes and reversals in the region. Three elements explain the government reactions in adjusting the initial pension reforms: (a) incomplete reforms, (b) tension between short-term and long-term priorities, and (c) institutional design.

Incomplete Reforms

Shortly after introducing the reforms, some of the countries followed economic policies that were inconsistent with the basic ideas that fostered the reforms. Countries like Hungry and Poland followed expansive fiscal policies over the decade, with sizable fiscal deficits and increases in private retirement savings. The subsequent effects on economic growth and capital market development did not materialize at the expected levels. As shown in figures 4.12 and 4.13, fiscal deficits in Hungary and Poland were above the 3 percent limit of the European Union's Stability and Growth Pact for almost the whole decade. The lack of fiscal discipline was an important impediment to

TABLE 4.5

Outcome of the Financial Crisis on Funded Defined Contributions to Pension Schemes, Selected European Economies, 2008–2013

Reversal	Hungary Permanent	8% 2nd-pillar contribution rate reduced to 0% in January 2011 and transferred to the 1st pillar/state PAYG system. Reversal is permanent.
Part reversal, part reduction	Poland Permanent	7.3% contribution rate cut to 2.3% in May 2011. While rate was expected to gradually increase to 3.5% by 2017, in August 2013 the government announced several measures that will significantly reduce the role of the mandatory funded system.
	Russian Federation Permanent	State Duma backed the plan to reduce rates from 6% to 2% in November 2012. Change is permanent and will go into force in January 2014.
Reductions in contributions	Slovak Republic Permanent	9% contribution was reduced to 4% in 2013. The funded scheme moved from an opt-out to an opt-in system.
	Estonia Temporary	6% (4% + 2%) rate cut to 0% between June 2009 and January 2011. Contributions shifted from 2nd to 1st pillar. Gradual increase from 2011. Rate set at 3% in January 2011 and 6% in January 2012. Rate may rise to 8% in 2014–17 to offset missed contributions.
	Latvia Temporary	8% contribution rate reduced to 2% in May 2009. Rates increased to 4% from 2013.
	Lithuania Temporary	5.5% contribution rate reduced to 2% in July 2009. Rates were further lowered in January 2012 to 1.5%. Increase to 2% is planned from January 2014.
	Romania Temporary	Reduction in planned growth path of contribution rate from 2% to 6%. Rate froze in 2010 at 2% but started to increase again in 2011 at annual rate of 0.5%.
No changes in 2nd pillar arrangements announced as of June 2012	Croatia	No changes; 2nd pillar contribution rate remains at 5%.
	Bulgaria	No changes; 2nd pillar contribution rate remains at 5%.
	Macedonia, FYR	No changes; 2nd pillar contribution rate remains at 7.42%.
	Kosovo	No changes; 2nd pillar contribution rate remains at 10% (additional voluntary contributions can add up to 20%).
Planned implementation of 2nd pillar continuing	Czech Republic	2nd pillar reform went into force on January 1, 2013. Contribution rate is set at 5%.

Sources: National regulatory authorities; Schwarz 2011; OECD 2012.

the sustainability of the funded systems on various fronts. In the case of Hungary, the fiscal deficits would have been above 3 percent even if the contributions to the mandatory funded scheme had been considered part of the social security revenues.[18]

Large fiscal deficits during the pre-crisis period resulted in unsustainable government debt stocks. These triggered concern when the crisis hit the region. At the time of the reversal, Polish and Hungarian government debt was close to 55 and 80 percent of GDP respectively. By netting the debt held by pension funds, the nationalization of the mandatory funded systems in Hungary implied a reduction in the debt stock by approximately $8 billion.[19]

FIGURE 4.12
Fiscal Balance of Hungary, 2001–2010

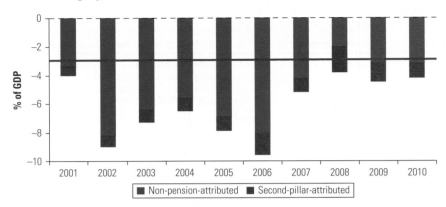

Sources: Central Bank of Hungary; IMF World Economic Outlook Database.
Note: The red line reflects the 3 percent fiscal deficit limit of the Stability and Growth Pact.

FIGURE 4.13
Fiscal Balance of Poland, 2001–2010

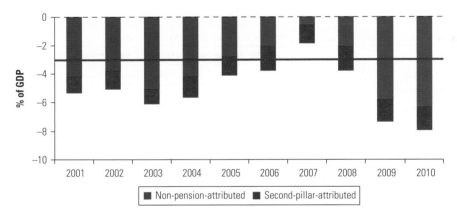

Sources: Polish Financial Supervision Authority (KNF); IMF World Economic Outlook Database.
Note: The red line reflects the 3 percent fiscal deficit limit of the Stability and Growth Pact.

Pension reforms in some countries were not backed by the whole political spectrum, and the first attempts to scale down the funded schemes took place shortly after approval of the reforms. In Hungary and the Slovak Republic, attempts to unwind the reforms started once the political parties (or coalitions) that opposed the pension reforms took office. The Slovak case illustrates these attempts. The Slovak mandatory funded system was created in 2005 as an opt-out system in which the default option for contributors was to split contributions between the public pension system and the manda-tory funded system. In 2008, legislation promoted by the new government was approved to turn it into an opt-in system. In this system, by default, workers contribute only to the public pension system, and therefore contributors need to make an explicit decision to enter the funded scheme. In 2012 the new government reinstituted the original opt-out scheme, but within a few months it was reversed again when yet another government took power. While at the beginning, the pension fund management industry fought back by increasing efforts to bring new contributors into the funded scheme, subsequent lowering of caps on management fees and increases in the level of guarantees provided by pension fund management companies eroded the industry's willingness to attract contributors.[20]

In addition, pension reforms in most countries were not followed by forceful policies to foster the development of domestic capital markets. The lack of development of the corporate bond market, mortgage bond markets, and infrastructure bond markets is not because pension funds lack interest in developing these markets, but in some cases is due to the lack of institutional development on the supply side that might facilitate the issuance of these instruments. For example, the development of the infrastructure bond market requires institutional capacity at the level of the government to bring the ideas of marketable infrastructure projects to concessionary companies, which may later issue infrastructure bonds to refinance these projects in the long term.

The development of a private long-term fixed-income market requires the development of a long-term government bond market. Issuers of private sector bonds require liquid benchmarks of long-term bonds for pricing long-term securities. As discussed below, investment regulations of pension funds would need to be revised to foster interest in this segment of the market. All of these elements require deliberated coordination with the private sector and within the government, which is unlikely to happen spontaneously.[21]

It takes more than a stock exchange and pension reform to develop the local equity market. Despite the fact that all countries in the region have stock exchanges, most of these markets are highly illiquid. Exchanges provide the infrastructure for issuing and trading instruments, and pension funds and other institutional investors provide potential demand for these securities. However, corporations consider a number of other elements when deciding whether to list their companies, including alternative sources of financing, growth prospects of the business, tax benefits, rule of law, and a set of rules and regulations that may protect the interests of the shareholders. Some countries face challenges in this area. For example, in the case of Russia, many companies prefer to be listed abroad rather than in the domestic market.

The strong presence of bank financing of businesses in the region before the crisis was a limiting factor for capital market development. At that time, a favorable economic cycle and banks' reliance on foreign funding for financing domestic projects did not create the conditions for domestic capital market development. Besides the problems of restrictive investment regulations for pension funds that inhibited investments in riskier assets, the weaknesses in banking regulation that allowed financing of local projects in foreign currency was an important impediment to the development of the capital market.

However, the availability of banking sector funding in the region is changing rapidly, and consequently institutional investors should start playing a more active role in the financing of economic growth. Since 2010, banks in Central and Eastern European countries have increasingly deleveraged their portfolios and moved into strategies of lending driven by deposit growth. Considering a narrower deposit base solely from domestic economies compared to the availability of funds before the crisis, the deleveraging of banks in the region will have consequences for the availability of funds for local companies and individuals. In this context, if incentives are properly placed, domestic pension funds and other institutional investors may start playing a larger role in the financing of economic growth in the region. Finally, the presence of local pension funds might be a stable source of domestic funding, for example, through bond issuance for subsidiaries of international banks that are increasingly required to have financial autonomy.[22]

Tension between Short-Term and Long-Term Priorities

Pension reforms involving the diversion of part of the social security contribution to a funded scheme require long and, most of the time, painful fiscal transitions. In most cases, these transitions have been partially or totally debt-financed, which has created constant budgetary tension in governments, especially in the years since the crisis. The introduction of funded schemes solves a long-term fiscal problem, but it also creates discomfort during the transition, often requiring additional fiscal efforts for at least a couple of decades. In the absence of a clear political consensus on the role that funded pension schemes play in the long term, and in the presence of large public pension deficits, it will be difficult to sustain funded schemes in the region.

This tension becomes more evident in periods of recession, as the fiscal deficit increases and financing deficits become more expensive. Shifting part of the contributions from the funded pillar into the PAYG component is an evident but short-term alternative. Unfortunately, reversing these pension reforms addresses the short-term problem at the cost of significantly worsening the long-term fiscal situation, reducing the future pensions of individuals, or a combination of both.

During the financial crisis, all the Baltic countries and Romania switched a portion of contributions from the mandatory funded scheme to the public pension system as a means of increasing revenues for paying other fiscal obligations.[23] As shown in table 4.6, the crisis in the region was severe, and in the case of the Baltic countries—with negative GDP growth of around 15 percent in 2009—there was some justification for temporary measures affecting the pension systems, including the funded component. Crises of this order of magnitude shift the balance toward resuming economic growth, and therefore temporary measures might be expected. Stabilizing the economies in order to resume economic growth in the medium term may require drastic measures to restore the credibility of the market. In fact, these countries did stabilize their economies,

TABLE 4.6

Real GDP Growth in Selected European and Central Asian Economies, 2007–2012

Country	2007	2008	2009	2010	2011	2012
Bulgaria	6.45	6.19	−5.48	0.39	1.67	0.78
Croatia	5.06	2.08	−6.95	−1.41	−0.01	−1.98
Estonia	7.49	−3.67	−14.26	2.26	7.64	2.45
Hungary	0.10	0.90	−6.80	1.27	1.70	−1.66
Kazakhstan	8.90	3.20	1.18	7.25	7.50	5.04
Kosovo	6.26	6.91	2.90	3.90	4.96	2.15
Latvia	9.60	−3.28	−17.73	−0.34	5.47	5.58
Lithuania	9.80	2.91	−14.84	1.44	5.87	3.62
Macedonia, FYR	6.15	5.00	−0.92	2.90	3.11	−0.27
Poland	6.79	5.13	1.63	3.87	4.32	2.05
Romania	6.32	7.35	−6.58	−1.65	2.45	0.33
Russian Federation	8.54	5.25	−7.80	4.30	4.30	3.40
Slovak Republic	10.49	5.75	−4.93	4.18	3.35	2.03

Source: IMF World Economic Outlook Database.

and economic growth resumed in the subsequent years. However, it is not clear whether the downsizing of mandatory funded systems will be transitory or permanent, as Latvia and Lithuania still have contribution rates to the mandatory funded system well below the pre-crisis rates.

The asymmetry in the treatment of explicit and implicit debt is at the heart of the incentives for reversing pension reforms. In funded schemes, to the extent that part of the transitional deficit is financed with debt, governments make explicit commitments to bondholders. In PAYG systems, by contrast, governments simply commit to pay future pensions to current contributors. While renegotiation of the terms of sovereign bonds is rare in countries that are not facing an imminent crisis, renegotiation of commitments of future pensions (in terms of, for example, retirement age or indexation rules) is common.

Explicit debt is subject to intensive market screening. Investors are willing to buy these bonds on the condition that they receive a market interest rate, which is a function of the expected probability of default. Independent agents, including financial institutions, banks, rating agencies, and general investors, buy these bonds and value these instruments on a regular basis. The interest rate fluctuates over time, depending on the market perception about default probability.

Implicit pension debt follows a different dynamic than explicit debt. Instead of being taken by bondholders, implicit pension debt is taken by the government (on behalf of future pensioners). It is therefore unsurprising that independent of its probability of default, the government is willing to take this debt at face value. Governments face an important conflict of interest, as they are both the issuers of and the representative of the holders of "implicit contracts" at the same time. In the absence of transparency about the volume of the implicit pension liabilities, and given the incestuous relationship between the issuer and the holder of the contractual obligations, governments may have incentives to oversize the amount of implicit liabilities (which have a more obscure method of accounting) at the cost of more modest and transparent figures of explicit debt.

To the extent that the cost of taking implicit debt for governments is flat and governments are not accountable for taking excessive implicit contracts, governments have incentives to limit the size of funded schemes. The sizable gap between the average duration of pension contracts and the duration of government mandates together with the lack of transparency on implicit pension obligations creates incentives to transfer these liabilities to future generations.[24]

In democratic countries, the horizon for government mandates is much shorter than the duration of pension obligations that the government is taking on behalf of workers. While governments' horizons are typically shorter than 6 years, as representatives of pension contract holders (implicit bondholders) they might be willing to take these long-term contracts related to the retirement age of the working population with low accountability.

The conflict of interest derived from the distortion created by the asymmetric treatment of implicit and explicit debt leaves mandatory funded pension systems in a vulnerable position for reversals. In the presence of fiscal needs, governments might prefer to take a long-term (undisclosed) liability and finance the deficit by downsizing the funded defined contribution, rather than by issuing explicit debt for financing the transitional deficit (or increasing taxes).

Rating agencies and investors, in general, may have only an indirect interest in the implicit pension liabilities. It is important to understand that the rating agencies' business is to evaluate the default probability of each specific debt instrument, and they receive compensation for this service. To the extent that the implicit commitments of governments have a potential effect on the probability of default on explicit debt, rating agencies and investors may have an interest in implicit pension liabilities; otherwise it is an additional parameter in the determination of the credit risk of the country.[25] Italy's 2011 pension reform was able to calm the market regarding the probability of default on explicit debt. The government's obligations were of such magnitude that a credible government commitment to reduce the implicit liabilities (by increasing the retirement age and reducing pension benefits) significantly reduced the default probability of the government and therefore its cost of debt financing.

In addition, as it does not consider implicit pension debt, the Maastricht treaty does not contribute to stable funded schemes. As transition countries see the possibility of accessing the euro area as a way of weathering the pressures on their currencies and stabilizing their economies, the incentives for maintaining the mandatory funded systems are less clear. As it only considers explicit debt and fiscal deficit, the Maastricht treaty unfairly penalizes countries with large funded schemes and creates incentives for downsizing them. By temporarily downsizing contributions to the mandatory funded system, Estonia was successful in complying with the parameters for accessing the euro area in 2011. Assuming that future pensioners in Estonia will not be affected by the temporary reduction in the mandatory funded system, if implicit and explicit liabilities had been treated symmetrically, such a change would not have been necessary.

A series of recent agreements and guidelines by the European Commission have had an impact on this dilemma but have not resolved it. Changes known as the "Six Pack" and the guidelines of the Economic and Financial Committee (EFC) of the European Union produced in September 2012 may have an effect on the future stability of funded pension schemes.[26] The EFC report discusses multipillar pension reforms and explains that the formula for setting the medium-term budgetary objective (MTO) for each member state explicitly includes a fraction of the adjustment needed to cover the present value of the future increase in age-related government expenditure. The report further states that multipillar reforms that include the transfer of contribution revenue previously recorded as government revenue to pension funds classified outside the general government sector are reasons for temporary deviations from the MTO. They thus allow these countries to have a safety margin with respect to the 3 percent GDP deficit reference value. For euro area member states, the safety margin is taken to be a deficit not exceeding 1 percent of GDP. However, the EFC report stipulates that temporary deviations from the normal adjustment path toward the MTO should be no more than 4 years.

The key issue for funded pension systems is whether the changes to the fiscal rules outlined above will still have the effect of getting countries to abandon, reverse, or reduce their mandatory funded schemes in favor of increasing liabilities in unfunded or only partly funded social security reserves. First, while the costs of aging are reflected in the MTO, it is not clear that the new guidelines make governments indifferent with respect to raising implicit or explicit debt.[27] The incentives of the MTO might be insufficient to persuade countries to prefer funded schemes over unfunded ones, so countries may still prefer to hide debt in the form of implicit pension liabilities. Second, the 4-year transition period for taking account of multipillar reforms in the EFC report contrasts with three to four decades for the transitional deficit of a funded system. Third, the maximum 1 percent deviation from the path also imposes a cap on the contribution rate that can be managed by mandatory funded schemes, which is unlikely to be higher than 3 percent of wages. Fourth, the timing of the EFC guidelines is a factor, as they were issued when most Central and Eastern European countries had already taken bold policy decisions about their funded pension schemes.

While the direction of the EFC guidelines is welcome, the measures are likely to be insufficient to ensure stability of mandatory funded schemes in countries with multipillar pension systems. Given that governments are making potentially damaging long-term decisions, it is clearly an area that needs further consideration.

Institutional Design

While fees in some Central European countries have reached more reasonable levels, there is a widespread perception that mandatory funded systems are expensive and manage poorly diversified pools of assets. The relatively high costs of the system are explained by the emphasis on individual selection, by provision of costly and misplaced guarantees by pension fund management companies, and by an industrial organization of the pension fund management industry that facilitates oligopoly behavior.

Pension reforms in the region placed great emphasis on individual choice in the selection of pension fund management companies.[28] This policy preference was not aligned with the low level of financial literacy of the average contributor or the track record of the management companies, nor were there standardized parameters that could help people make an objective selection. The launching of funded pension schemes was accompanied by multimillion-dollar marketing campaigns run by pension fund management companies and supported by massive sales forces that played a deceptive role in allocating contributors among pension fund management companies. While the costs of these campaigns were undisclosed, prices for recruiting contributors ranged between 10 and 150 euros per contributor at the beginning and end of the recruiting period respectively. A cost-benefit analysis may suggest that temporary allocation of contributors among a small group of eligible pension fund management companies would have brought the same outcome—supply-driven selection—at a much lower cost.

While the authorities knew about these expensive campaigns, their actions were focused on preventing use of malpractice to attract clients, such as offers of gifts or other incentives by the pension fund management companies. Since these marketing campaigns were financed by the private sector, the government perceived the campaigns as beyond their interest; moreover, the regulations imposed caps that would avoid excessive fees. In practice, individual selection resulted in the supply-driven selection of pension fund managers and big expenditures by management companies.

In the years that followed the reform, pension fund management companies tried to recover some of the initial expenses through fees. In most countries in the region, they still charge the maximum fees authorized. A few years after the reform, the authorities realized that the caps on fees were not low enough and decided to change regulations to lower them. While pension fund management companies in countries like Poland had enough time to recover their initial expenses, others, for example in the Slovak Republic, did not. In the latter case, the industry reacted by cutting costs to the minimum while continuing to charge the maximum fee allowed in the regulation, which has resulted in poor asset allocation.

In the presence of an uninformed demand, the model of open competition for allocating new contributors is suboptimal. The principle of voluntariness in the selection of a pension fund management company can also be achieved by making an initial random allocation of contributors among a predefined number of companies, and then—after 2 years or so, when pension funds may show some differentiation—allowing contributors to switch between companies. However, this model would require a strict licensing process and a predictable fee scenario. In addition, while improvements in financial literacy may help increase the elasticity of the demand for management of pension funds, this is a slow process, and it may take decades before the average contributor can make an informed selection of a pension fund manager.

Guarantees of relative performance create distortions in portfolio allocation and increase the cost of funded schemes. Pension fund management companies are required to guarantee that returns are aligned with the average return of the industry. As shown by Castañeda and Rudolph (2010), these relative guarantees create incentives to move to suboptimal asset allocations, with an excessive focus on short-term returns. Consequently, the competition derived from such a scheme is not welfare-improving in terms of the expected replacement rates at retirement age. The minimum return guarantee is an ineffective instrument for ensuring that contributors receive adequate pensions at retirement age. In addition, these guarantees are expensive to manage and consequently serve to increase the fees charged to contributors.

Proper strategic asset allocation is the best guarantee of good pensions in the future. Investment regulations driven by minimum return guarantees are not only an important source of distortion for asset allocation and management costs, but also provide short-term protection that contributors do not need. These misplaced guarantees support a vicious cycle of undiversified portfolios, low performance, high fees, and discomfort among participants. This combination may endanger the stability of the funded scheme, as in the case of the Slovak Republic. The short-term guarantee only prevents volatility.

Volatility might even be good for young contributors as they may benefit more than older individuals from investing in risky portfolios.

The design of a defined contribution pension system that is welfare-improving for society also requires changes in the industrial organization of the companies. Pension fund management companies in the region are typically hybrids between account management (record keeping) and portfolio management (asset management). Account management is a business with scale economies and therefore there is not much room for competition. The lowest administration costs for portfolio management are achieved at a level that opens room for multiple asset managers.

The combination of these two businesses in one entity, namely the pension fund management company, creates incentives to acquire market share. In a market with little growth in the labor force, pension fund management companies have incentives to steal contributors from competitors. As it is largely supply driven, this form of competition is wasteful and can hardly be considered welfare-improving. In order to avoid a war of attrition, pension fund management companies typically reach some sort of agreement that allows them to keep their relative market shares and maintain high fees. These arrangements can include cartels. The need for a sizable sales force and physical presence (office space for attending clients) serves to deter potential new entrants and facilitate the creation of oligopoly structures.

Full separation between the asset management and account management businesses, with centralized account management and competition in portfolio management, is a way of introducing efficiency to both functions. As the businesses become clearer and more straightforward, it becomes easier to impose tariffs on the account management and portfolio management separately. The introduction of blind accounts, as in Sweden, where the asset managers do not know the identities of the contributors, reduces the incentives for direct sales and keeps costs low, helping to focus the portfolio management business on its core objective. Most importantly, blind accounts are efficient in lowering the barriers to potential entry of new competitors, which in turn helps reduce fees.

Finally, as shown by Rudolph et al. (2010), portfolio benchmarks that follow life-cycle strategies are the most effective way to ensure that investments of pension funds are consistent with the optimization of the expected future pensions of individuals. Benchmarking portfolios of pension funds against a set of explicit market indexes is a necessary step. Since market interactions by themselves are not conducive to portfolios that optimize the future pensions of individuals, it is essential to rely on exogenous portfolio benchmarks that pension funds can use to guide their investments. To avoid manipulation of the assets, portfolio benchmarks should be based on market indexes and designed to optimize the expected value of the pensions at retirement age. This implies the use of life-cycle strategies with higher components of equity for young contributors, and more long-term fixed income for older contributors.[29] As funded schemes are expected to provide a sizable part of future pensions, these portfolio benchmarks would need to be validated in society.

In order to build confidence in the system, risk-averse policy makers may want to introduce some sort of guarantees of the value of the contributions at retirement age. Viceira and Rudolph (2012) provide some estimates of the cost of these guarantees in relation to the real or nominal value of contributions, but it is important to note that the cost of guarantees is a function of the underlying pension portfolios. In their analysis, life-cycle strategies minimize the cost of the guarantee and optimize the expected replacement rate for individuals. In order to make them effective, the guarantees need to be priced at market value, and the guarantor who writes the guarantees needs to be independent from the pension fund management companies.

With the weakening of public pension schemes as a consequence of the inverting pyramid, savings for retirement will be essential to ensure consumption smoothing. However, the introduction of pension reform in the region, which includes the creation of funded schemes, needs to be accompanied by sound macroeconomic and financial sector policies.

Notes

1. The payoff of the portfolio of the funded component is higher when the government capacity to pay pensions, for example, as a consequence of the inverting pyramid, is lower.
2. To the best of the authors' knowledge, there are no studies that quantify the impact of these reforms on savings, investments, and economic growth in the region. However, Corbo and Schmidt-Hebbel (2003) estimated the contribution of pension reform for the case of Chile in the period 1981–2003. Chile's pension reform has features similar to the reforms in Europe and Central Asia. The study suggests that the combination of these factors increased the rate of national savings, domestic investment, and economic growth by 2.3 percent, 2.1 percent, and 1.2 percent of GDP, respectively.
3. Total factor productivity measures a combination of changes in efficiency in the use of factor inputs in the production function of the economy and technological changes.

4. Pension funds based on revenues from commodity endowments are an exception.

5. Exceptions are Norway and to some extent Sweden. However, Norway's Government Pension Fund Global has objectives that go beyond financing pension expenditures.

6. It is interesting to note that prior to the crisis, Ireland's National Pensions Reserve Fund was used as an example of governance, but the magnitude of the crisis was such that the fund was sacrificed to stabilize the country's failed banking system.

7. The Czech Republic implemented a mandatory funded scheme in 2013.

8. For more discussion on nationalization, see Price and Rudolph (2013).

9. Some countries, such as Chile, have been able to increase coverage of the voluntary scheme, but these plans do not require maintaining savings until retirement.

10. Examples of auto-enrollment plans include the National Employment Savings Trust in the United Kingdom and KiwiSaver in New Zealand. See IOPS (2013) for more details on these programs.

11. For a discussion about the impact of bounded rationality on retirement savings behavior, see Benartzi and Thaler (2007).

12. Madrian and Shea (2001) document a 50 percent increase in savings plan participation by newly hired employees at a large employer after a switch from an opt-in to an opt-out automatic enrollment regime.

13. Different parties and coalitions in the Slovak Republic take different approaches toward the role of mandatory funded systems in the overall pension system.

14. While automatic enrollment is efficient in getting people started, employees can be stuck with insufficient saving rates. Auto-enrollment requires employees to be automatically signed up at a certain saving rate; as these rates need to be low enough not to deter people from participating in the program, they can sometimes be insufficient to generate enough savings for retirement. Benartzi and Thaler (2013) propose the use of automatic escalation, meaning that individuals are invited to commit at sign-up to increase their saving rate later, but those increases will be linked to salary increases.

15. This section is based on Vittas, Rudolph, and Pollner (2010).

16. In Central Asia, Kazakhstan in 1998 followed the Chilean model of a single mandatory funded system.

17. Bulgaria, Croatia, Estonia, Hungary, Kosovo, Latvia, Lithuania, the former Yugoslav Republic of Macedonia, Poland, Romania, the Russian Federation, and the Slovak Republic.

18. The red bars in figures 4.12 and 4.13 reflect the value of the contributions to mandatory funded schemes that theoretically are diverted from the social security agency.

19. It is not simple to separate the impact of the pension fund nationalization from other elements that affected the cost of funding the Hungarian government. While nationalization had an effect in reducing the government debt stocks, it did not help reduce the cost of funding the government. While in the period right after the nationalization, the spread of government debt increased by 125 basis points, additional reductions followed, which might be a consequence of multiple regional

and idiosyncratic factors. Further research might be needed to clarify this point.

20. It is interesting to note that in all countries where pension funds were nationalized, including Argentina, Bolivia, and Hungary, the pension fund management industry has not played a role in defending the system. Typically, it is not in the interest of these institutions to confront governments, as they have to protect their brands and the possibility of attracting other potential business in the country. Pension fund management companies have typically reacted to threats of policy reversal by lowering operational costs and minimizing losses.

21. One reason for the success of the Chilean pension reform in fostering the development of the domestic capital market has been the active role of the government and regulatory agencies in supporting the institutional development needed to facilitate the supply of innovative instruments to the market.

22. This point is strongly made by Impavido, Rudolph, and Ruggerone (2013).

23. In the case of Romania, it was a slowdown in the programmed path of increases of the contributions to the mandatory funded system.

24. For a working population with an average age of 40 years and a retirement age of 65, the average duration of the implicit commitment might be greater than 20 years, while the government mandate is typically below 6 years.

25. It would be interesting to analyze whether rating agencies would be willing to rate the probability of default on implicit debt of different governments.

26. On the Six Pack, see European Commission (2011). For the EFC guidelines, see European Commission (2012), available on the "Relevant Legal Texts and Guidelines" page of the European Commission Economic and Financial Affairs website, http://ec.europa.eu/economy _finance/economic_governance/sgp/legal_texts/.

27. The August 2013 announcements by the Polish government regarding the future of the mandatory funded system provide evidence of the preference for implicit debt.

28. The institutional design adopted in these countries for mandatory funded schemes followed Chile's 1981 pension reform.

29. Individuals should be allowed to select the portfolios that are aligned with their preferences, but experience suggests that only a small proportion of contributors will make explicit selections.

References

Benartzi, Shlomo, and Richard Thaler. 2007. "Heuristics and Biases in Retirement Savings Behavior." *Journal of Economic Perspectives* 21 (3): 81–104.

_____. 2013. "Behavioral Economics and the Retirement Savings Crisis." *Science* 339 (6124): 1152–53.

Calderón, César, and Klaus Schmidt-Hebbel. 2003. "Learning the Hard Way: Ten Lessons for Latin America." Central Bank of Chile, Santiago.

Castañeda, Pablo, and Heinz P. Rudolph. 2010. "Portfolio Choice, Minimum Return Guarantees, and Competition." In *Evaluating the Financial Performance of Pension Funds*, edited by Richard Hinz, Heinz P. Rudolph, Pablo Antolín, and Juan Yermo, 97–118. Washington, DC: World Bank.

Corbo, Vittorio, and Klaus Schmidt-Hebbel. 2003. "Macroeconomic Effects of Pension Reform in Chile." In *Pension Reforms: Results and Challenges*, edited by Federación Internacional de Administradoras de Fondos de Pensiones. Santiago: CIEDESS.

Corsetti, Giancarlo, and Klaus Schmidt-Hebbel. 1997. "Pension Reform and Growth." In *The Economics of Pensions: Principles, Policies and International Experience*, edited by Salvador Valdés-Prieto, 127–59. New York: Cambridge University Press.

European Commission. 2011. "EU Economic Governance 'Six-Pack' Enters into Force." Memo/11/898 (December 12). Brussels.

———. 2012. *Specifications on the Implementation of the Stability and Growth Pact and Guidelines on the Format and Content of Stability and Convergence Programmes*. Brussels: European Commission.

Feldstein, Martin, and Charles Horioka. 1980. "Tax Policy and International Capital Flows." *Economic Journal* 90 (358): 314–29.

IMF (International Monetary Fund). World Economic Outlook Database. http://www.imf.org/external/pubs/ft/weo/2013/01/weodata/index.aspx.

Impavido, Gregorio, Heinz P. Rudolph, and Luigi Ruggerone. 2013. "Bank Funding in Central, Eastern and South Eastern Europe Post Lehman: A 'New Normal?'" IMF Working Paper WP/13/148, International Monetary Fund, Washington, DC.

IOPS (International Organization of Pensions Supervisors). 2013. "Supervising Auto-Enrollment." Paper presented by IOPS Technical Committee at IOPS Conference, Paris, June 5, 2013.

Kasek, Leszek, Thomas Laursen, and Emilia Skrok. 2008. "Sustainability of Pension Systems in the New EU Member States and Croatia: Coping with Aging Challenges and Fiscal Pressures." World Bank Working Paper 129, World Bank, Washington, DC.

Madrian, Brigitte C. 2013. "Matching Contributions and Savings Outcomes: A Behavioral Economics Perspective." In *Matching Contributions for Pensions: A Review of International Experience*, edited by Richard Hinz, Robert Holzmann, David Tuesta, and Noriyuki Takayama, 289–309. Washington, DC: World Bank.

Madrian, Brigitte C., and Dennis Shea. 2001. "The Power of Suggestion: Inertia in 401(k) Participation and Savings Behavior." *Quarterly Journal of Economics* 116 (4): 1149–87.

OECD (Organisation for Economic Co-operation and Development). *Global Pension Statistics Database*. http://www.oecd.org/finance/private-pensions/globalpensionstatistics.htm.

———. 2012. *OECD Pensions Outlook 2012*. Paris: OECD.

Price, William, and Heinz P. Rudolph. 2013. "Reversal and Reduction, Resolution and Reform: Lessons from the Financial Crisis in Europe and Central Asia to Improve Outcomes from Mandatory Private Pensions." Working Paper 77779, World Bank, Washington, DC.

Rudolph, Heinz P., Richard Hinz, Pablo Antolín, and Juan Yermo. 2010. "Evaluating the Financial Performance of Pension Funds." In *Evaluating the Financial Performance of Pension Funds*, edited by Richard Hinz, Heinz P. Rudolph, Pablo Antolín, and Juan Yermo, 1–23. Washington, DC: World Bank.

Rudolph, Heinz P., and Roberto Rocha. 2007. "Competition and Performance in the Polish Second Pillar." World Bank Working Paper 107, World Bank, Washington, DC.

Schwarz, Anita. 2011. "New Realities of Pension Policy in Central Europe." Human Development Group, Europe and Central Asia Region, World Bank, Washington, DC. http://www.ebrd.com/english/downloads /research/news/Schwarz_paper.pdf.

Thaler, Richard H., and Cass R. Sunstein. 2008. *Nudge: Improving Decisions about Health, Wealth, and Happiness*. New Haven, CT: Yale University Press.

Viceira, Luis, and Heinz P. Rudolph. 2012. *The Use of Guarantees on Contributions in Pension Funds*. World Bank, Washington, DC.

Vittas, Dimitri, Heinz P. Rudolph, and John Pollner. 2010. "Designing the Payout Phase of Funded Pension Pillars in Central and Eastern European Countries." Policy Research Working Paper 5276, World Bank, Washington, DC.

Walker, Eduardo, and Augusto Iglesias. 2010. "Financial Performance of Pension Funds: An Exploratory Study." In *Evaluating the Financial Performance of Pension Funds*, edited by Richard Hinz, Heinz P. Rudolph, Pablo Antolín, and Juan Yermo, 39–95. Washington, DC: World Bank.

World Bank. 2012. *Program Document on a Proposed Loan in the Amount of EURO 750 Million to the Republic of Poland*. Report 68697-PL. Washington, DC: World Bank.

———. Private Pensions (internal database). Capital Markets Practice, Financial and Private Sector Development, World Bank, Washington, DC.

CHAPTER 5

Financing Pensions in Europe and Central Asia

Introduction

Pension benefits are already the largest public spending item in most European countries. As shown in chapter 2, pension spending has increased steadily in recent decades, as both the number of pensioners and the generosity of pension benefits have expanded. Today, approximately 130 million people (about 17 percent of the population) receive pension benefits in European and Central Asian countries. Governments tend to spend about a quarter of their revenue on pensions, equal to about 9 percent of gross domestic product (GDP). However, the latter proportion varies widely across countries, from 3.5 percent of GDP in Kazakhstan to over 15 percent in Austria and Ukraine, reflecting differences in demographics, pension coverage, and generosity.

With aging populations, pension spending will continue to grow. Increasing life expectancy and the approaching retirement of the baby boomers will continue to strain pension finances. Over the next four decades another 75 million people will reach pension age, exerting additional fiscal pressure on pension spending. The European Union (EU) expects average pension spending by its member states to rise to about 12.8 percent of GDP by 2050. Similar—or even larger—increases can be expected in other countries in the region, especially in many countries of the former Soviet Union (FSU) that face similar or, in some cases, more pronounced demographic transitions.

The growing financial burden of pension benefits and how it is financed matters not only for fiscal sustainability but also for employment, competitiveness, and income distribution. While much attention has focused on measures to contain spending pressures related to aging, the revenue side is equally important.

The current model of financing social security outlays, notably pensions, primarily through labor taxes has important implications. First, in terms of fiscal sustainability, the growth in pension spending is only a concern to the extent that pension obligations grow faster than the contribution base. Since labor taxes are the predominant source of financing for most pension systems in the region, aging not only will increase pension spending but simultaneously will exert pressure on revenues, with fewer taxpayers paying social security contributions (SSCs). Second, the large tax burden, especially on labor, can have detrimental impacts on (formal) employment and competitiveness in an increasingly global economy (see chapter 6). This will constrain the choices available to countries seeking to increase revenue from payroll contributions to improve the fiscal balance of social protection and pension systems. Third, these labor market constraints, together with growing fiscal pressures in social security systems, imply that noncontributory revenue sources, including general government revenue, are likely to become more important in financing social protection and pensions.

The Current Financing of Pension Systems in Europe and Central Asia

Countries in the region have adopted different social security financing models, but most are based on labor taxes. At present, the vast majority of pension systems in Europe and Central Asia rely heavily on labor taxes paid by active workers to finance pensions and other social benefits. These are usually collected in the form of payroll contributions on gross wages (or self-employment income), with contributions shared between employees and employers. Unlike other labor taxes, the payment of SSCs is principally—albeit in some cases weakly—linked to specific benefit entitlements, of which pensions are typically the most significant financially. If taxpayers perceive this link to be actuarially fair and credible, they may see SSCs as a form of deferred consumption or forced savings, which would mitigate distortionary effects on employment compared to other forms of direct taxation. There is little evidence, however, that behavioral responses to SSCs differ from responses to other direct taxes. Moreover, aging will further weaken the contribution-benefit link, forcing public schemes to reduce benefits to maintain financial sustainability.

While contribution-based financing is the most prevalent model, there are alternative approaches in a few countries. For example, Denmark, Georgia, and Ireland have largely or fully eliminated payroll contributions. They finance public pay-as-you-go (PAYG) systems with flat, social pension benefits through general government revenue while relying on funded, private pensions for additional retirement income support.[1]

SSC systems vary widely across countries in terms of contribution rates and tax bases (figure 5.1). The average statutory payroll contribution rate, comprising both employer and employee contributions, in countries of Europe and Central Asia is around 32 percent,

FIGURE 5.1

Statutory Social Security Contribution Rates in Selected European and Central Asian Economies, 2011

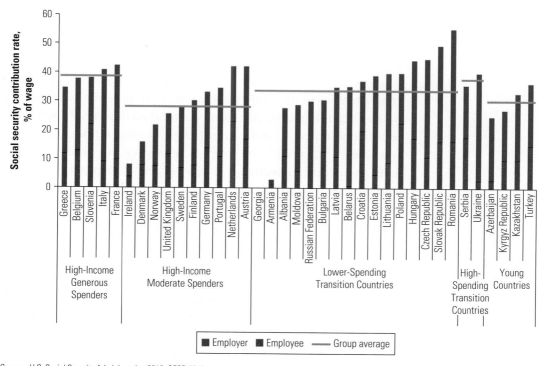

Sources: U.S. Social Security Administration 2012; OECD 2013; country-provided data.
Note: Since not all countries specify separate rates for individual benefits, e.g., pension, unemployment, etc., the reported rates are the aggregate rates for social contributions. For countries that apply differentiated rates, the reported rate is the highest marginal contribution rate.

significantly higher than the 24 percent average for non-European countries of the Organisation for Economic Co-operation and Development (OECD). While this makes the region as a whole a high-tax area, there is wide variation, from a low of 3 percent in Armenia to a high of 55 percent in Romania. Several countries apply differential (either regressive or progressive) rate schedules to employee SSCs. For example, France applies four different rates; the Slovak Republic has three different rates; while Germany, the Czech Republic, and Poland each have two different rates. Most countries also apply maximum income thresholds beyond which income is exempted from employee SSCs. As a result, the incidence of SSCs is regressive in most countries but progressive in some, and in still others it combines regressive and progressive features.

SSC systems vary in terms of covered earnings and incidence.[2] There is a substantial degree of complexity in the design of contribution systems and specifically in the taxable earning base. Many countries apply minimum and/or maximum income thresholds, differential rates, and exemptions, all of which affect not only the size of the tax base but also the distributional impact of payroll taxes. In a majority of countries, employee SSCs are capped at a certain income level, making employee SSCs regressive.[3] However, these thresholds are set at vastly different levels in the overall income distribution.

Figure 5.2a, shows the upper threshold at which SSCs are capped in relation to the average gross earnings across a number of countries. While the upper threshold is set at 70 percent of average gross earnings in the Netherlands, it is set at more than 600 percent in the Czech Republic. This results in marked differences in the distributional impact. In many of the High-Income Moderate Spender countries, SSCs tend to be strongly regressive. As shown in figure 5.2b, the average effective SSC rates in the Netherlands, Sweden, Germany, and Denmark drop sharply for higher gross earnings. For example, the effective average contribution rate for a single taxpayer with gross earnings of 167 percent of average gross earnings in the Netherlands is 9.3 percent, compared to 15.4 and 21.1 percent for taxpayers with average gross earnings and 67 percent of average gross earnings, respectively. In contrast, comparatively high upper thresholds result in essentially flat SSC rates in most transition countries (see figure 5.3 for a comparison of the effective contribution rates at different levels of income in Germany, the Bulgaria, and Czech Republic).

In contrast, only a few countries apply minimum income thresholds below which SSCs are not payable, implying some progressivity

FIGURE 5.2

Distributional Features of Social Security Contribution Systems in Selected European Economies, 2011

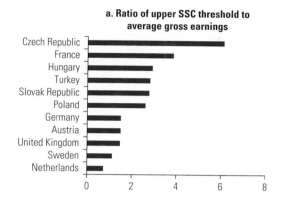

a. Ratio of upper SSC threshold to average gross earnings

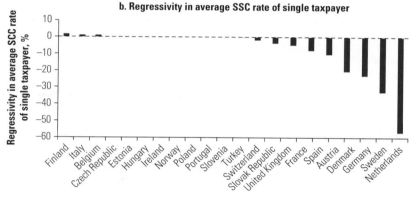

b. Regressivity in average SCC rate of single taxpayer

Source: OECD 2013.

Note: Panel b shows the difference in the average SCC employee contribution rate for a single person at 167 percent of average wage and a single person at 67 percent of average wage.

in employee SSC. This is the case with all forms of employee SSCs in Austria, Belgium, Germany, Ireland, Norway, Sweden, and the United Kingdom, as well as with pension contributions in Hungary. While some of these countries generally exempt income below the minimum threshold (which in some countries is linked to minimum wages), exemptions in others only benefit taxpayers with total gross earnings below the threshold. Taxpayers who earn more usually are subject to contributions on their first unit of earnings. This is the case, for example, with pension contributions in Norway and Sweden. Very few countries, most notably Belgium and Italy, apply progressive rate schedules similar to progressive personal income taxes (PITs) for employee contributions, making contributions in these countries generally progressive.

FIGURE 5.3

Effective Social Security Contribution Rates in Germany, the Czech Republic, and Bulgaria, 2010

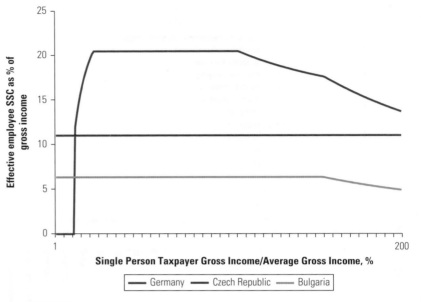

Source: OECD 2013.

The fiscal importance of SSC revenue has grown steadily over the past four decades. While comprehensive historical data are not available for all countries, data from Western European countries and Turkey show that SSC revenue on average more than doubled as a share of GDP between 1970 and 2011 (figure 5.4). For example, while SSC revenue in Germany in 1970 accounted for only 8.5 percent of GDP (and 26 percent of government revenue), it grew rapidly until the late 1990s, more than doubling to over 15 percent of GDP (and 39 percent of consolidated general government revenue) in 2000. It has since remained at this level. A similar trend can be observed in France, where SSC revenue grew from around 12 percent of GDP (34 percent of consolidated general government revenue) in 1970 to about 17 percent in 2010. These sharp increases resulted from expansion of the contribution base (more people entering the labor force and higher social insurance coverage) together with rate increases in several countries, as described in chapter 2.

Today, SSCs yield, on average, about 10 percent of GDP in revenue, accounting for about a quarter of government revenue (figure 5.5). Alongside differences in rates, tax bases, and tax compliance, the yield from payroll contributions varies across countries, ranging from 1.9 percent of GDP in Denmark to 18.7 percent of GDP

FIGURE 5.4

Social Security Contribution Revenue as a Percentage of GDP in Selected European Economies, 1970–2010

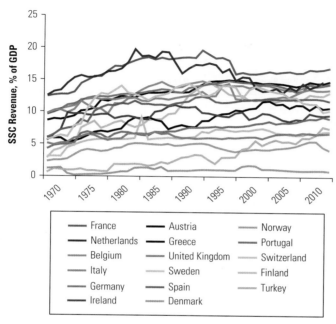

Source: OECD revenue statistics.

FIGURE 5.5

Revenue Yield of Social Security Contributions as a Percentage of GDP, Selected European and Central Asian Economies, 2011

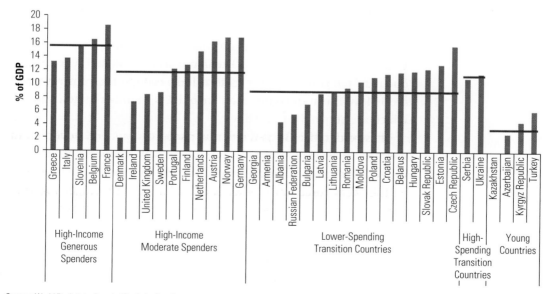

Sources: World Bank data; Eurostat Statistics Database.

FIGURE 5.6

Social Security Contribution Rates and Revenue Yield, Selected European and Central Asian Economies, 2011

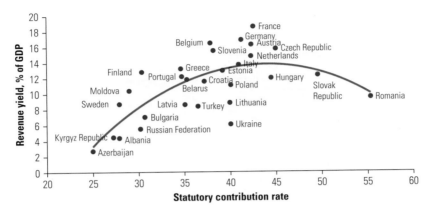

Sources: World Bank data; Eurostat Statistics Database.
Note: R² = 0.5266.

in France. In terms of share in total revenue, payroll contributions account for about 25 percent across countries on average, again with much variation, from just above 4 percent in Denmark to almost 40 percent in the Czech Republic and the Slovak Republic.

However, the productivity of contribution systems varies across countries. As can be seen in figure 5.6, the relationship between contribution rates and revenue yield tends to be U-shaped. The figure suggests that revenue yield declines for contribution rates above a certain level. Romania, for example, has the highest statutory contribution rate, but its revenue yield is close to the average across countries. Higher contribution rates may induce labor supply responses, including higher degrees of informality, which may harm revenue yield rather than increase it.[4] The figure also shows that revenue productivity tends to be lower in transition economies, most of which are below the trend line, than in old EU member states, most of which are above the trend line.

These differences in SSC revenue productivity are related to differences in the level of informal economic activity across countries, making social security financing especially challenging in environments with low tax compliance. Among other factors, revenue productivity is affected by tax compliance.[5] Transition economies tend to face particularly low tax compliance, as the informal sector accounts for a large share of economic activity. According to estimates from Schneider, Buehn, and Montenegro (2010), the average shadow economy size in Europe and Central Asia (excluding Western Europe) was 36.5 percent of official GDP in 2005, compared to 13.5 percent in

FIGURE 5.7

Relationship Between Informality and Revenue Productivity of Social Security Systems, Selected European and Central Asian Countries, 2011

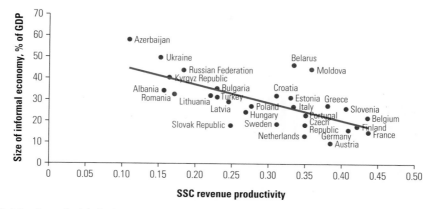

Sources: World Bank data; Eurostat Statistics Database.
Note: R² = 0.4571.

high-income OECD countries. These large informal sectors erode the tax base, especially for labor taxes. Figure 5.7 shows that revenue productivity is in fact inversely correlated with the estimated size of the informal economy across countries. As also discussed in chapter 6, finding the right balance between incentives for participation in the formal labor market and financing of social security obligations is an especially difficult task in environments with low tax compliance.[6]

While payroll contributions are the primary source of financing for social protection spending in the region, revenue coverage is insufficient in most countries, requiring general government revenue to partially fund social benefits. On average, noncontributory financing of social benefits accounts for about 30 percent of total social protection spending, equal to about 3 percent of GDP. As shown in figure 5.8, there are widespread variations from country to country, reflecting differences in the scope and coverage of social benefits and differences in the mix between contributory and noncontributory social benefits in different countries. The share of social protection spending financed by noncontributory revenue, such as general taxation, is particularly large in countries such as Denmark, Ireland, and Georgia, which by design rely on general taxation to finance their social protection systems. But most countries with payroll tax financing also face large (and growing) financing gaps, originating from fiscal imbalances in the public pension PAYG system.

At the same time, SSCs drive high labor taxes in the region, accounting for about 65 percent of nonwage labor costs on average. Taken together, labor taxes, including PITs and SSCs, account on

FIGURE 5.8

Social Protection Spending in Relation to Social Security Contribution Revenue, Selected European and Central Asian Economies, 2011

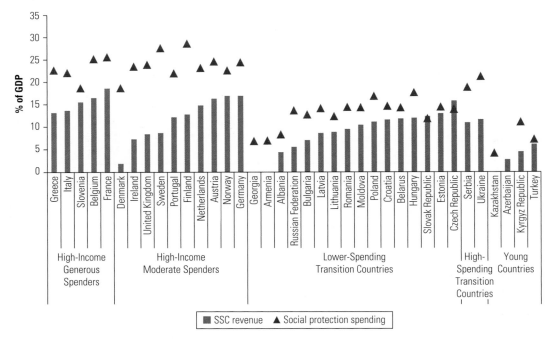

Sources: World Bank data; Eurostat Statistics Database.

average for about 40 percent of total gross labor costs, compared to 34 percent on average in OECD countries. If a worker receives the equivalent of 100 euros in net earnings, the employer incurs a labor cost of 167 euros on average. There is, however, significant variation among countries (figure 5.9), with the tax wedge being highest in Belgium (55.8 percent) and lowest in Georgia (19.4 percent).[7] SSCs are the largest part of the tax wedge except in Ireland, Denmark, and Georgia, where PIT by design accounts for the main portion of the tax wedge. The tax wedge tends to increase with the aging of the population, which results in larger social security financing needs supported by fewer contributors (figures 5.10 and 5.11).

Given the already large tax burden on labor, addressing pension financing needs by increasing revenue from SSCs is constrained by the potential negative impacts of high labor taxes on employment and competitiveness. By increasing the cost of labor, labor taxation may have an impact on labor demand. However, the relationship is complex and depends on, among other things, the rigidity of wages—that is, whether increased nonwage labor costs can be passed through to employees. This varies across countries and within countries across

FIGURE 5.9

Contribution of Labor Taxes to Gross Labor Costs in Selected European and Central Asian Economies, 2011

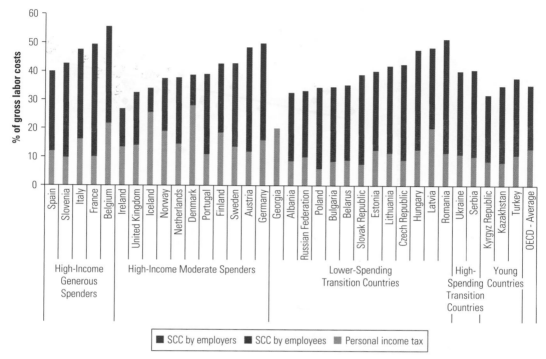

Sources: U.S. Social Security Administration 2012; OECD 2013.

FIGURE 5.10

Labor Tax Wedge in Relation to Social Protection Spending, Europe and Central Asia, 2011

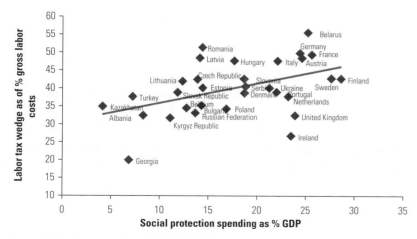

Sources: U.S. Social Security Administration 2012; OECD 2013.
Note: $R^2 = 0.2115$.

FIGURE 5.11

Labor Tax Wedge in Relation to Old-Age Dependency Ratio, Europe and Central Asia, 2011

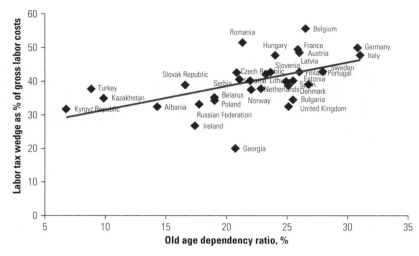

Source: World Bank staff estimates using World Bank, OECD, and UN data.
Note: R[2] = 0.2916.

different groups of employees.[8] Higher labor costs may erode international competitiveness and discourage investment and job creation. Finally, a larger tax wedge may also encourage economic activity to shift to the informal sector, with respective fiscal implications, as discussed earlier in this chapter.

Moreover, going forward, a shrinking labor force will put further pressure on revenue from payroll taxes. Together with rising expenditures on pensions, the reliance on payroll contributions of active workers is central to the demographic impact on the financial sustainability of social security systems in general and pension systems in particular (see box 5.1 for a review of the potential economic impact of changing demographics). Since labor taxes are the main financing source of social security and pension systems in Europe, demographic change will simultaneously affect pension spending and contribution revenue. The key problem is that over the next several decades, the number of retirees is expected to grow rapidly, while the number of workers who will make the payroll contributions will decline (or grow at a much slower pace).

As can be seen in figure 5.12, a majority of countries will experience substantial declines in their labor force through 2050. On average, the labor force will contract by about 20 percent of today's labor force, with the decline expected to be most severe in the eastern part of the continent: among Central European EU members, some FSU

BOX 5.1

The Inverting Pyramid and Economic Growth

At the microeconomic level, there are strong life-cycle effects on the decisions to work, save, and invest. Since individuals attempt to maximize their lifetime utility, they tend to work and save more at younger ages in order to enjoy a higher level of leisure time and consumption at older ages. In a simple growth-accounting framework, the changing age structure of the population— that is, the inverting pyramid—is expected to have a direct effect on aggregate labor supply and on savings behavior, which, together with prevailing production technologies, will determine the long-term growth potential of any economy (Bloom, Canning, and Fink 2011). However, the potential drag on economic growth created by an aging population could be at least partially offset by higher productivity, increases in labor quality, or increased labor force participation. Moreover, the specific sources of the shift in age structure do matter, as aging is the result of simultaneous declines in fertility rates and increases in life expectancy. While increases in lon- gevity can be seen as growth enhancing (Romer 1990), fertility decreases are generally expected to lower growth potential. In reality, the overall impact of aging may therefore depend on the rel- ative change between fertility and mortality, whether it is associated with increasing or decreas- ing long-run economic growth (Jones 1995).

Savings and Capital Accumulation

The standard consumption-smoothing motive predicts that at the individual level the highest savings rate will take place in the midlife period in anticipation of the need to provide for con- sumption expenditures during retirement, when incomes are expected to decline (see, for example, Jappelli and Modigliani 2005). Higher savings may in turn imply deepened capital mar- kets, productivity-enhancing investments, and hence high per capita incomes (Börsch-Supan and Winter 2001). Rising longevity may induce individuals to increase their savings rates further during their economically active years (Bloom, Canning, and Sevilla 2003; Mason 2005). How- ever, a shift in the age structure that results in a larger share of older (retired) individuals would be expected to lead to a decrease in aggregate savings, thus reducing the speed of capital accu- mulation (see, for example, Lindh and Malmberg 1999).

Labor Supply

Aging presents a shock to aggregate labor supply. Some empirical estimates have quantified the impact of declining workforces in OECD countries, showing reductions in annual growth rates of 0.2 to 0.5 percentage points in France and Germany and 0.8 percentage points in Japan (Martins et al. 2005). The extent to which demographic change will affect labor supply will depend on labor participation rates, which vary substantially across countries (Burniaux, Duval, and Jaumotte 2004).

continued

BOX 5.1 *continued*

Productivity

Changes in age structure may also affect productivity. On the one hand, increases in the life expectancy of individuals may render investments in human capital more profitable (Hazan and Zoabi 2006; Cervellati and Sunde 2009). Lower fertility may reinforce incentives for human capital investments among women (Becker, Murphy, and Tamura 1994). At the same time, shifts in the age structure mean that the labor market becomes more reliant on mature and older workers to meet new and emerging skill needs, while these workers may face weak incentives for further human capital investments (Hazan and Zoabi 2006).

FIGURE 5.12

Growth of the Working-Age Population, 2010–2050, in Selected European and Central Asian Economies

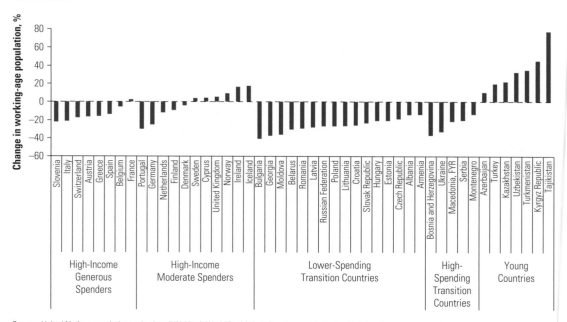

Sources: United Nations population projections (UN 2011); World Bank World Development Indicators (database).

countries (except in Central Asia), and the countries of the Balkans. In all of these, population aging is compounded by outmigration.

Finding Alternative Sources of Pension Financing

The demographic and labor market realities described above are testing the labor tax–based model of social security financing. As noted in chapter 3, in the long run, countries with aging populations will need to mobilize between 4 percent and 6 percent of annual GDP to cover the additional financing needs of their pension systems. While taming the growth in pension spending is key to restoring sustainable finances, in most countries revenue measures will have to play a role in preserving long-term fiscal health (as no government will leave its retirees destitute). But raising additional financing from the existing labor taxes will be harmful to labor markets, job creation, and growth. These longer-term pressures have been reinforced by the more acute concerns about simultaneous deterioration of fiscal accounts and soaring unemployment in the aftermath of the global financial crisis. In these circumstances, governments are seeking wider tax reform options that can contribute to fiscal consolidation in the short term while addressing long-term fiscal pressures related to prospective demographic change, minimizing distortionary effects on decisions to work, save, and invest.[9]

Europe will have to cope with aging-related fiscal pressures in the pension system on top of an already sizable public sector footprint. The average tax burden in European and Central Asian countries is around 38 percent of GDP (2011), but this average masks wide differences across the region (figure 5.13). While the Young Countries tend

FIGURE 5.13

Tax Burden as a Percentage of GDP in Selected European and Central Asian Countries, 2011

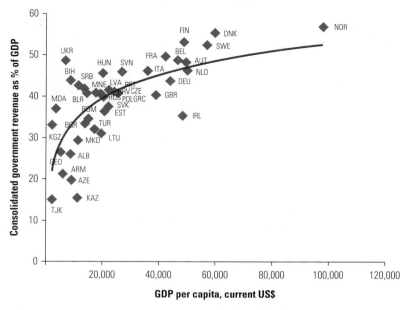

Sources: World Bank staff estimates using OECD government revenue statistics; World Bank World Development Indicators (database).
Note: $R^2 = 0.4955$.

to have smaller governments and may have room for additional revenue mobilization, the tax burden is especially large in European countries, many of which face the most severe demographic pressures. The
space for expanding the size of government in these countries is
severely limited, as additional tax increases would be harmful to long-
term growth prospects. Already, today, social protection spending is a
main driver of public spending in Europe, accounting for 42 percent
of general government expenditures on average. In addition to
increased pension spending, aging is also expected to increase the
need for spending on health and long-term care. The room for additional growth in revenues and rationalization of expenditures is therefore small, putting an additional constraint on pension reforms.

Current tax structures in Europe and Central Asia rely mainly on
consumption and income taxes and on social security contributions
(figure 5.14). Direct taxes account for 58 percent of tax revenue on
average, equal to 18 percent of GDP, split about equally between

FIGURE 5.14
Composition of Government Revenue in Selected European and Central Asian Economies, 2011

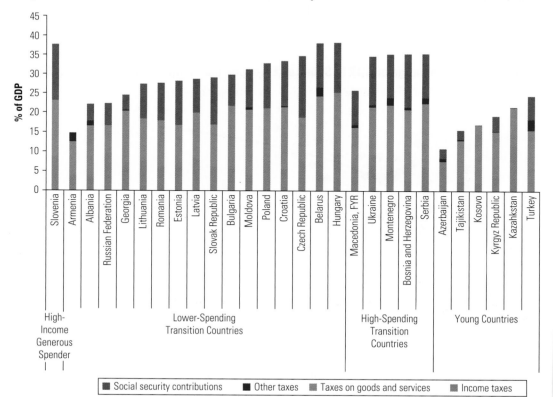

Sources: World Bank staff estimates using OECD; World Bank data.

income taxes (both corporate and personal) and SSCs. Indirect taxes, including most importantly the value-added tax (VAT), account for about 37 percent of tax revenue (12 percent of GDP). Other taxes, including property taxes, contribute about 5 percent of tax revenue (1.5 percent of GDP). There are notable differences across different groups of countries, in terms of both composition of revenue and underlying tax systems. Income taxes tend to be more important in Northern Europe, where they account for 40 percent of tax revenue (15 percent of GDP). In contrast, income taxes account for a smaller share of tax revenue in central Europe and the FSU, largely due to the prevalence of low flat tax initiatives; the average PIT rate for Central European and FSU countries is 16.7 percent, less than half that of other European subregions.

The following sections explore options for increasing fiscal space, including raising consumption and property taxes, using fiscal savings from natural resource revenue, and rationalizing other expenditures.

Raising Consumption Taxes

Raising consumption taxes, and especially VAT, is often considered a primary option for mobilizing additional fiscal revenue. Compared to income taxes, consumption taxes are generally seen as less distortionary and more efficient sources of tax revenue (see, for example, Myles 2009). Shifting the financial burden of growing pension spending to consumption taxes offers several potential advantages:

- *Improving competitiveness.* Income taxes, including SSCs, are origin-based, meaning that they are levied on domestic production while imports are not included in the tax base. In contrast, consumption taxes are destination-based, meaning that domestic consumption of both nontraded and imported goods is included in the tax base, while exports are zero-rated (and as such are excluded from the tax base). As a result, a tax shift from labor taxes to VAT implies a change in relative prices, lowering the cost of exports while increasing the cost of imports. It has been argued that tax shifts can, therefore, contribute to fiscal devaluation and help adjustments in the context of external imbalances through containment of imports and boosting of exports (de Mooij and Keen 2012 show this theoretically and empirically). There is also some empirical evidence that a tax mix that relies more heavily on consumption taxes, rather than income taxes, is associated with higher rates of economic growth— at least in OECD countries (Kneller, Bleaney, and Gemmell 1999).

- *Broadening the tax base.* Consumption provides a broader base than labor income. Consumption is financed not only by income from labor, but also by other sources of income, including pensions and other government transfers, corporate profits, and savings. A broader base allows for similar revenue generation at a lower rate, and since distortionary effects tend to increase disproportionally with increases in the tax rate, this can mitigate the distortionary effect of the tax system.

- *Mitigating the revenue impact of demographic change and enhancing intergenerational equity.* Since the two tax bases, consumption and labor income, may grow at different rates, tax shifts may have important long-term revenue implications. While aging will have a substantial impact on the composition of domestic consumption, for example by increasing consumption of health services, demographic change will affect the overall level of consumption less than it will affect labor income. Raising additional revenue from consumption taxes means that taxpayers receiving a major share of their income from sources other than labor and those financing consumption out of savings will carry a larger burden: they will pay higher consumption taxes without receiving the benefit of reduced labor income taxes. This group of taxpayers includes pensioners, among others, and increased consumption taxation may therefore help offset the intergenerational inequities associated with the intergenerational redistribution of PAYG systems.

Current VAT systems vary widely in terms of rates and revenue yield. Table 5.1 summarizes the main features of VAT systems across European countries. While the standard VAT rates vary from a low of 12 percent in Kazakhstan to a high of 27 percent in Hungary, the vast majority of countries have standard VAT rates between 19 percent and 23 percent. In addition, many countries apply reduced rates and/or VAT exemptions to certain categories of goods and services, such as medicines, basic foodstuffs, hotel services, and others.

Since the global financial crisis, many countries have increased VAT rates as part of their fiscal consolidation programs, raising their standard statutory VAT rates and to a lesser extent their reduced VAT rates. VAT increases were implemented in 13 of the 27 EU member states, with the average standard VAT rate increasing from 19.4 percent in 2007 to 21.0 percent in 2011.[10] A few countries have undertaken VAT increases in conjunction with SSC reductions (box 5.2).

TABLE 5.1

VAT Systems and Performance across European and Central Asian Economies

	VAT standard rate (%)	VAT reduced rate (%)	VAT revenue as % of GDP	VAT revenue as % of final consumption	C-efficiency (%)	Additional revenue from improving C-efficiency by 10 percentage points (% of GDP)
Albania	20.0	10.0	9.3	9.5	47.6	1.9
Austria	20.0	10.0/12.0	7.8	10.7	53.5	1.5
Belarus	20.0	0/0.5/10.0	10.0	14.9	74.6	1.3
Belgium	21.0	0/6.0/12.0	7.0	9.1	43.4	1.6
Bulgaria	20.0	9.0	9.2	12.1	60.7	1.5
Czech Republic	20.0	14.0	7.3	10.2	50.9	1.4
Denmark	25.0	0	9.9	12.9	51.5	1.9
Estonia	20.0	9.0	8.5	12.4	62.1	1.4
Finland	23.0	0/9.0/13.0	8.9	11.2	48.6	1.8
France	19.6	2.1/5.5/7.0	7.0	8.5	43.4	1.6
Georgia	18.0	n.a.	10.6	11.6	64.2	1.7
Germany	19.0	7.0	7.3	9.6	50.4	1.5
Hungary	27.0	5.0/18.0	7.9	10.7	39.8	2.0
Italy	21.0	4.0/10.0	6.2	7.7	36.4	1.7
Kazakhstan	12.0	0	3.1	5.8	47.9	0.6
Latvia	21.0	12.0	6.1	7.8	37.3	1.7
Lithuania	21.0	9.0/5.0	6.6	8.0	38.0	1.7
Netherlands	19.0	6.0	7.2	9.9	52.3	1.4
Poland	23.0	5.0/8.0	7.6	9.6	41.8	1.8
Portugal	23.0	6.0/13.0	7.8	9.0	39.3	2.0
Romania	24.0	9.0/5.0	7.5	9.9	41.2	1.8
Russian Federation	18.0	10.0	5.5	8.0	44.5	1.2
Slovak Republic	20.0	10.0	6.8	9.0	44.8	1.5
Slovenia	20.0	8.5	8.2	10.5	52.5	1.6
Sweden	25.0	0/6.0/12.0	9.5	13.0	51.9	1.8
Turkey	18.0	1.0/8.0	6.1	7.1	39.7	1.5
Ukraine	20.0	0	9.5	11.3	56.4	1.7
United Kingdom	20.0	0/5.0	7.3	8.5	42.3	1.7

Sources: World Bank staff estimates using World Bank and OECD data; IMF 2012.
Note: n.a. = not applicable.

BOX 5.2

Tax Shifting in European Countries

Denmark

Many observers consider Denmark as the prime example of noncontributory financing of social security. In 1987 Denmark introduced wide-ranging tax reform to improve the viability of the social security system while strengthening competitiveness. Average marginal effective tax rates on labor income for fully employed individuals declined from about 58 percent in 1986 to 54 percent in 2002. Initially, the employer payroll tax for unemployment and disability insurance was phased out and replaced by a VAT-like tax on consumption. That tax was later merged into the general VAT by increasing the VAT rate from 21 percent to 25 percent. In parallel, excise duties on energy products (petroleum products, electricity, gas, coal) were raised gradually. To mitigate the regressive nature of VAT and excise financing of social security benefits, the tax system has a progressive personal income tax with one of the highest marginal tax rates in the world.

Georgia

Georgia eliminated payroll contributions entirely in 2008 as part of a comprehensive tax reform, shifting social insurance benefits, including a flat pension benefit, to general government revenue.

Germany

Germany introduced a 3 percentage point increase in the standard VAT rate (from 16 percent to 19 percent) and a simultaneous reduction of 1.8 percentage points in employer social security contributions (SSCs) in 2007. It simultaneously reduced the unemployment insurance contribution by 2.3 percentage points and increased the pension contribution by 0.5 percentage points.

Hungary

In 2009 Hungary implemented a simultaneous 5 percent reduction in employer SSCs and a 5 percent increase in VAT.

However, like any tax increases, VAT rate increases trigger behavioral responses by taxpayers, up to and including evasion. Rate increases beyond a certain level may therefore harm rather than increase revenue yield. Some estimates have placed the revenue-maximizing VAT rate at below 25 percent (Agha and Haughton 1996; Matthews 2003). Room for future rate increases may therefore be limited.

As a result, further VAT revenue reforms will increasingly have to rely on base broadening and on improvements in compliance. As can be seen from table 5.1, C-efficiency, which measures the revenue yield at any given statutory rate, is on average 49 percent across countries in the region (varying from 36 percent in Italy to 75 percent in Belarus). For a fully compliant country with a single VAT rate, C-efficiency would be 100 percent. The gap reflects differences in policy (e.g., reduced rates and exemptions) and compliance. Reining in reduced rates and exemptions and curbing evasion through enhanced tax administration can increase C-efficiency. The potential revenue gains that could be realized by improving C-efficiency are quite substantial, as can be seen in the last column of table 5.1. On average, a 10 percentage point increase in C-efficiency would yield around 1.6 percent of GDP across the countries covered here.

However, tax shifts to consumption taxes may have important distributional impacts. Consumption taxes are, in principle, distributionally neutral when assessed against lifetime income (provided constant tax rates and no inheritances, so that all lifetime income is eventually spent on consumption). However, governments may be more concerned about the immediate redistributional impact on current household income and consumption. Consumption taxes tend to be regressive when assessed relative to current household incomes (figure 5.15). This is because lower-income households tend to spend a higher share of their income on current consumption, while the saving rate tends to increase with higher incomes. In particular, eliminating reduced VAT rates to improve C-efficiency is likely to have significant distributional impacts because the consumption of poorer households tends to include a larger share of goods that are VAT-exempted or taxed at reduced rates. If VAT increases are combined with reduction in SSCs, then the net distributional impact of the reform also depends on the initial incidence of SSC (which varies substantially across countries, as described earlier in this chapter). In addition, rather than assessing VAT increases in isolation, the focus should be on the overall equity in fiscal policy. There may be more efficient ways than reduced VAT rates to achieve desirable redistribution, for example, through progressive income taxation or targeted social assistance spending.

To assess the fiscal impact of tax policy options, an overlapping generations model is used for two countries, Poland and the Slovak Republic (Keuschnigg, Davoine, and Schuster 2013).[11] The model and policy simulations are discussed in more detail in chapter 6.

FIGURE 5.15

VAT Payments as a Percentage of Disposable Household Income in Five European Countries, 2013

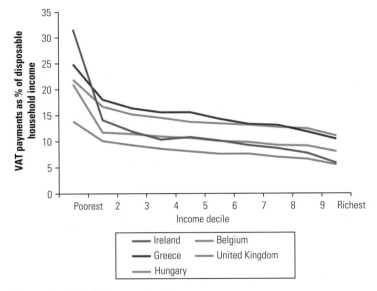

Source: European Commission 2013.

Here the focus is on simulating the impact of revenue measures: specifically, the model is used to assess and compare the impact of SSC and VAT increases. In both cases, the targeted revenue increase equals 3 percent of initial GDP. The results are expected to answer three interrelated questions. First, what is the impact of aging on VAT and SSC revenue? Second, what contribution to fiscal sustainability can be achieved through revenue policy measures? And third, which of the two revenue instruments (SSC or VAT) is more efficient?

The model captures behavioral responses of households to changes in tax policy and pension benefits, and how these responses in turn affect government finances. It reflects endogenous labor supply decisions by households in an overlapping generations structure with two generations. All households from the first generation (the young) decide to participate in a labor market or not; and if they decide to participate, they join either the formal or the informal labor market. The young also decide how much to consume in the first period and how much to save for the second period. Households from the second generation (the old) choose their retirement date, and before retiring, they choose to work in the formal or the informal market. Importantly, both VAT and SSC affect labor supply

FIGURE 5.16

Simulation of Long-Term Fiscal Impact of Increases in Social Security Contributions (SSC) and VAT Tax, Poland and the Slovak Republic, 2010 and 2050

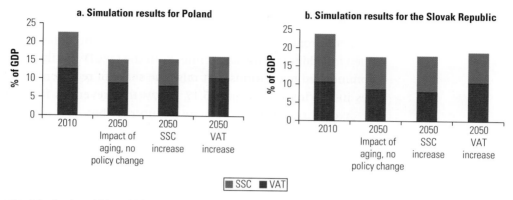

Source: Keuschnigg, Davoine, and Schuster 2013.

decisions and tax compliance. The results of this exercise suggest the following (see figure 5.16):

- Aging affects consumption tax revenue and labor tax revenue differently. The simulation results for Poland (figure 5.16a) and the Slovak Republic (figure 5.16b) show that aging populations affect both revenue from consumption taxes and SSC. However, SSC will decline more sharply as a result of a declining contributor base.

- Revenue mobilization can help improve the fiscal position, but its contribution will be relatively small compared to reforms of benefit entitlements. The model results suggest that tax increases deliver some fiscal benefits, but in a limited fashion (around 1.0 percent of GDP in Poland and 1.4 percent of GDP in the Slovak Republic), and with much less impact than pension benefit reductions.

- Because they lead to increased rates of informality, Social Security Contribution (SSC) rate increases are a relatively inefficient means of raising additional revenue. Lower compliance in turn affects revenue yield. Due to these behavioral responses, the increase in SCC revenue is lower than 1 percent of GDP in both countries (0.77 percent in Poland and 0.43 percent in the Slovak Republic).

- VAT increases also increase informality, but the revenue is higher than with SSC rate increases, mainly due to the broader tax base. Behavioral responses to VAT increases include both lower labor supply and lower compliance, which reduce the overall revenue impact. However, because consumption is a larger tax base, the revenue impact is greater (1.44 percent in Poland and 1.85 percent in the Slovak Republic).

Raising Property Taxes

Recurrent property taxes are another potential source that could be tapped for additional fiscal revenue. Both the OECD and the EU have recommended tax reforms that raise the share of recurrent property taxes in the tax mix. Figure 5.17 shows that revenues from property taxes vary substantially across countries, but overall, revenue yield tends to be relatively low in most European countries.[12] While there are considerable differences in the tax treatment of properties, this is the result of both low tax rates and tax assessment based on undervalued properties in several countries.

While property taxes affect investment decisions, taxing immobile wealth, such as buildings and land, is generally considered less distortionary and harmful to growth than taxing income.[13] Property taxes also tend to be progressive (with the notable exception of the United Kingdom), although undervaluation of the tax base may undermine

FIGURE 5.17

Property Tax Yield as a Percentage of GDP in Selected European and Central Asian Economies, 2010

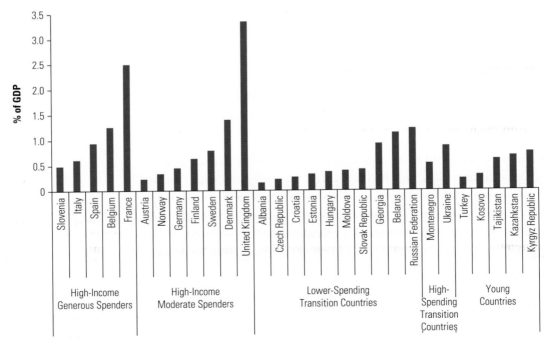

Sources: World Bank data; OECD government revenue statistics.

progressivity. Finally, as in the case of consumption tax financing, a shift from labor to property tax financing may also have impacts on intergenerational equity, especially as retired property owners may enjoy the income effect of fully owned housing that is taxed at relatively low rates.

Tapping Natural Resource Revenues

Fiscal savings from natural resource revenue may provide additional financing for pension obligations in resource-rich economies. Azerbaijan, Kazakhstan, Norway, and the Russian Federation possess significant proven oil reserves and have established sovereign wealth funds. They have done so not only to stabilize fiscal accounts in view of volatile revenue inflows, but also to accumulate long-term savings, typically invested in offshore financial assets.

These funds operate with different rules, and the asset values vary substantially. In principle, the financial returns on the fund assets as well as withdrawals of the principal could be used to finance future pension liabilities. In fact, both Norway and Russia have linked their savings funds explicitly to pension obligations. As can be seen from table 5.2, the level of proven reserves, the maturity of the extraction cycle, and the accumulated financial assets vary across countries. But if managed responsibly, fiscal savings generated from natural resources could provide additional future fiscal revenue, at least in some countries.

Reducing Other Expenditures

Finally, governments should consider rationalizing nonpension expenditures to cope with increased pension spending. If pension reform measures are insufficient to ensure actuarial sustainability of

TABLE 5.2

Asset Accumulation in Four Oil-Exporting Countries

Country	Proven reserves (billions of barrels)	Oil production (thousands of barrels/day), 2011	Reserves-to-production ratio	Asset value of oil fund (US$, billions, 2011)	Asset value of oil fund (% of GDP)
Norway	6.9	2,039.3	9.2	235	48
Azerbaijan	7.0	1,033.0	18.6	30	52
Kazakhstan	39.8	1,681.6	64.9	62	30
Russian Federation	74.2	10,032.1	20.3	87	4

Sources: World Bank staff estimates using World Bank data; data provided by the finance ministries of Norway, Azerbaijan, Kazakhstan, and Russian Federation; BP 2013.

the pension system, governments need to seek measures to reduce spending on a wider front, especially given the already high level of taxation. Assessing the room and specific options for expenditure rationalization is a highly country-specific endeavor. It is inherently linked not only to specific policy objectives but also to the design and efficiency of the current public spending program in a particular country.

While an in-depth analysis of these issues is beyond the scope of this chapter, some very general trends can be observed (figure 5.18). Given the significance of social welfare spending, reforms of social welfare systems are central to fiscal reforms. Aside from curtailing pension spending, which is addressed in chapter 3, countries will also have to deal with the challenging task of containing health care costs, which are expected to rise as a result of aging and the increasing availability of expensive care. For other social assistance transfers there may be options for improved targeting and means testing, although these need to be assessed in light of equity and efficiency

FIGURE 5.18

Components of Public Spending as a Percentage of GDP in Selected European and Central Asian Countries, 2011

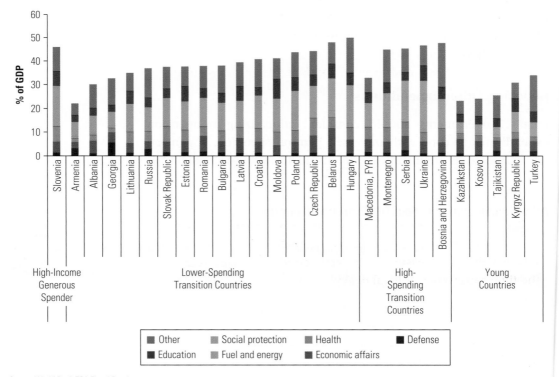

Source: World Bank ECA Fiscal Database.

concerns, which again will be country-specific. Outside the welfare system, there may be room to improve efficiency and cut spending in a number of areas, including energy subsidies, which remain significant in a number of countries. These subsidies are costly, they tend to be regressive, and they may encourage inefficiency in energy consumption.

Policy Options

Maintaining sustainable public finances while securing adequate old-age income support will require a combination of policy measures. Aging will place significant constraints on fiscal policies for years to come. Reforms of public pension schemes, including increases in the statutory and effective retirement age and reduced generosity of pension benefits, remain essential. However, governments may also have to consider a broader range of fiscal reforms that could contribute to closing the long-term financing gap. Generally, the room to redress pension-financing imbalances within the general government budget is relatively limited, given the already large size of the tax burden in most countries in the region. Simulations suggest that revenue measures taken individually will be insufficient to achieve sustainability, but they may constitute important elements in a comprehensive policy response necessary to tackle aging-related fiscal challenges.

While circumstances and available options vary across countries, this chapter has looked at the broad contours of available fiscal policy choices:

- *Maintaining fiscal discipline.* The daunting fiscal implications of aging reinforce the need for prudent fiscal management with a medium- to long-term perspective. Since today's policy choices and even relatively modest changes to the primary balance may have large dynamic effects in the long term, countries need to anchor fiscal policy in measures of long-term sustainability. Adopting such measures in a formalized fiscal framework, such as, for example, the sustainability gap measure in the Netherlands, could help improve the time consistency of fiscal policy.

- *Reforming SSC systems to broaden the tax base and improve work incentives.* High SSC rates limit the room for revenue-enhancing increases in these rates in most countries, but there may be scope in several countries for revenue-neutral or even revenue-enhancing reductions in marginal rates and improvements in progressivity in social contribution systems. Low compliance appears to undermine collection efficiency, particularly in transition economies. Countries like Romania and Ukraine seem to be trapped in high rate–low collection equilibria and may therefore have considerable room for additional taxpayers and more transactions coming into the system.

There are different options for strengthening compliance, including improved tax administration as well as changes in policy that could improve incentives for tax compliance. The latter could include reductions in marginal rates, especially for low-income wage earners with relatively high labor supply sensitivity. In addition, changes to the earning base could improve revenue yield and increase progressivity, for example by raising the contribution limit of covered earnings. This broadening of the tax base is different from an across-the-board increase in the payroll tax rate, because it restricts the tax increase to those with the highest earnings. However, such policy changes need to take into account the implied increases in benefits that are linked to covered earnings in most countries and may therefore offset revenue increases, at least partially.

- *Shifting social security financing to consumption taxes and property taxes.* Broad-based consumption taxes are generally viewed as more efficient and less distortionary than labor taxes. Shifting the tax burden from labor taxes to consumption taxes may therefore help meet long-term financing needs and enhance efficiency while reducing adverse effects of labor taxes on employment and growth. The VAT already constitutes a significant revenue source in most countries. Most tax policy changes in recent years have involved increases in the standard statutory VAT rate and to a lesser extent in reduced VAT rates. Since rate increases beyond a certain level may depress rather than increase revenue yield, room for future rate increases may be limited.

Further increases in revenue through VAT reforms will increasingly have to rely on base broadening and on improvements in compliance. VAT C-efficiency, which measures the revenue yield at any given statutory rate, is on average 49 percent across countries in the region, suggesting that significant potential revenue gains could be achieved by reining in reduced rates and exemptions and curbing evasion through enhanced tax administration. Such policy measures could achieve, on average, around 1.6 percent of GDP in additional revenue. Since shifts to consumption taxes may increase regressivity of the tax system, such reforms will need to be assessed carefully from an equity perspective. In addition, property taxes may offer another potential revenue source that is seen as relatively harmless to growth and tends to be progressive.

• *Rationalizing expenditures.* If pension reform measures are insufficient to ensure fiscal sustainability of the pension system, governments will need to seek measures to reduce spending on a wider front, especially in light of the already high levels of taxation. Given the significance of social welfare spending, reforms of social welfare systems are central to fiscal reforms. Along with curtailing pension spending, as discussed in chapter 3, countries will also have to deal with the challenging task of containing health care costs, which are expected to rise as a result of aging and the availability of increasingly expensive care. Outside the social welfare system, there may be room to improve efficiency and cut spending in a range of areas, including energy subsidies, which remain significant in a number of countries. Fiscal rules constraining expenditure growth may also be useful in ensuring creation and preservation of fiscal space on the spending side.

Shifts of pension financing to general government revenue need to be embedded in wider reforms of the pension system. Since shifting the financing burden to general government revenue eliminates the link between individual contributions and benefits, changes on the revenue side will most likely need to be accompanied by changes to the determination of pension benefits. Public schemes that are largely financed from general taxation will most likely concentrate public retirement provision on basic income support rather than paying earning-related pension benefits while relying on private savings for additional income support (as discussed in chapter 4). This is the case both in Denmark and Georgia. Of course, some countries will need to change the philosophy underlying their pension systems if they are to move in this direction, but the alternative of increasing cross-subsidization from the general budget of rising deficits in contributory public pension schemes is likely to involve greater inequities and fiscal costs.

Notes

1. In Denmark, social contributions of both employers and employees are lump-sum charges, covering mostly unemployment insurance, while pensions are financed from the general budget. The social security rate for Danish employees is a monthly lump-sum contribution

(DKr 90 in 2012), while employers contribute to a number of funds (approximately DKr 8,000–10,000 per employee per year). The reported SSC rate for Denmark is the effective rate for the average wage earner.

2. The incidence of SSC payments, however, should not be assessed in isolation. Rather, the overall distributional impact of any social security and/or pension system will depend on the impact of tax and spending instruments combined.

3. These thresholds are typically set below the income level at which the top statutory personal income tax (PIT) rate begins to apply, implying that SSC rates do not increase the marginal personal tax rate (encompassing PIT and employee SSC) beyond the top statutory PIT rate. In addition, several countries, including France, Germany, Poland, and the United Kingdom, apply regressive rate schedules in which contribution rates decline for higher-income brackets.

4. There is extensive research on the so-called Laffer curve, which underpins the U-shaped relationship between tax rates and revenue yield. Much of this literature is concerned with the behavioral response to tax rates and its impact on the tax base. In addition, more recent literature has stressed the effect of tax rates on compliance behavior. Of particular relevance in this context is the work of Sanyal, Gang, and Goswami (2000), who show how a Laffer curve may arise under informality, and Papp and Takáts (2008), who focus on the relationship of tax rates, compliance, and revenue yield.

5. Differences in productivity across countries are also related to policies such as coverage (for example, the treatment of self-employed people) and to the underlying tax base upon which contributions are levied.

6. Informality also decreases pension obligations under PAYG systems, because informal activity does not accrue pension rights. However, fiscal pressure will remain, as governments will find themselves compelled to provide at least minimum old-age income support to the uninsured.

7. The tax wedge is the difference between gross labor costs and net take-home pay of the employee, expressed as a share of gross labor costs.

8. This has been confirmed by several empirical studies, most recently by Packard, Koettl, and Montenegro (2012) and Andrews, Caldera Sánchez, and Johansson (2011).

9. An analysis of the key fiscal policy challenges and possible reform options faced by countries in Europe and Central Asia after the recent financial crisis is provided by Islam and Smits (2013).

10. At the onset of the crisis, in late 2008 and early 2009, some countries postponed plans to increase VAT rates (the Netherlands, 19 to 20 percent) or reduced the standard VAT rate (Ireland, 21.5 to 21.0 percent in 2010; Portugal, 21 to 20 percent; the United Kingdom, 17.5 to 15.0 percent) to boost domestic demand during the initial downturn. Later on, in 2009 and 2010, many countries began to raise their VAT rates. They included Ireland (21.0 to 21.5 percent); from mid-2009, Hungary (20 to 25 percent), Estonia (18 to 20 percent), the Czech Republic (19 to 20 percent), and Latvia (21 to 23 percent); from mid-2010, Lithuania (21 to 23 percent), Spain (16 to 18 percent), Portugal (back to 21 percent), Greece (21 to 23 percent), Finland (22 to

23 percent), and Romania (19 to 24 percent); and in early 2011, the United Kingdom (17.5 to 20.0 percent).

11. Both countries face similar challenges of aging, but they vary in terms of their pension finance outcomes. Poland currently spends more on pensions but is expected to experience a decrease in pension expenditures, according to projections from the European Commission (2012)— from 11.8 percent of GDP in 2010 to 9.6 percent in 2060. In contrast, the European Commission estimates an increase in pension expenditure for the Slovak Republic, from 8 percent of GDP in 2010 to 13.2 percent in 2060. This is mainly because the Polish PAYG system relies on defined contribution notional accounts and hence adjusts benefits to changes in life expectancy, even after retirement, while benefits in the Slovak PAYG pillar are calculated according to points earned during time before retirement.

12. In fact, net property taxation is negative in several countries because of tax-deductible mortgage interest payments.

13. Conceptually, property taxation can be treated either as wealth taxation or as a consumption tax on the imputed rent in owner-occupied housing.

References

Agha, Ali, and Jonathan Haughton. 1996. "Designing VAT Systems: Some Efficiency Considerations." *Review of Economics and Statistics* 78 (2): 303–8.

Andrews, Dan, Aida Caldera Sánchez, and Åsa Johansson. 2011. "Towards a Better Understanding of the Informal Economy." OECD Economics Department Working Paper 873, Organisation for Economic Co-operation and Development, Paris.

Becker, Gary S., Kevin M. Murphy, and Robert Tamura. 1994. "Human Capital, Fertility, and Economic Growth." In *Human Capital: A Theoretical and Empirical Analysis, with Special Reference to Education*, edited by Gary S. Becker, chapter 12. Chicago, IL: University of Chicago Press.

Bloom, David E., David Canning, and Günther Fink. 2011. "Implications of Population Aging for Economic Growth." PGDA Working Paper 64, Program on the Global Demography of Aging, Harvard University, Cambridge, MA.

Bloom, David E., David Canning, and Jaypee Sevilla. 2003. *The Demographic Dividend: A New Perspective on the Economic Consequences of Population Change.* Santa Monica, CA: RAND.

Börsch-Supan, Axel H., and Joachim K. Winter. 2001. "Population Aging, Savings Behavior and Capital Markets." NBER Working Paper 8561, National Bureau of Economic Research, Cambridge, MA.

BP. 2013. *Energy Outlook 2030.* http://www.bp.com/en/global/corporate /about-bp/statistical-review-of-world-energy-2013/energy-outlook -2030.html.

Burniaux, Jean-Marc, Romain Duval, and Florence Jaumotte. 2004. "Coping with Ageing: A Dynamic Approach to Quantify the Impact of Alternative

Policy Options on Future Labour Supply in OECD Countries." OECD Economics Department Working Paper 371, Organisation for Economic Co-operation and Development, Paris.

Cervellati, Matteo, and Uwe Sunde. 2009. "Life Expectancy and Economic Growth: The Role of the Demographic Transition." IZA Discussion Paper 4160, Institute for the Study of Labor (IZA), Bonn, Germany.

de Mooij, Ruud, and Michael Keen. 2012. "'Fiscal Devaluation' and Fiscal Consolidation: The VAT in Troubled Times." IMF Working Paper 12/85, International Monetary Fund, Washington, DC.

European Commission. 2012. *The 2012 Ageing Report: Economic and Budgetary Projections for the 27 EU Member States (2010–2060)*. Brussels: European Commission, Directorate-General for Economic and Financial Affairs.

———. 2013. *Employment and Social Developments in Europe 2012*. Brussels: European Commission.

Eurostat Statistics Database. European Commission, Brussels. http://epp .eurostat.ec.europa.eu/portal/page/portal/statistics/search_database.

Hazan, Moshe, and Hosny Zoabi. 2006. "Does Longevity Cause Growth? A Theoretical Critique." *Journal of Economic Growth* 2 (4): 363–76.

IMF (International Monetary Fund). 2012. *World Economic Outlook 2012*. Washington, DC: IMF.

Islam, Roumeen, and Karlis Smits. 2013. "Fiscal Recovery in ECA? Managing in a Risky World." World Bank, Washington, DC.

Jappelli, Tullio, and Franco Modigliani. 2005. "The Age-Saving Profile and the Life-Cycle Hypothesis." In *The Collected Papers of Franco Modigliani*, vol. 6, 141–72. Cambridge, MA: MIT Press.

Jones, Charles I. 1995. "R&D-Based Models of Economic Growth." *Journal of Population Economics* 103 (4): 759–83.

Keuschnigg, Christian, Thomas Davoine, and Philip Schuster. 2013. "Aging and Pension Reform: A General Equilibrium Approach." Background paper for this report, World Bank, Washington, DC.

Kneller, Richard, Michael F. Bleaney, and Norman Gemmell. 1999. "Fiscal Policy and Growth: Evidence from OECD Countries." *Journal of Public Economics* 74: 171–90.

Lindh, Thomas, and Bo Malmberg. 1999. "Age Structure Effects and Growth in the OECD, 1950–90." *Journal of Population Economics* 12 (3): 431–49.

Martins, Joaquim Oliveira, Frédéric Gonand, Pablo Antolin, Christine de la Maisonneuve, and Kwang-Yeol Yoo. 2005. "The Impact of Aging on Demand, Factor Markets and Growth." OECD Economics Department Working Paper 420, Organisation for Economic Co-operation and Development, Paris.

Mason, Andrew. 2005. "Demographic Transition and Demographic Dividends in Developed and Developing Countries." Paper presented at the United Nations Expert Group Meeting on Social and Economic Implications of Changing Population Age Structures, Mexico City, August 31–September 2.

Matthews, Kent. 2003. "VAT Evasion and VAT Avoidance: Is There a European Laffer Curve for VAT?" *International Review of Applied Economics* 17 (1): 105–14.

Myles, Gareth D. 2009. "Economic Growth and the Role of Taxation: Aggregate Data." OECD Economics Department Working Paper 714, Organisation for Economic Co-operation and Development, Paris.

OECD (Organisation for Economic Co-operation and Development). 2013. *Taxing Wages 2013.* Paris: OECD.

Packard, Truman, Johannes Koettl, and Claudio E. Montenegro. 2012. *In from the Shadow: Integrating Europe's Informal Labor.* Washington, DC: World Bank.

Papp, Tamás K., and Előd Takáts. 2008. "Tax Rate Cuts and Tax Compliance: The Laffer Curve Revisited." IMF Working Paper 08/7, International Monetary Fund, Washington, DC.

Romer, Paul M. 1990. "Endogenous Technological Change." *Journal of Political Economy* 98 (5): 71–102.

Sanyal, Amal, Ira N. Gang, and Omkar Goswami. 2000. "Corruption, Tax Evasion and the Laffer Curve." *Public Choice* 105 (1–2): 61–78.

Schneider, Friedrich, Andreas Buehn, and Claudio E. Montenegro. 2010. "New Estimates for the Shadow Economies All Over the World." Background Paper for *In from the Shadow: Integrating Europe's Informal Labor* (Washington, DC: World Bank, 2012).

UN (United Nations). 2011. *World Population Prospects: The 2010 Revision.* New York: United Nations, Department of Economic and Social Affairs, Population Division. CD-ROM.

U.S. Social Security Administration. 2012. *Social Security Programs throughout the World.* http://www.ssa.gov/policy/docs/progdesc/ssptw/.

World Bank. ECA Fiscal Database (internal database). World Bank, Washington, DC.

World Bank. World Development Indicators (database). http://data.worldbank.org/data-catalog/world-development-indicators.

CHAPTER 6

Working More, Longer, and More Productively

Introduction

As argued in chapters 2 and 5, a key factor straining pension systems is a shrinking labor force, a result of the inverting of the working-age population pyramid. This process uncovers the unsustainability of past generous expansions of old-age benefit provisions: more and more pensions are paid, for longer periods of time, and have to be financed from the contributions of fewer and fewer workers, who spend less of their longer adult lives in employment. This chapter focuses on ways to mitigate the effects of a declining labor force on pension systems in the aging countries of the Europe and Central Asia region.

There is considerable scope for increasing employment levels, and achieving this could significantly ease pressures on pension financing and reduce poverty risks for both current and future cohorts of older people. However, improving labor market performance is far from a simple task, especially in the current economic climate. The financial crisis and its aftermath in Europe have led to large employment losses and a significant rise in unemployment. New European Union (EU) member states and other countries closest to the euro area have experienced the largest job losses, while the Russian Federation, Turkey, and some of the former Soviet Union (FSU) countries bounced back more quickly. However, the region as a whole had weak employment performance prior to the financial crisis as a result of structural factors. In many countries, low labor force participation (LFP) and a decline in the share of people working in formal sector jobs, where they pay social security contributions, are of particular concern for achieving the sustainability and adequacy of pension systems.

Creating more and better jobs calls for a multisectoral policy agenda that goes beyond the scope of this chapter. Above all, there is a need for policies that facilitate a sustained economic and labor market recovery that lays the groundwork for sustained creation of jobs individuals, and that help individuals prepare for these new jobs. These issues are analyzed in great detail in a new World Bank report that discusses solutions to the overall employment problem in the region, including youth joblessness (Arias and Sánchez-Páramo 2013). This chapter focuses more specifically on the obstacles to achieving longer and more productive working lives and the policies that can help confront the barriers faced by older workers in the region.

The remainder of the chapter is organized in four parts. A first section examines the employment challenges resulting from low LFP, high unemployment, and informality, factors prevalent in many countries in the region. Using projections of demographic trends, it then analyzes how population aging will affect the size and composition of the labor force in coming decades. The results show that inducing more women to join the labor force and encouraging older workers to remain in the labor force are key for safeguarding old-age income provisions. It is also clear, though, that there is only so much that can be achieved by increasing the participation of the domestic working-age population. Beyond these limits, only immigration of younger workers can help stem the demographic decline.

The second section discusses the barriers to achieving greater work attachment and higher productivity (and hence fiscal contributions) of older workers. This requires us, first of all, to confront several widespread myths and misperceptions about employment at older ages: that older workers prefer retirement to working, that older workers are less productive and difficult to employ, and that keeping older workers in the active labor force prevents the young from finding jobs. The chapter argues that once past these misperceptions, policy makers can focus on devising strategies that confront the real barriers faced by older workers.

The third section sets forth policy options, highlighting four key sets of measures that can make a notable difference in helping to achieve longer and more productive working lives. First, governments should review taxes and social benefits, notably those that give people strong incentives to remain out of the labor force. The objective is to encourage a more gradual transition from work into retirement—for example, by allowing older people to work part-time while collecting a partial pension. Second, governments should reform labor regulations that impede flexible work, and they should tackle wage-setting mechanisms that are based on seniority rather than rewarding productivity. Third, employers should be encouraged and enabled to make proactive adjustments to the workplace that prepare their operations for an aging workforce, raise the productivity and comfort level of older workers, and tap the benefits of age-diverse working teams. Fourth, employers, governments, and workers need to invest in appropriate training strategies that enable mature workers to learn new skills cost-effectively.

The final section explores the consequences of successful reforms more directly. It presents new results from a comprehensive modeling exercise that accounts for links between real-world pension parameters and benefits, tax burdens, and formal and informal employment choices. The analysis suggests that more active, productive, and longer working lives are no panacea, but they can contribute substantially to mitigating any short-term adverse impacts of unavoidable reforms in the pension system.

In particular, expanding the base of contributors can only ease or delay reforms of pension systems. Greater formalization of the workforce or an influx of immigrants, for instance, only provides a temporary mitigation of the strain on pension systems. Since these "new" workers become entitled to future pensions, pension systems will become even more unsustainable over time as long as they do not balance contributions and pension promises in a realistic and sustainable way. Each additional worker, each additional year and hour of work, and each additional contribution made to the pension system widens the pension gap if the relationship between contributions and benefit accrual is fundamentally flawed. Having more people work and work longer will help ease the transition to a more sustainable pension system by spreading out the costs of reforms to more people over a longer period of time, but it is no substitute for pension reform itself.

Labor Force Challenges: Low Participation, High Unemployment, and Informality

Between 2000 and 2007, transition countries in the Europe and Central Asia region experienced rapid income growth, increased productivity, and reduced poverty. As discussed by Arias and Sánchez-Páramo (2013), many countries successfully integrated into the global economy, restructured enterprises, improved conditions for doing business, and modernized labor markets and social benefits systems. But these actions did not always translate into higher aggregate employment, as economic restructuring in some countries meant that jobs were both created and destroyed. Economic and labor market performance was heterogeneous. Some countries experienced strong economic and productivity growth with higher employment levels, while others did not.

Following the 2008 financial crisis, job destruction accelerated in many countries and the unemployment situation worsened sharply, particularly among youth and older workers. Since then, the strength and speed of the economic and labor market recovery has varied significantly across countries. For instance, countries like Poland and Turkey have weathered the employment impacts of the crisis better, while labor markets in the western Balkans and the Baltic countries remain very weak, with employment rates still below their pre-crisis peak.

Overall employment rates in the region are much lower than in Western Europe and in the non-European countries of the Organisation for Economic Co-operation and Development (OECD), particularly among women and older workers. The economic transition of the early 1990s made it difficult for older workers to stay employed. Moreover, those who continued working through the transition often dropped out of the labor force relatively early in their lives. Once older workers leave the labor market, it becomes increasingly difficult to bring them back.

Figure 6.1 compares recent employment rates across the country clusters used in this report. In 2010, over one-third of men and over half of women in the age group 55–64 were not employed. Relative to the High-Income Moderate Spender countries, employment rates among older women are around 15 to 25 percentage points lower in the Lower-Spending and High-Spending Transition Countries, while the gap is 5 to 10 percentage points for women aged 25–54. These employment gaps are even larger in the Young Countries. The employment rates among older men in Lower-Spending and High-Spending Transition Countries and Young Countries are nearly 10 to 15 percentage points lower than among their peers in the High-Income Moderate Spenders, while the gap is 5 to 10 points among men aged 25–54. The gaps in male employment rates are somewhat lower in the Young Countries and more pronounced for women in the Balkans and Turkey, following a similar age pattern.

FIGURE 6.1

Employment Rates by Gender and Age Group, Selected European and Central Asian Economies with OECD Comparators, 2011

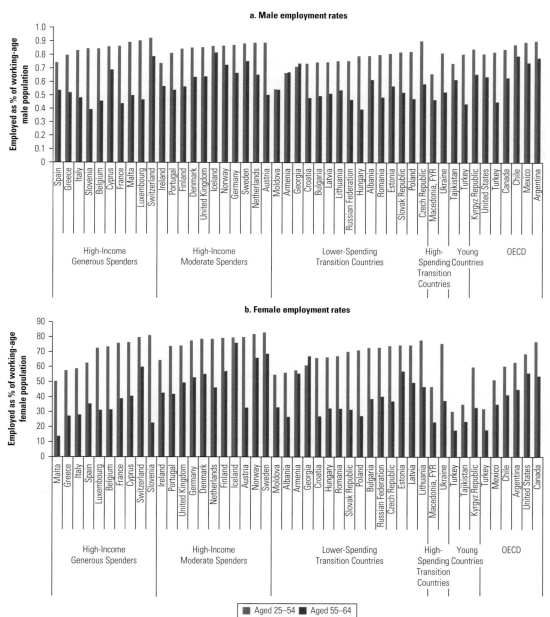

Source: World Bank and Eurostat estimates from labor force and households surveys, latest years available.

Looking closely, the employment problem in Europe and Central
Asia reflects low LFP and high levels of unemployment and informality. As shown in figure 6.2, this also has distinct age and gender
dimensions. About one in four individuals do not actively seek jobs
and stay outside the labor force. Nearly one in 10 of those in the labor
force are unemployed. And roughly one in three of those who are
employed have an informal job, whether as self-employed or as
employees not making contributions to social security. Older workers,
and older women in particular, exhibit low labor market attachment.

FIGURE 6.2

**Employment Status over the Life Cycle in Countries of Europe and Central Asia, by Gender,
circa 2009**

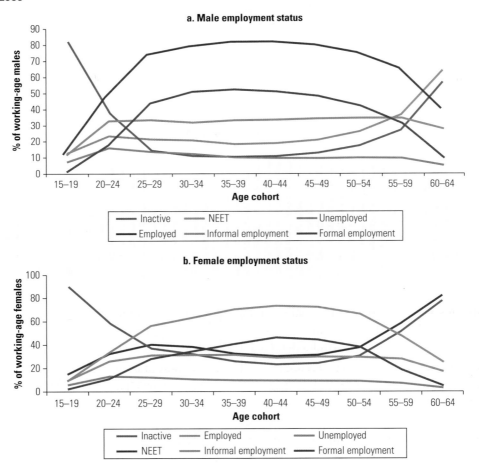

Source: World Bank estimates based on labor force and household surveys, latest years available.
Note: Based on simple average for available countries: Albania, Armenia, Bulgaria, the Czech Republic, Estonia, Georgia, Hungary, the Kyrgyz Republic, Latvia,
Lithuania, the former Yugoslav Republic of Macedonia, Moldova, Poland, Romania, the Russian Federation, the Slovak Republic, Slovenia, Turkey, and Ukraine. For
formal/informal breakdown, the sample does not include Armenia, Georgia, Lithuania, Moldova, Romania, and Russia. Note that all rates are presented as a percentage of working-age population. Some rates, like the informality rate, when expressed as a percentage of total employment would display quite different profiles over
age groups. NEET = not in education, employment, or training.

The problem of joblessness is particularly acute among youth (aged 15–24), having reached dramatic levels in Armenia, Greece, the former Yugoslav Republic of Macedonia, and Spain (20 to 33 percent). Informal employment is actually more prevalent than formal work among youth and older workers. The compound effect of the resulting "unused work capacity" and smaller base of contributors is an enormous strain on contributory pension systems in the region.

Ensuring the adequacy and sustainability of old-age pensions in the region hinges especially on the ability to increase the labor market attachment of women and of workers beyond age 55. For youth, there is a trade-off between getting them quickly into the workforce and allowing them time to develop the skills needed to support longer careers in an increasingly demanding and changing labor market. The rapid aging of the population implies that keeping older workers longer in work is a key strategy to stem the impact of a shrinking labor force.

In this respect, the gaps in LFP in Europe and Central Asia are unique in the world. LFP rates are lower (average 57 percent in 2011) than in most non-European OECD countries, particularly among women. The gap in LFP among women, measured in relation to OECD levels, ranges from nearly 10 percentage points in Central and Southern Europe to about 20 percentage points in the Balkans and the Young Countries. For men, the participation gaps range from only 3 or 4 percentage points in Southern Europe and the Young Countries to 8 percentage points in Central Europe to nearly 10 percentage points in Russia and other countries of the FSU. The gaps in LFP are widest among older workers. The average participation rate among older workers, 58 percent, is far below the average for the OECD (73 percent) and other middle-income regions (between 60 and 65 percent in Latin America and Asia).[1]

Countries could increase their labor force significantly if older workers reached their participation potential. Older populations across the region are increasingly healthy, making it feasible to achieve longer working lives. Figure 6.3 shows the potential to increase the labor force in four older age groups, taking the participation rate of prime-age adults (aged 40–44) in each country as the benchmark. By this yardstick, the majority of Lower-Spending and High-Spending Transition Countries could increase their workforce of individuals aged 45–64 by at least 15 percent; Hungary and Poland could increase it by up to one-third. The High-Income Moderate Spenders could achieve participation gains of 15 to 20 percent. Given the gender gap in participation profiles, the lion's share of these gains would come from drawing more women into the labor force.

FIGURE 6.3

Potential Labor Force Gain in the Population Aged 45–64, by Age Group, in Selected European and Central Asian Economies

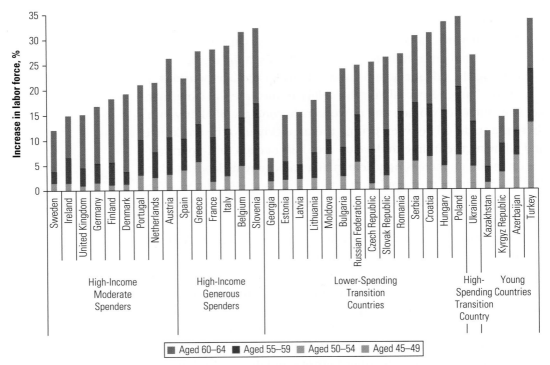

Source: World Bank estimates based on World Development Indicators and labor force and households surveys, latest years available.
Note: Potential gain is calculated as the projected increase in the size of the workforce aged 45–64 if the population aged 45–64 had the same participation rate as the 40–44 age group in each country. Data are for 2008 for all countries except Georgia, Moldova, and Ukraine (2005) and the Kyrgyz Republic (2006).

The next section examines the demographic arithmetic and various scenarios for stemming the projected shrinking of the working-age population. It quantifies the scope to do this through higher LFP (mainly of women and older people) and longer working lives, along with possible labor relocation to leverage youth bulges in the Young Countries.

The Scope for Curbing the Inverting Population Pyramid

Since pension systems in the region are mostly pay-as-you-go systems, financed through labor taxation, the sustainability of these systems depends crucially on the size of the labor force. Hence, it is important to assess the impact of the region's demographic trends in this regard. As discussed in chapter 2, old-age dependency ratios[2] are already high in the region and are projected to increase dramatically over the next 50 years. Today, in most countries of the region, there are about 20 to 30 people aged 65 or older for every 100 people aged 15–64. This ratio is expected to increase to up to 70 per 100 over the next decades (for example, in Albania and in Bosnia and Herzegovina). These demographic dynamics are leading to an inverting population pyramid: the size of the labor force will shrink drastically while the number of pensioners will increase significantly.

In order to better understand the interaction between the demographic transition and the evolution of the size of the labor force, a detailed analysis of LFP rates across age, gender, and countries combined with demographic trends was carried out. This analysis used data from the United Nations Population Division on projected future demographic developments in combination with data from the International Labour Organization on current and future LFP rates by gender and age group; this allowed a detailed assessment of the impact of the demographic transition on the size and the structure of the labor force.[3] In addition, assuming alternative developments for LFP profiles offers insights on how increasing the participation rates of the population—in particular of young workers, older workers, and women—could potentially stem the decline of the labor force.

With no changes in LFP profiles, Europe and Central Asia— including EU and European Free Trade Association countries—will lose 54 million workers between 2010 and 2060. Figure 6.4 depicts projected changes in the size of the labor force over the next five decades by age group. During the current decade, the 2010s,

FIGURE 6.4

Projected Change in the Labor Force in Europe and Central Asia, by Age Group and Period, 2010s through 2050s

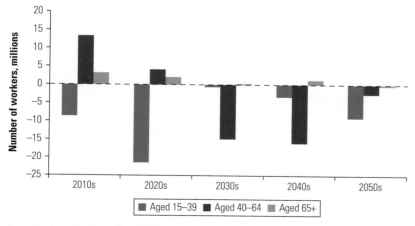

Source: Based on methodology in Koettl 2008.
Note: Includes all countries of Europe and Central Asia, including all EU and EFTA countries.

no major changes will be felt yet. Although the younger labor force will start to decline, losing 9 million workers aged 15–39, the prime-age labor force aged 40–64 will still grow significantly. By far the biggest change will happen during the 2020s, with a projected decline of 22 million young workers. Although the prime-age labor force will still increase slightly, the 2020s will be the first real decade of aging, with dramatically fewer young workers entering the labor market. The result will be massive declines in the prime-age labor force during the 2030s and the 2040s. The 2040s will see the largest overall decline in the labor force, with a loss of 18 million workers in that decade alone. The 2050s will see a slight slowdown in the overall decline, but the "demographic echo" of ever-smaller age cohorts will speed up the decline of the young labor force and lead to further declines of the overall labor force beyond 2060.

Looking at the country clusters shows that these overall regional trends vary significantly across countries and subregions (figure 6.5). The High-Income Generous Spenders in aggregate are still experiencing a significant increase in their prime-age labor force, which is projected to gain 5.5 million workers during the 2010s. During the 2020s these countries will experience a strong decrease in the labor force, but the drop will be less steep than in the High-Income Moderate Spenders, which face a considerably starker demographic decline. In the latter group of countries the decline will be "front-loaded," with an earlier onset and the biggest drop (a loss of 5.1 million overall) coming during the 2020s. Declines for this group continue in the 2030s through the 2050s but become gradually less severe. This gives hope that once countries face their most severe labor force declines during the 2030s, they will be able and willing to carry out reforms to address the unsustainability of their pension systems, as many of the High-Income Moderate Spenders have already done over the last decade.

Worryingly, though, such contrasting demographic pictures cannot be observed in the High-Spending Transition Countries and the Lower-Spending Transition Countries. Both clusters are already experiencing declines in the labor force during the 2010s, driven by significant decreases in younger workers. This trend will continue during the 2020s, translating into substantial decreases in the labor force aged 40–64 during the 2030s and 2040s. Despite the bleak demographic outlook, some countries seem to have opted for considerably more generous pension systems than others.

As for the Young Countries, they will continue to enjoy labor force increases well into the 2050s. Only then will the demographic transition start to be felt, with vast decreases in the younger labor force

FIGURE 6.5

Projected Change in the Labor Force in Europe and Central Asia, by Country Cluster, Age Group, and Decade, 2010s through 2050s

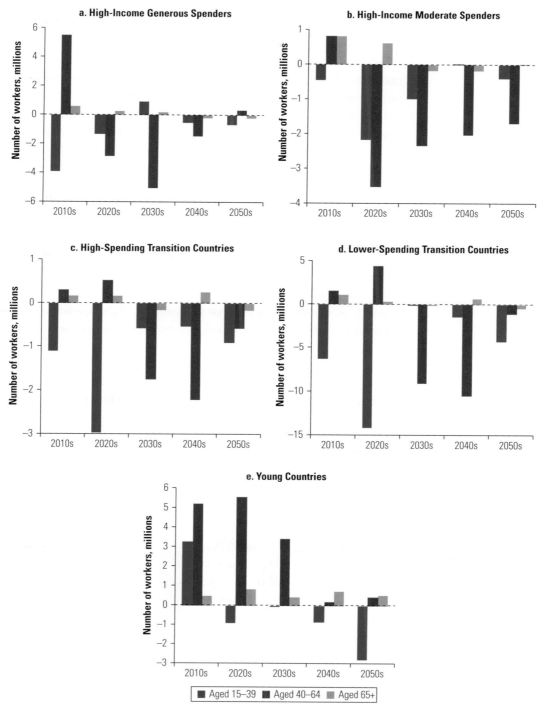

Source: Based on methodology in Koettl 2008.

that will eventually put these countries in the same situation as their older European peers today.

Can the inverting of the working-age population pyramid be halted through increases in LFP? Figure 6.6 shows the projected impact of four alternative scenarios (in addition to the baseline scenario just discussed). They are based on simulations of the effects of achieving different goals for LFP rates across age, gender, and countries. The scenarios do not focus on one particular policy goal, but rather on a combination. Increases in LFP of women, youth, and, most importantly, older workers are part of each scenario, but the emphasis is different in each. The main overall finding from these simulations is that significant increases in participation rates in many countries, especially among women, youth, and older workers, could indeed stem some of the decline in the labor force. It is informative to examine the results in detail.

Scenario 1, constant participation rates, serves as a baseline and corresponds to the projections presented above. Scenario 2, convergence to benchmark countries, simulates an overall increase in participation rates to levels similar to those observed today in countries with the highest participation rates among the 50+ population: Iceland, Norway, Sweden, and Switzerland. This scenario implies increases in LFP across the board, but especially among women and

FIGURE 6.6

Projected Change in the Labor Force in Europe and Central Asia under Different Scenarios, by Age Group, 2010–2050

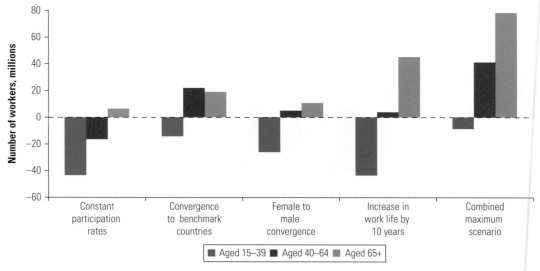

Source: Based on methodology in Koettl 2008.

older workers, who exhibit the largest participation gaps. Scenario 3, female to male convergence, simulates a convergence of the female participation profile to the male profile in each country. This also implies a considerable increase in female LFP at older ages. Scenario 4, increase in work life by 10 years, simulates an increase of a decade in the average length of the working life, country by country and gender by gender.

Scenario 5—the maximum scenario—combines all three alternatives to give a sense of the maximum potential for stemming the decline in the labor force by increasing LFP. In such a scenario, participation in all countries would increase to the average of the profiles seen today among the male population in Iceland, Norway, Sweden, and Switzerland, with an additional increase of 10 years in work life. This implies LFP rates above 80 percent even among people aged 70–74. It should be kept in mind that achieving the policy goals in all of these scenarios would require major pension reforms (such as, for example, higher statutory retirement ages) in tandem with many other labor market, tax, and skills policy reforms to enable such increases in participation and extension of working lives.

The biggest impact would come from a convergence to the LFP rates observed in benchmark countries (Iceland, Norway, Sweden, and Switzerland). Not only could the decline by 54 million workers be stemmed, but such a development would actually yield an increase of nearly 27 million workers in the overall labor force—an 80 million net increase compared to the base scenario. The decline in the younger labor force, though, could not be avoided; the potential to activate more workers is mostly among prime-age women and older workers. An increase in work life of 10 years could also stem the labor force decline by bringing in more than 40 million workers aged 65 and older. Combining the various scenarios of increasing overall LFP, in particular among women, and lengthening work life would substantially increase the labor force in Europe and Central Asia by more than 100 million workers. Yet even in this unrealistically optimistic scenario, the decline in the younger labor force—and subsequent decline in the overall labor force—could not be prevented.

When considering these various scenarios, looking only at aggregate numbers obscures important differences between countries (figure 6.7). The country cluster disaggregation reveals that most of the increases in the younger labor force would be achieved in the Young Countries. For the region as a whole to benefit from these increases would require an integrated labor market and efficient allocation of labor throughout the whole region. In other words,

FIGURE 6.7

Projected Change in the Labor Force in Europe and Central Asia under Different Scenarios, by Country Cluster and Age Group, 2010–2050

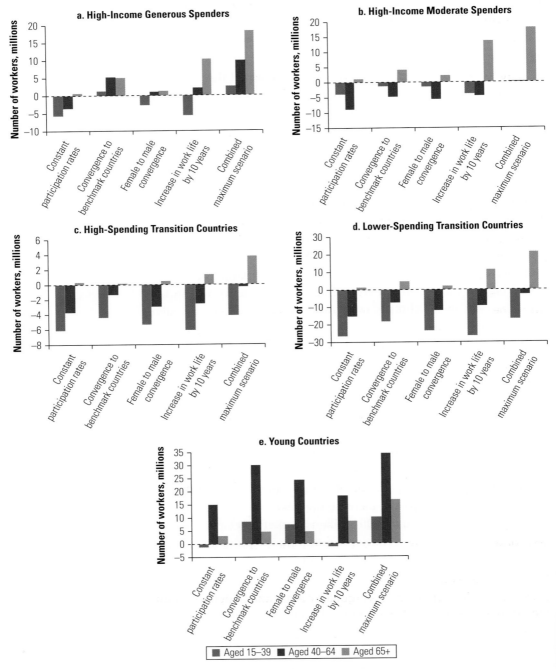

Source: Based on methodology in Koettl 2008.

intraregional migration would have to increase considerably, namely from the younger to the aging countries.

For example, in the High-Income Moderate Spenders, where participation rates are already high, there is little potential to increase them further, except among those aged 65 and older. Among the High-Income Generous Spenders, on the other hand, there is considerable potential to increase overall participation rates, which could possibly even stem the decline among the young and prime-age labor force. In the transition countries, both low and high spenders, however, the decline among young and prime-age workers is unlikely to be contained: the only potential here is to significantly increase participation among older workers. Finally, in the Young Countries, there is enormous potential to increase the LFP of young and prime-age workers, especially among women. For Europe and Central Asia as a whole to benefit from these favorable conditions in the Young Countries of the region—and especially in Turkey, the largest young country—the region will have to integrate its labor market much more.

Immigration, therefore, offers a natural way to counter the decline of the labor force. Bringing in more workers from other countries to cover the gap left by a shrinking workforce can complement other reforms and increase overall LFP. It spreads out the costs of reforms over more people and in this way can help decrease the political costs of reforms. Of course, increased migration itself might pose new political challenges beyond those of pension reform, especially in a subdued economy and a sluggish labor market. The key is to strengthen the link between immigration policies and labor market needs to ensure that those workers entering the country's labor market from outside have the skills that are in demand. Most countries in the region have just begun to design immigration policies, and as immigration starts to increase, it will be important to ensure that the right talents and skills are attracted (Gill and Raiser 2012).

In sum, there seems to be considerable potential to stem—or at least slow down—some of the inverting of the working-age population pyramid and the ensuing decline in the labor force over the next 50 years. This would require first and foremost, of course, that these workers be able to find jobs. As argued by Arias and Sánchez-Páramo (2013), to get more people back to work, countries need to regain the momentum that existed before the crisis to carry out economic and institutional reforms. This would mean, first of all, pushing reforms to establish the fundamentals to create jobs for all workers by laying an enabling environment for existing firms to grow, become more productive, or exit the market, and by tapping entrepreneurship potential so that new firms emerge and succeed or fail fast and cheap. It would also require implementing policies to support workers so they are prepared to take on the new jobs being created: workers need the right skills, appropriate incentives, access to work, and readiness to move to places with the highest job-creation potential.

Policies and reforms to remove impediments that keep older workers from staying longer in the workforce are crucial to efforts to stem labor force decline. Many of these impediments come from pension systems themselves, which discourage people from lengthening their work lives and participating in the labor force at older ages. There are many other areas, though, outside of the pension system—like tax and benefit systems, labor regulations and institutions, training, and workplace adjustments—that also need reforms to enable and encourage people to work longer and more productively.

A growing number of older workers are in good health, have valuable skills and experience, and are willing to stay longer in the labor market. However, to realize this potential, it is necessary to confront a number of barriers faced by older workers, including ill-adapted workplaces, stereotypes about older workers, and attitudes and social norms about work at older ages.

Myths and Misperceptions about Older Workers

As a first step, societies and employers must confront some of the most common myths and misperceptions about older workers, namely that they prefer retirement over work, that they are less productive and not employable, and that they take away jobs from the young.

Figure 6.8 summarizes results from a Eurobarometer survey conducted in 2011 on active aging in the then EU-27 member states and five non-EU countries: Croatia (at that time was not yet an EU member), FYR Macedonia, Iceland, Norway, and Turkey (Eurobarometer 2012).[4] Respondents were asked to rate the importance of commonly accepted reasons why the population 55 and over may stop working. The presentation of results compares the responses in the EU-15 (the 15 EU members in Western Europe) and the EU-11 (new member states including Croatia), highlighting, when relevant, differences for Turkey and FYR Macedonia and across demographic groups, drawing on Eurobarometer (2012).

A lack of gradual retirement options, exclusion from training, and negative perceptions about older workers on the part of employers are thought to be the main reasons that older people stop working.

FIGURE 6.8

Why Older Workers Stop Working: Perceptions in the European Union, 2011

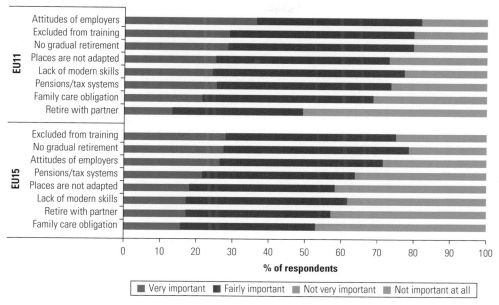

Source: Eurobarometer 2012.

These three obstacles were seen as fairly or very important by seven in 10 respondents across most of the EU member countries in 2011. Only 4 to 6 percent viewed these reasons as unimportant across the EU. Respondents in the EU-11 rated these obstacles more highly important than those in the EU-15 countries. About six in 10 respondents also highlighted a lack of skills for the modern workplace, disincentives in the pension and tax systems, and workplaces that are ill adapted to the needs of older workers. Family-related reasons, such as obligations to care for grandchildren or the desire to retire at the same time as a partner, were less likely to be viewed as important, although women were more likely to feel that family care obligations were an important obstacle (56 percent vs. 52 percent of men). On most other obstacles, men and women held similar views, while, interestingly, the age of the respondents was not linked to significant differences in responses.

These results reveal three salient myths or misperceptions about older workers, outlined briefly below. They also highlight real barriers facing older workers, which need to be confronted to pave the way for longer working lives (see annex 6A for a more detailed discussion).

Myth number 1: Workers, particularly at older ages, prefer to retire rather than continue working.

Fact: Most workers prefer to have the option of combining work and retirement, although in some countries attitudes and social norms do not favor longer working lives.

According to the Eurobarometer (2012) results, just over half of EU-27 respondents (54 percent) and EU-11 respondents (52 percent) do not want to continue working once they are entitled to a pension. A third want to continue working, and the rest are unsure. The proportion of individuals who would like to continue working once they reach pensionable age is actually higher (41 percent) among older workers.

A closer examination of work and retirement preferences reveals that about two-thirds of respondents in most countries, especially at older ages, would prefer to have or allow others the flexibility to combine partial retirement with longer working lives. Also, most citizens (61 percent) think people should be able to work past the official retirement age if they so desire. Similarly, a slight majority (53 percent) disagree with the entire notion of a compulsory retirement age. There is significant variation in revealed preferences and attitudes toward retirement across countries, and in some countries attitudes and social norms do not favor longer working lives (see annex 6A).

Importantly, empirical evidence suggests that responding to preferences for a more flexible approach to retirement would improve the quality of life in old age (see annex 6A for more details). Thus, reforms that foster LFP at older ages not only help ensure the sustainability of pension systems but may also lead to positive health benefits for older individuals.

Myth number 2: Older workers are less productive than younger workers and are difficult to employ.

Fact: Most older workers can remain very productive over longer careers, yet many do face barriers in the workplace and when looking for work.

In reality, individuals and employers have mixed views about older workers. In the Eurobarometer (2012) survey, shown in figure 6.8, six in 10 respondents in the EU-15 and nearly eight in 10 in the EU-11 perceive the lack of skills for the modern workplace to be a strong obstacle that inhibits people 55 years and older from working. However, when asked to compare the workplace qualities of older and younger workers, the vast majority of respondents actually believe that older ones have more advantages. For one thing, 38 percent see older workers as more productive than younger workers, while 41 percent see them as equally productive. Not surprisingly, virtually all respondents perceive older workers to be more experienced, and an overwhelming majority (80 percent or more) see them as either equal or superior to younger employees in terms of reliability, independent decision making, problem solving, handling stress, and working with other people.

Seven of 10 survey respondents believe that employers' negative perceptions of older employees constitute an important barrier that keeps people 55 years and over from working, a view more commonly held in the EU-11 countries. Surveys of employers reveal that while they recognize strengths in older workers, many harbor negative views as well. In its report on aging and employment policies covering 21 countries, the OECD (2006) cites evidence that employers often have mixed views of older workers, including negative perceptions about their flexibility and ability to adapt to changes in technology and business.

Are these ambivalent perceptions and attitudes supported by facts? Overall, the scientific evidence does not support the inevitability of a significant fall in productivity with aging, at least not before very old age and not for tasks that do not require physical strength. Numerous studies in occupational medicine, developmental psychology, and gerontology find that physical capacities (like muscle strength and eyesight) and some mental capacities (like memory and cognitive ability) can start weakening as early as age 25. However, as discussed further in annex 6A, such early onset of decline is far from universal. Depending on the task or job, mild deficits often can be offset by the older worker's accumulated knowledge and experience in performing tasks.

The micro-empirical literature on whether older workers are less productive is mixed. While some studies claim to find a fall in productivity at older ages, those with stronger designs find either no fall, a slight fall, or an increased variance in labor productivity at older ages. In studies where aging dampens productivity, the decline is to a level that is still above productivity in midlife and younger ages. A recent study using the Survey of Health, Ageing and Retirement in Europe, a household panel of nationally representative population samples for several European countries, finds that retirement per se accelerates cognitive decline. This effect is heightened by low education, with less educated individuals experiencing more significant age-related decline in cognitive abilities (Mazzonna and Peracchi 2012).

Myth number 3: Older workers keep younger ones from finding jobs.

Fact: The "lump of labor" is nothing but a fallacy.

The long-standing public perception of an alleged trade-off between employment of younger and older workers is known as the lump-of-labor fallacy.[5] In a Eurobarometer (2009) survey on inter-generational solidarity covering the 27 EU countries, 56 percent of respondents said they thought that if older people worked longer there would be fewer jobs for young people.[6] Respondents over age 55 (57 percent) were more likely to agree with this idea than respondents aged 15–24 (51 percent).

Although the lump-of-labor notion permeates the policy debate about encouraging older workers to work longer, it has been refuted by both simple observations and serious analysis of the data. Time and again, the evidence has shown that if anything, the opposite is true. Comparison of employment rates of older individuals (aged 55–64) and of young people (aged 20–24) across countries in the Europe and Central Asia region actually yields a positive statistically significant relationship; the same result holds for the changes in the employment rates of both groups over the 2000s (Arias and Sánchez-Páramo 2013). Gruber and Wise (2010) provide the most thorough analysis debunking claims of a trade-off between older workers and youth employment. Analyzing long time-series data from the 1960s to the 2000s in 12 OECD countries (including nine in Western Europe),[7] they found in each country a strong positive correlation between employment of older (55–64) and younger (20–24) workers, and even those in prime age. Moreover, results from within-country "natural experiment" comparisons in Denmark, France, and Germany—exploiting reforms that induced older workers to leave the labor force but were unrelated to the employment of youth—yield no evidence that reducing the employment of older persons provides more job opportunities for younger persons or that increasing the LFP of older persons keeps youth out of work.

The lump of labor across ages is indeed a fallacy. If anything, the weight of the evidence suggests that increasing the employment of older workers provides more job opportunities for youth and reduces their unemployment rate. As more workers of any age are employed, the growing segments of the economy tend to create more job opportunities for all workers, including youth. It should be noted, however, that in economies with sclerotic labor markets, such as those heavily dominated by public sector employment, there could indeed be trade-offs between the employment of different groups. In such situations, early retirement is, nevertheless, not the way to promote higher youth employment. Instead, reforms are needed to tackle the root causes of labor market sluggishness.

Summing up, the three myths about older workers—their alleged resistance to longer working lives, their low productivity, and their displacement of youth—lack a solid empirical basis. Once policy makers in the region move past these misperceptions, they can then confront real barriers that hinder the labor participation of older workers. As discussed below, disincentives rooted in the design of the tax and social benefits system, including pensions, and labor market regulations too often limit hiring or flexible work schedules, do not make work pay, and discourage participation in the social security system.

Policy Measures to Remove Impediments and Encourage Employment of Older Workers

Improving the overall rates of formal employment requires strengthening incentives for individuals of all ages to (a) move out of inactivity or unemployment to take on a formal job; (b) opt for and remain in formal rather than informal employment (for those already in the labor force); and (c) stay longer in employment (in the case of older workers).

In the first two cases, disincentives can arise when the design of taxes and social benefits does not make work pay for both the employee and the employer. These include employment-related benefits such as unemployment and family allowances, as well as benefits from social assistance programs. Disincentives can also arise from the way pension systems are designed, especially in case of retirement provisions or benefit formulas that induce early exit from the labor force. Recent findings in behavioral economics also show that contextual factors, including norms and institutions, and individual cognitive and noncognitive traits affect the responses to incentives and attitudes about participation in pension schemes. Finally, labor market regulations and institutions, like employment protection legislation (EPL), provisions governing part-time work, or seniority wages, may create disincentives for firms to hire formal workers, even though such measures are intended to provide protection or prevent discrimination of older workers.

This section discusses policies to increase participation in the labor market, both overall and of older workers in particular, through two broad sets of measures: first, reforms to improve incentives to participate in the (formal) labor markets through better design of taxes, benefits, and labor regulations; and second, measures to improve the productivity of older workers through workplace adjustments and skills development so that employers are encouraged to hire them and keep them employed longer. Older workers can enjoy longer productive working lives if the design of taxes, benefits, and labor regulations do not discourage work, businesses make smart accommodations in the workplace, and training strategies are age-informed so that older workers can enhance their valuable experience with new skills.

Tax and Benefit Reforms to Make Formal Work Pay at All Ages

Designing taxes and benefits is a balancing act between achieving redistribution and ensuring adequate incomes for jobless people, on the one hand, and maintaining strong incentives for formal sector employment, on the other. The main conclusion from recent studies is that work disincentives arising from the design of tax and social benefits in the region are especially severe for low-wage and secondary earners (Koettl and Weber 2012; Arias and Sánchez-Páramo 2013). These groups consist of exactly those workers whose participation in the formal labor market overall is lagging: young, low-skilled, female, and older workers, who are often looking for part-time opportunities to work while studying or to supplement income from a spouse or a pension.

This section looks more closely at work incentives, especially for older workers, stemming from labor taxation and social benefits design, including pensions. Disincentives for formal work currently appear substantial in many countries in the region, especially for low-productivity workers. Applying a micro-econometric analysis, Koettl and Weber (2012) show that there is a negative correlation between the incidence of formal employment and tacit work disincentives at the individual level. Crucially, this correlation is twice as strong when the sample is restricted to low-wage earners, suggesting a more decisive impact of work disincentives in the low-wage segment.

For workers in the new EU member states with very high effective taxes on formal work, the benefits of formal jobs, such as employment-related benefits and protection, would have to be large enough to offset their opportunity costs, mainly higher taxes and social security contributions and the withdrawal of some social assistance benefits. Formal jobs, especially low-paying, part-time jobs, may not be an economically viable option for low-productivity job seekers and their employers in these countries. The tax and benefit structures of some non-EU countries, in particular in the Balkans or Turkey, have similar features that can make low-paying, part-time formal work unappealing. Yet it might be exactly these so-called "mini" and "midi" jobs—casual part-time jobs at low-to-medium wage levels, often in the service or retail sector, with uncertain work hours—that could be filled by older workers who either already draw a pension or would like to work while drawing a partial pension. Data from the European Union Statistics on Income and Living Conditions confirm that informal employment in the new member states is indeed most prevalent in the low-wage sector, especially for those jobs that earn less than 50 percent of average wage (Packard, Koettl, and Montenegro 2012).

At the individual level, work disincentives vary significantly by income level and family type. Figure 6.9 depicts potential work disincentives for formal work for an archetypical single person with no children in Bulgaria and Romania in comparison to Australia and the United States in 2008. Work disincentives are quantified by the so-called formalization tax rate (FTR), which measures how much informal income would be "taxed away" through taxes, social contributions, and reduced social benefits if the same job were done formally.[8] In Bulgaria and Romania (figure 6.9a), the opportunity costs of formal work as measured by the FTR can be as high as 70 percent. That is, at low wage levels, informal workers would lose up to 70 percent of their informal income (wages and benefits) from formalization. The corresponding benefits that come with formalization would have to be unreasonably high to make up for the costs. Other countries, like Australia and the United States, design their tax and benefit systems differently—providing, for instance, an earned income tax benefit. In these two countries the opportunity costs of formal work are much lower (up to about 40 percent) for low-wage earners.

Building on these results, figure 6.10 shows disincentives for low-wage earners across age groups in various European countries. These are average work disincentives, as measured by the FTR and the marginal effective tax rate, faced by people in five different age groups in 10 countries. By and large, work disincentives in most countries are highest for the oldest workers (aged 55–64) and display a U-shaped curve with age. Thus, these potential disincentives might be a factor behind the higher rates of informal employment among older workers.

How can policy makers ease some of these disincentives to formal work? The key is to target low-wage earners, many of whom work today in informal jobs or casual part-time jobs in order to supplement household income from pensions or earned by the main breadwinner of the family. These types of jobs frequently do not pay off when done in the formal sector.

FIGURE 6.9

Opportunity Costs of Formal Work as Measured by the Formalization Tax Rate in Bulgaria, Romania, Australia, and the United States, 2008

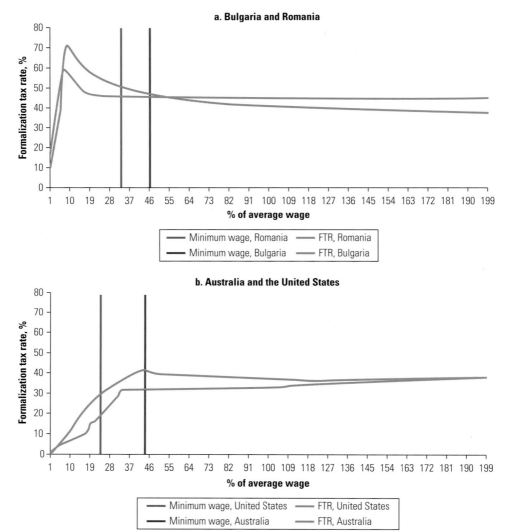

Source: Koettl and Weber 2012.
Note: The formalization tax rate (FTR) measures the percentage of informal income that would be "taxed away" through taxes, social contributions, and reduced social benefits if the same job were done formally. The figure shows the FTR for an archetypical single person with no children.

Packard, Koettl, and Montenegro (2012) and Arias and Sánchez-Páramo (2013) suggest two main avenues for changing work disincentives: (a) improve the design of social benefits like social assistance, unemployment compensation, and family and housing benefits in such a way as to reward or at least not penalize formal work; and (b) reduce labor taxation, with a focus on low-wage earners. The former entails reforms that make formal work pay and

FIGURE 6.10

Work Disincentives (Formalization Tax Rate and Marginal Effective Tax Rate) for Low-Wage Earners across Age Groups, Selected European Economies, 2008

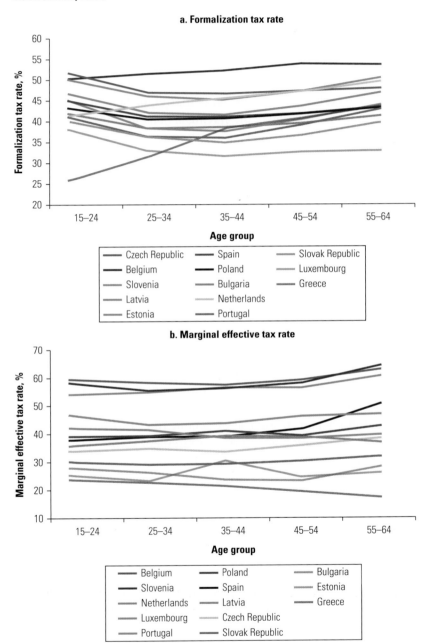

Sources: World Bank staff calculations based on EU-SILC 2008; and OECD Tax-Benefit Model 2008.
Note: Calculations for a sample restricted to low-wage earners earning 50 percent of the average wage or less.

allow for a phased withdrawal of benefits. That is, as work income increases, social benefits are not withdrawn abruptly but instead are reduced gradually in order not to penalize formal work. Those taking up a new formal job can be allowed to keep some of their benefit entitlements for a certain period. The reduction of labor taxes entails shifting taxation away from labor to other types of income, consumption, or property and assets. Targeting labor tax reductions to low-wage earners has proven more effective than making across-the-board tax reductions in the past.[9] This could be done through tax credits or so-called in-work benefits that grant benefit entitlements or tax breaks conditional on having a job, like the U.S. Earned Income Tax Credit (Immervoll and Pearson 2009). Chapter 5 discussed the scope for these and other fiscally neutral reforms, taking into account their consequences for both equity and efficiency.

While incentives are important, recent research in behavioral economics warns that they do not necessarily translate immediately to changes in behavior. Work decisions also depend on psychological and social features of the workplace environment, including employee morale, job security, and the perceived fairness of one's pay. As noted by Perry et al. (2007) and Packard, Koettl, and Montenegro (2012), survey evidence reveals that mistrust and dissatisfaction with public institutions may cultivate a social norm of noncompliance with taxes and divert participation in institutions like pension schemes. It is well known that attitudes toward risk on the part of young workers, who have to pay contributions now, influence how they value the resulting future entitlements and whether they see these entitlements as certain or uncertain.[10] In this context, as noted in chapter 4, the use of default rules can have substantial effects on participation in voluntary retirement savings plans.[11] Thus, policies to encourage participation in formal employment should factor in ways to cultivate social norms and attitudes that favor participation in pension schemes.

Finally, looking at why older workers may not stay longer in the workforce, we turn to disincentives stemming from the pension system itself. Clearly, the level of pension benefits and the ensuing social security contributions alter incentives for formal employment and affect labor and economy-wide productivity.[12] The disincentive effects on the labor supply of older people are well documented for many industrialized countries. For instance, in their comprehensive study that included nine Western European economies, Gruber and Wise (1999, 2004) found that pension benefit rules—and the resulting "implicit tax on continued work"—are a crucial determinant of the timing of retirement across several countries. They estimate that a reform that increases the pension age by 3 years would likely reduce the proportion of inactive men aged 56–65 by up to 36 percent. Likewise, high contributions, and a perceived uncertainty of eventual retirement benefits, can erode people's incentives to work or, more precisely, to contribute to the pension system.

Data availability has precluded the study of labor supply and retirement effects of pension systems in emerging economies, including in the transition economies of Europe and Central Asia.[13] An exception is a recent study by Danzer (2010), who uses a natural experiment from Ukraine to estimate the causal effect of a threefold increase in the legal minimum pension on labor supply and retirement behavior at older ages. Applying difference-in-difference and regression discontinuity methods to two independent, nationally representative data sets, he finds that higher pension incomes have strong disincentive effects on the labor supply decisions of older individuals. The income effect from the new pension policy leads to a 37–47 percent increase in retirement at the statutory retirement age for men, and to a 30–39 percent increase for women. Those women who remain in the workforce reduce their yearly working hours by 15 percent, while men have no significant response. The estimated effects are much stronger for less educated workers. Danzer (2010) concludes that although the substantial pension increase had positive impacts in terms of averting old-age poverty, it provided strong disincentives to work and put a heavy fiscal burden on Ukraine.

Issues related to disincentives stemming from the pension system and the trade-offs with adequacy are addressed in more in depth in chapter 7.

Labor Regulations and Institutions that Enable Longer Working Lives

Labor regulations can also create disincentives for formal work. In some countries, incumbents might be favored at the expense of new entrants, including older workers out of work. A study by the OECD (2011) shows that in 2004, there was indeed a negative correlation across countries between the employment and hiring rates of men aged 50–64 on the one hand and the strictness of EPL on the other. There is, however, inconclusive evidence on the causal mechanisms behind this correlation.

Deelen and Bourmpoula (2009), constructing an EPL index specifically for older workers and applying panel regression to 28 OECD countries, confirm this finding more rigorously. In particular, they find that strict EPL is negatively related to participation and employment rates and to the inflow into unemployment of older workers. At the same time, it is positively related to long-term unemployment. These effects seem more pronounced with older women. However, Langot and Moreno-Galbis (2008) find that EPL negatively affects employment rates of younger workers across OECD countries, but for older workers the effect seems to be the inverse. Thus, as in the literature on the role of labor regulations in hindering overall employment, the emerging evidence on the effect of EPL on employment of older workers is mixed.[14] What is important is for countries to set labor regulations in a range where impacts on employment or productivity are modest and distributional impacts minimized, so that labor markets remain contestable.

Meanwhile, Neumark and Song (2012) find for the United States that stronger state-level age discrimination protections actually increase employment and hiring of older workers. Since their result is for workers who are caught by recent increases in the retirement age, their evidence points to important policy complementarities between pension age reforms and employment protection policies to lessen barriers to the employment of older workers.[15] They also point out that the deterrent effect of stringent employment protection—the implicit increase in hiring costs due to higher firing costs—could be less severe for older workers, especially those close to retirement age, because of a foreseeable exit of the hired workers into retirement.

One aspect of regulations and labor institutions that does seem crucial is provisions for flexible work arrangements to enhance opportunities for gradual retirement of older workers and LFP of women of all ages. Today's workplace and labor regulations have been mainly designed for prime-age male workers who can work full-time, have limited family and household responsibilities, have completed their formal education, and have significant work experience. As a result, these regulations do not necessarily fit the needs of older workers transitioning into retirement, of women who take time off for maternity leave and child care, or of men and women who would like to balance family and work throughout their careers.

Part-time work could benefit employers by giving them more flexibility to adjust work hours in the economic cycle. Yet part-time employment in the Europe and Central Asia region is less common than in Western Europe, covering less than 10 percent of the employed. Constraints to flexible work schedules are sometimes embedded in labor legislation, but they can also arise from norms and attitudes in the workplace. In most countries, it is a statutory right of employees to increase (or decrease) their working hours, but in some places it is more difficult. For example, in Montenegro, part-time work cannot be less than one-fourth of a full-time engagement, or 10 hours per week. In a survey of employers in 21 EU countries, on average only 27 percent of managers reported that part-time employees could easily get a full-time job: 43 percent said that this could happen only exceptionally and the rest said there was "no chance" of this happening (Eurofound 2011). Constraints also arise from the interaction with the tax and benefit systems. For instance, in Serbia, minimum social contributions of those earning less than 35 percent of the average wage are not adjusted for hours worked, amounting to a double penalty for anyone working less than full-time (Koettl 2013).

Seniority wages, arising from collective bargaining or performance-pay rules based on experience, could be another potential disincentive for employing older workers. If wages of older workers are based on seniority—that is, years with the company—independent of actual productivity levels, they can drive up labor costs of older workers beyond what employers are willing to pay for such workers. There seems to be strong negative correlation across countries between hiring rates and wage levels of older workers (OECD 2011). However, as de Hek and van Vuuren (2011) conclude in their review of the literature, seniority wages need not imply that older workers are overpaid. From a company perspective, it can very well pay off to "backload" wage increases to later years to tie valuable employees— in whom the employer might have invested substantial training resources—to the company. However, if regulations undermine employers' ability to decrease wages for those employees whose productivity has fallen over the years, then separation or early retirement might be the only option. As with all other age groups, the key is to allow employers sufficient flexibility to adjust wages to productivity levels. For older workers, this might be even more important, as research has shown that the variance in productivity levels across individuals increases significantly with age (see annex 6A).

Keeping Older Workers Productive through Workplace Interventions and Skills Development

An important question is how older workers fare in terms of employment prospects and productivity levels in a changing and globalizing economy. As noted, one of the concerns about older workers is that employers are less willing to hire them or keep them in employment because they are less able to adapt to new technologies. If this is true, overall productivity in an aging economy may suffer. Are older workers indeed less able to adapt to new technologies, and if so, what can firms and countries do to adjust when faced with an aging workforce?

Langot and Moreno-Galbis (2008) show that in the United States, employment rates of workers below age 55 are inversely related to total factor productivity growth. They speculate that as technology advances, firms tend to rely on younger workers to adopt newer technologies, while older workers are made redundant. Specifically, they argue that for young workers, the time during which a firm can recoup costs of updating production technology is longer than for older workers.

Therefore, the optimal strategy for a firm introducing a new technology may be to keep younger workers in the affected jobs while removing older workers. This process would result in young workers being positioned at the technological frontier, while older workers stay in jobs that are becoming technologically obsolete. Empirical findings of Abowd et al. (2007), Ahituv and Zeira (2011), and Borghans and Weel (2002) confirm that this is indeed happening. However, firms may opt to retain older workers whose productivity can remain high, and it may even pay off for firms to invest in skills training of older workers rather than destroying the jobs they occupy. Moreover, at the enterprise level there is evidence of a complementarity between older and younger workers that positively affects firm productivity. Enterprises can reap the potential benefits of an aging workforce through the use of age-diverse working teams. This highlights the importance of individual productivity levels and investments in skills development for the retention of older workers.

Experience in a number of companies has shown that making changes to business practices to adapt to an aging workforce is a smart business strategy (Hodin and Hoffmann 2011). A prominent example is the German automaker BMW, which found ways to keep older workers productive by making physical accommodations in the workplace (box 6.1)

The drugstore chain CVS in the United States has also taken innovative steps to maximize the productivity of older workers (Hodin and Hoffmann 2011). In retail, as opposed to manufacturing, customer service is at the core of productivity. CVS's innovation was to introduce new initiatives and programs to attract and retain older workers, put them in positions to mentor younger employees and help older customers, create flexible work programs to accommodate their lifestyles and needs, and reward them for their life experiences. CVS has more than doubled the number of employees over age 50 in recent years.

BOX 6.1

Adapting the Workplace for an Aging Workforce: BMW's "2017 Assembly Line"

German luxury automaker BMW has gone beyond talk to test ways to accommodate an aging workforce. BMW's highly specialized and well-trained workforce is aging quickly. Traditional approaches to dealing with an aging workforce, like dismissals or early retirement, are not an option for BMW, which prizes itself on being a dependable employer and committed to its loyal workers. In addition, because BMW is one of the largest employers in Bavaria, large-scale dismissals of older workers would be perceived as discriminatory and would have political repercussions. Instead, through an experiment at its Dingolfing plant, BMW tried to address the coming challenges of aging proactively.

The average age of workers at the plant was expected to increase from 39 in 2007 to 47 in 2017. Because of more frequent and longer sick leaves and decreased physical ability of older workers, management feared that the plant's productivity levels would decrease and its competitiveness erode. The experiment consisted of staffing a particular assembly line—one making rear-axle gearboxes for medium-sized cars—with a team of workers who fit the expected average worker profile of 2017. The line was relatively small, only 42 workers, but very labor intensive. Almost 40 percent of workers on the so-called "2017 line" were 50 or older, while only 20 percent were that age on a typical 2007 line.

In the course of one year, through a series of 70 interventions, the productivity level of the 2017 line increased by 7 percent, bringing it up to par with the plant's average. Quality defects quickly decreased to expected levels and, later on, decreased even further. Absenteeism due to sick leave and rehabilitation dropped from an above-average 7 percent to 2 percent, well below average.

Key to the success of the intervention was the process that was applied. Plant management initiated the project, creating the environment in which solutions could be developed, but it was the workers themselves who found those solutions. Management turned to the Workers' Council at the plant for initial consultations. The council referred management to a study on the issue previously conducted at the same plant that provided a basic framework for proposed changes along five dimensions: health management, skills development, workplace adjustments, work-time adjustments, and change management. The study also showed that although productivity of workers on average seems to decrease with age, the variance in productivity levels also increases significantly. The challenge was to find out why some workers seem to be able to keep their productivity levels high while others do not.

After considerable initial resistance—the project line was referred to as the "pensioners' line" among staff—management was able to win over enough young and old workers to staff the project line by creating ownership and applying a hands-on approach. In various workshops, staff came up with a list of 70 specific interventions, most of them physical changes at the workplace

continued

BOX 6.1 *continued*

that reduced wear and tear on workers' bodies. These ranged from installing wooden flooring to reduce strain on joints to using chairs, orthopedic footwear, adjustable work tables, angled monitors, magnifying lenses, large-handled gripping tools, stackable containers, and manual hoisting cranes. These workplace adjustments were complemented by job rotations that ensured that the physically most demanding tasks were limited to three hours per shift. Workers engaged in stretching and strength exercises with a physiotherapist at the beginning of shifts and during breaks.

All of these interventions came at the negligible cost of 40,000 euros, half of which went toward salaries of staff attending workshops, while the other half paid for equipment and salaries of an ergonomist and a physiotherapist. For BMW, the experiment was a big success, as it showed that productivity challenges coming from its aging workforce could be addressed successfully. Follow-up projects were successfully implemented in many other plants throughout the automaker's global production chain.

Source: Based on Loch et al. 2010.

The BMW and CVS examples give hope that through targeted interventions, productivity levels of an aging workforce can be sustained. The question is whether the success of these experiments is driven by specific interventions that could be replicated elsewhere or whether it also reflects idiosyncrasies—related, for example, to motivation of workers, enthusiasm of project participants, or successful industrial relations—in these particular firms. More importantly, among the many interventions implemented at BMW and CVS, which ones really delivered results, and which ones are irrelevant?

Recent research, also from Germany, shows that in aggregate, specific measures for older employees do indeed have an impact on their productivity. Importantly, though, this research suggests that not all such measures have the same impact, or any impact for that matter. Using a large matched employer-employee survey, Göbel and Zwick (2009) compare plant-level productivity profiles of workers in specific age groups in firms that use such measures and in those that do not. They categorize these measures in five groups: (a) workplace adjustments; (b) reassignment to age-specific tasks; (c) mixed-age working teams; (d) reduced work time; and (e) training. Within the representative sample of German companies, about 50 percent used at least one of these measures for older workers in 2002. Interestingly, there does not seem to be much correlation between the different measures, suggesting that firms do not apply the whole range of instruments.

The findings of Göbel and Zwick (2009) suggest that there is indeed a drop in productivity—albeit relatively small—for workers aged 50 and older. Overall, the productivity profile across ages seems surprisingly flat. Moreover, firms that use at least one age-specific measure register significantly higher levels of productivity among their older workers than firms that do not adopt such measures. The first three categories of measures significantly increase the productivity of older workers. There are some spillover effects from these investments to prime-age workers: in companies with workplace adjustments for older workers, the relative productivity not only of older workers but also of workers aged 40–45 is significantly higher than in companies that do not invest in such adjustments. This productivity spillover seems lower for workers aged 55–59 than for those aged 40–45. Reassignment to age-specific jobs has a statistically significant impact on this oldest group of workers, but not for younger groups. The adoption of mixed-age work groups, finally, has a significant positive effect not only on the oldest group of workers, but also on the relative productivity of younger workers aged 20–30. This points to important complementarities in term of knowledge and experience between older and younger workers.

Among the five categories of measures discussed, reduced work time and additional training do not seem to have a significant effect on the productivity levels of older workers. The findings on work time could be explained by the fact that in Germany, the majority of workers do not choose "bridging pensions"—that is, reduced work hours while drawing a partial pension—but opt for "block pensions," meaning early retirement after working full-time. As discussed below, the findings on training raise questions about how to upgrade the skills of older workers. For example, is classroom training really the right measure for older learners, or do "aging brains" require a different form of learning?

Many older workers in the Europe and Central Asia region, educated prior to the transition, are likely to suffer from skills obsolescence. However, there are promising avenues to address weaknesses in current training and adult education systems in order to develop relevant skills of adults in a constantly changing labor market.

Over the last two decades, the rapid pace of change in technologies and business organization has in turn changed the key labor competencies needed in a dynamic labor market. Many jobs have become less routine and more interactive, particularly in the service sector, with implications for skills requirements. A seminal study by Autor, Levy, and Murnane (2003), looking at the United States, documented the rise of jobs that require nonroutine cognitive, analytical, and interpersonal skills, which they call "new economy skills." There was a concomitant decline in jobs requiring mostly routine cognitive skills as well as routine and nonroutine physical skills, many of which can be easily automated or offshored. These trends have also been observed in many Western European economies and some emerging economies (Handel 2012).

Arias and Sánchez-Páramo (2013) offer evidence that the economic transition in Europe and Central Asia may have rendered obsolete the skills of many older workers. Looking at the most modern economies in the region, those with a relatively skilled labor force, the study finds that—consistent with changes observed in OECD economies—the demand for "new economy" skills increased while the demand for skills associated with manual tasks remained sluggish or declined. These changes were more pronounced in new member states that became more integrated with external markets after EU accession. Importantly, the demand for new skills is stronger or in some cases only evident among younger cohorts, while job intensity in manual skills falls or is flat for older cohorts.

Thus, older workers have not benefitted as much from the expansion of jobs that require higher-order skills, and they are losing out as jobs requiring traditional skills disappear. Countries lagging in policy reforms have not yet experienced significant changes in the skills intensity of jobs, but as they embark on the pending reforms agenda they may experience similar age-differentiated changes in skills demand that could leave some older workers shortchanged. These trends will affect the labor market prospects not only of today's older workers but also of people currently in their thirties and forties, whose work lives extend over the next couple of decades.

These trends in skills demand and the rapidly advancing demographic outlook in many countries in the region further underscore the need to develop effective adult education and training systems. Currently, the participation rates in continuous education in the region are much lower than in the EU-15. Only about 10 to 20 percent of employees participate in continuous vocational training activities in Estonia, Hungary, and Poland, whereas the lowest share for the EU-15 is 26 percent in Italy. Similar proportions can be observed if the share of the working-age population participating in any educational activity is considered. Hungary has the lowest rates of participation, with only 4.4 percent of the population aged 55–64 continuing to learn, while in the EU-15 this share varies from 22 percent in the United Kingdom to 35 percent in Italy. But more importantly, the relatively few rigorous evaluations of these programs

increase enormously, from 19.0 to 45.7 in the Slovak Republic and from 22.7 to 46.0 in Poland. The size of the working-age population would fall by over 25 percent.

Before delving into specific results, we highlight five main findings.

- Tackling informality is not a solution to pension deficits in the long run. Although in the short run a reduction in informality would help cut pension deficits, those gains are wiped out later on, as the (new) formal workers retire and start collecting pension benefits.
- Increases in the retirement age would be essential to restore the financial sustainability of pension systems while maintaining adequate old-age income protection.
- Among the reforms considered, reductions in pension benefits would have the biggest impact on reducing aging-related pension deficits; such reductions are more effective than increases in contribution rates in achieving a better balance between fiscal and pension adequacy goals.
- Higher productivity growth leads to a very modest improvement in pension deficits as pension benefits are normally partly indexed to wages and thus increase with productivity.
- Feedback effects from the labor market are very significant for assessing the likely impact of reforms on pension financing and the economy more broadly.

Consistent with the analysis in chapter 2, pension deficit in the Slovak Republic, which starts from a balanced position, is predicted to climb to 5.4 percent of GDP by 2100 in the absence of any reforms. Although workers in the model can choose to retire somewhat later to finance consumption in old age, this effect is small, and the imbalance between the number of contributors to the pension system and the number of beneficiaries creates the sizable deficit. Without any other government action, the overall government per capita consumption is calculated to fall by more than 50 percent as a result of the negative impacts of the shrinking and aging of the population on employment and economic growth. This is a stark indication of the severe fiscal adjustment that would be required to avoid significant cuts in spending on essential public goods (e.g., infrastructure) and social services (e.g., education, health) in fast-aging economies. It underscores the urgent need for reforms that partly offset the impacts on the economy of the decline and aging of the labor force.

A first notable finding is that over the long run, formalization in itself does not reduce the social security deficit, although it delivers some short-term gains. Figure 6.11 illustrates this result over the entire period of the policy simulations (again for the Slovak Republic).

TABLE 6.1

Policy Simulations of Pension, Labor, and Tax Reforms: Nine Scenarios

	Baseline 2010	(1) Aging	(2) Constant human capital	(3) Constant informality	(4) Retirement + 2 years	(5) Social security contribution increase	(6) Pension flat benefit decrease	(7) Pension earnings-related decrease	(8) Social assistance decrease	(9) Productivity growth
Absolute numbers										
Population (age 15+, normalized, 2010 = 100)	100	81	81	81	81	81	81	81	81	81
Dependency ratio	19.2	45.7	45.7	45.7	45.7	45.7	45.7	45.7	45.7	45.7
Pensioners (% of population)	24.9	40.3	40.2	40.3	37.7	40.5	40.0	40.5	40.3	40.3
Unemployment rate (%)	14.7	14.4	14.0	14.6	14.2	15.0	14.4	15.0	14.9	14.7
Effective employment (yearly hours per capita)	793	667	685	640	699	614	681	617	706	629
Low-skilled (% of working-age population)	9.1	9.7	9.1	9.7	9.7	9.8	9.9	9.8	9.6	9.7
Medium-skilled (% of working-age population)	75.2	77.2	75.2	76.3	77.1	77.6	77.1	77.6	77.1	77.5
High-skilled (% of working-age population)	15.8	13.1	15.8	14.0	13.2	12.6	13.1	12.7	13.4	12.8
Informality rate (% of participants)	12.7	9.3	7.6	12.7	9.7	14.6	8.1	14.2	4.3	14.4
Increase from basis (%)										
Labor costs (low-skilled)	—	-3.5	-0.3	-4.8	-5.4	-2.7	-4.0	-2.4	-13.7	-10.1
Labor costs (medium-skilled)	—	-3.0	0	-3.8	-2.8	-2.4	-3.2	-2.4	-3.0	-9.2
Labor costs (high-skilled)	—	13.8	1.4	16.7	15.1	15.3	14.7	15.1	14.7	6.7
Pension payment per beneficiary	—	-1.4	1.8	-5.8	3.1	-11.8	-37.9	-46.7	3.5	1.5

TABLE 6.1
Continued

	Baseline 2010	(1) Aging	(2) Constant human capital	(3) Constant informality	(4) Retirement +2 years	(5) Social security contribution increase	(6) Pension flat benefit decrease	(7) Pension earnings-related decrease	(8) Social assistance decrease	(9) Productivity growth
GDP per capita	—	−14.5	−11.3	−18.1	−10.5	−21.1	−13.1	−20.7	−10.3	8.7
Consumption per capita (formal and informal goods)	—	0	1.6	0.2	2.5	−4.3	−4.6	−5.8	−0.1	8.4
Government consumption per capita	—	−56.1	−52.9	−59.0	−45.7	−47.1	−18.7	−27.0	−52.5	−7.0
Assets per capita	—	33.9	35.4	35.2	34.0	32.7	39.6	40.6	31.9	10.8
% of basis GDP										
Pension expenditure	7.10	9.19	9.46	8.77	8.99	8.25	5.74	4.98	9.64	7.52
Pension expenditure (constant population)	7.10	11.34	11.67	10.83	11.10	10.19	7.08	6.15	11.91	9.28
Social security deficit	0.08	5.08	5.08	5.01	4.45	3.29	1.45	1.46	5.11	4.40
Social security deficit (constant population)	0.08	6.27	6.27	6.19	5.50	4.06	1.79	1.80	6.31	5.44
Pension social security deficit	0.04	4.40	4.51	4.18	3.95	3.02	0.84	0.51	4.60	3.29
Pension social security deficit (constant population)	0.04	5.43	5.57	5.16	4.88	3.72	1.04	0.63	5.67	4.06

Source: Keuschnigg, Davoine, and Schuster 2013.

Note: The results of these simulations are based on parameters of the pension system of the Slovak Republic but are meant to be illustrative for other Eastern European and Central European countries. The nine scenarios are as follows: (1) aging: pure population aging until 2100, no reforms; (2) constant human capital: aging, no reforms, constant human capital decisions; (3) constant informality: aging, no reforms, constant informality decisions; (4) retirement +2 years: aging, increase in retirement age of 2 years; (5) social security contribution increase: increase in social security contribution rates by 3 percent of GDP; (6) pension flat benefit decrease: decrease in flat benefit portion of pension benefits by 3 percent of GDP; (7) pension earnings-related decrease: decrease in earnings-related portion of pension benefits by 3 percent of GDP; (8) social assistance decrease: decrease in welfare benefits by 0.5 percent of GDP; (9) productivity growth: increase in exogenous productivity growth rate by 20 percent. — = not available.

FIGURE 6.11

Change in Pension Deficit as a Result of Policy-Induced Reductions in Informal Employment in the Slovak Republic, 2011–2061

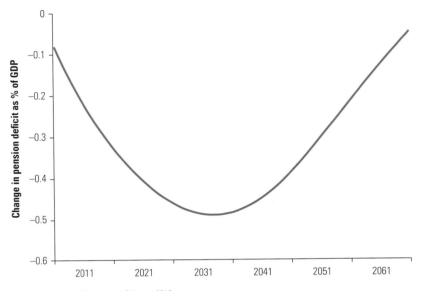

Source: Keuschnigg, Davoine, and Schuster 2013.
Note: This is the projected time evolution of the difference in the pension deficit between two scenarios of aging and no reforms (scenarios 1 and 3 in table 6.1).

It plots the difference in the pension deficit between two scenarios, both combining aging and no reforms but with distinct labor supply responses (scenarios 1 and 3 in table 6.1). In scenario 1 ("aging"), people are able to make choices about formal and informal work; informality falls over the long haul, since workers invest more in skills as they live longer and are more likely to land formal jobs. In scenario 3 ("constant informality"), people are not allowed to choose the type of work, so the occupational structure of formal/informal work by age groups remains the same as in the baseline. As people respond to incentives and enter the formal sector, the pension deficit falls in the short run (20 years or so) by up to 0.5 percent of GDP. But this gain is wiped out in the longer term (about four decades later), when these new formal workers start to retire and collect pension benefits according to the current benefits schedule. Indeed, simulations under constant informality show that the pension deficit would reach 4.18 percent of GDP, which is *lower* than the 4.40 percent obtained when allowing individuals to make informality decisions.

This runs against the conventional wisdom that sees informal workers as a main drag on pension financing. Although they do not contribute to financing, informal workers only receive non-earnings-related benefits, which are far lower than average earnings-related benefits. This is a result of the strong earnings-related link present in the pension system of the Slovak Republic, as well as in other countries. The immediate benefit of lower informality is higher social security contributions, but this eventually leads to higher expenditures in the form of larger pension payments. For public finances in the long run, the crucial factor is the sustainability of current schemes in terms of their ability to finance longer retirement periods at current benefit levels.

A related finding is that population aging alone, without any reforms, would reduce the rate of informality by as much as 30 percent in the Slovak Republic (from 12.7 percent to 9.3 percent). Two effects explain this. First, as workers live longer it becomes more beneficial for them to train and increase productivity over the life cycle in the formal sector (as, essentially, they get to enjoy the payoff from these investments for longer). Productivity increases as a result, and so do wages in the formal sector and social contributions and (later) pension benefits. Second, as people live longer, post-retirement income and thus access to formal pension benefits become more important. As a result, participation in the formal sector becomes overall more attractive.[19] These mechanisms illustrate the importance of accounting for labor and skill decisions of individuals over the life cycle when analyzing the outlook of pension finance.

Policy reforms of taxes, social assistance, and increases in the retirement age would help offset the demographic-driven social security financing gap, but by themselves they would be quite insufficient to eliminate it. As expected, postponement of the retirement age by 2 or 4 years, from 58 to 60 or 62 (scenario 4 in table 6.1), would lead to an improvement in the financing of pensions. However, the magnitude of the impact is modest (0.6 percent of GDP in the 2-year case, 1.4 percent in the 4-year case) and is insufficient to address the impending deficit. The impact of postponing the retirement age, which *ceteris paribus* lowers pension outlays, is dampened by the adjustments in the labor market: more workers stay in the formal labor force, pressing down formal sector wages and thus decreasing social security contributions revenue. Nevertheless, as this diminishes the aging-driven reductions in yearly hours per capita and per capita growth, the increases in the pension deficit can be contained by about 30 percent in the Slovak Republic and 50 percent in Poland. Hence, an increase in the effective retirement age by 4 years, which amounts to approximately 40 percent of the projected increase in life expectancy during the period of the analysis, is insufficient but can significantly contain the rise in the pension and general social security deficit for given tax and contribution rates.

Reforms to delay retirement have other beneficial effects. They contain the fall in per capita output and government consumption while increasing household consumption, thus reducing the chance of old-age poverty. In summary, further increases in the retirement age would be essential to restore the financial sustainability of pension systems while maintaining adequate old-age income protection and the overall fiscal capacity to provide public services to the population.

Increases in pension (social security) contributions could contain the pension deficit by more, but they would also lead to lower growth and employment. Raising contributions by an (ex-ante) equivalent of 3 percent of GDP (scenario 5) could reduce the aging-driven deficit by 1.8 percent of GDP, but it has negative impacts on growth, overall labor effort, and formal employment. This leads to a pension financing surplus in the first years after the reform but is not sufficient to contain the deficit in the long run. As a result, this reform ends up collecting far lower revenues than intended. Because of the induced reduction in employment, working hours, and formality, average pensions per beneficiary also drop, and overall household consumption per capita (a proxy of welfare) falls modestly. Therefore, an increase in contributions entails important fiscal, efficiency, and welfare trade-offs, which would need to be resolved on the basis of the main policy goals of the reforms.

Reducing the flat (universal) component or the earnings-related component of pension benefits (scenarios 6 and 7) can cut significantly the shortfall in pension financing without large negative impacts on growth, welfare, and formal employment. Cutting either of these benefit components by 3 percent of GDP reduces the pension deficit by 3.6 percent of GDP (pure-aging scenario) and thus to a more manageable level. In the case of the earnings-related component, the ensuing reductions in growth, hours of work, and formal employment are comparable to those obtained from increases in contribution rates, but household welfare (per capita consumption) declines by more (-5.8 percent compared to -4.4 percent). Reducing the flat component actually improves working hours and formality somewhat. Most of the gains from decreasing pension benefits come from the targeted aggregate expenditures reduction, and as a result, they also mitigate much more than the aging-induced decline in government consumption per capita. Reductions in pension benefits are a more effective policy tool to tackle the pension deficits due to aging than increases in contribution rates, as they achieve a better balance between fiscal and welfare policy goals of the reforms.

Unexpectedly, lowering social assistance benefits by 0.5 percent of GDP (scenario 8) has little impact on the pension deficit, despite positive impacts on employment and the economy. In fact, the deficit increases slightly despite a drop in informality (as work incentives improve) and a subsequent short-term increase in contributions revenue. This again reflects the negative long-term impact on pension expenditures as more households have access to earnings-related pension benefits.

Could higher productivity be the answer? Contrary to common expectations, higher productivity growth leads to a very modest (0.6 percent) improvement in the pension deficit (0.7 percent of initial GDP). To assess this scenario, the analysis simulates the impacts of a sizable (20 percent) exogenous increase in productivity growth (scenario 9). This can also be seen as equivalent to an increase in the economy's long-term potential growth rate. The result is by the type of pension indexation and by the assumption that productivity in the informal and formal sectors grows at the same rate and translates directly into higher wages in both sectors.[20] Pension benefits are partially indexed to wages and thus to productivity growth. Therefore, part of the increase in productivity translates into higher pension entitlements, and another part translates into sizable increases in consumption of both households (through higher wages) and government (through higher taxes).[21]

Summing up, the policy simulations illustrate the impact of population aging on the financing of pensions, with deficits growing by more than 5 percentage points of GDP in constant population terms until 2100. They show that informality alone is neither a cause of nor a solution to pension deficits over the long term. Of the various reforms considered, a reduction in pension benefits is the most effective means to curtail pension deficits due to aging; however, it leads to lower household consumption and thus increases the risk of old-age poverty. An increase in social security contributions can also help finance the pension system in the long run, but it leads to about half of the reduction in the deficit achieved by cuts in the earnings-related part of pension benefits. Increasing the retirement age is a quintessential policy to balance the objectives of financial sustainability, reduction in informality, prevention of old-age poverty, and economic efficiency.

These results are intended only to illustrate the interaction between reforms and labor market feedback over the long term. Keuschnigg, Davoine, and Schuster (2013) also examined scenarios that combine different policy reforms. Solutions for individual countries will depend on their specific circumstances and the demographic challenges they face. In every setting, it is crucial to define the appropriate balance between the multiple goals of reforms according to societal preferences and political economy considerations. Chapter 7 will discuss some specific policy options for pension reform, depending on countries' prototypical circumstances and pension systems.

Conclusions

This chapter has considered two ways to mitigate the effects on pension systems of the inverting population age pyramid and the ensuing decline in the labor force. The first is by increasing LFP in order to stem the shrinkage of the labor force—by having more people in work, having more people work longer, and having more people contributing to pension systems, as well as by expanding the contributory base through immigration. The second option is to enable people to work more productively so they stay in the labor force and so that each worker produces more, earns more, and contributes more to the pension system. More active, productive, and longer working lives are no panacea, but they can contribute substantially to mitigating the impacts of indispensable reforms in the pension system.

While there is some scope in some countries to increase women's participation in employment, in most countries a majority of men *and* women are already actively involved in job markets throughout their prime working years. For younger workers, there is a trade-off between getting them quickly into the workforce and strengthening their educational base to support longer careers. The main scope for adding to the base of contributors is therefore among older workers, aged 55 and above. Successful reforms in this respect will slow the decline in the labor force. But in the absence of very substantial immigration of young workers, the labor force is going to age significantly.

With an older workforce, removing policy barriers to remaining active in the labor market will be crucial. This requires confronting a number of damaging stereotypes that are based on myth rather than reality. There is the myth that older workers prefer retirement to working, when in fact a majority prefer to have the option of combining work and retirement. Another myth holds that older workers are less productive and difficult to employ, when in reality older workers can remain very productive over longer careers and can add to the productivity of others by being part of age-diverse teams. Finally, there is the prevalent myth that keeping older workers in the workforce prevents the young from finding jobs, when evidence shows time and again that strong LFP of old and young go hand in hand and reinforce each other. In a fluid labor market, greater employment levels among any age group strengthen demand and economic growth, meaning that more jobs are created for both older and younger generations.

A firm commitment to employment-friendly reforms will be crucial for tackling policy-related barriers that have inhibited formal employment in general and among older individuals in particular. This includes boosting work incentives and support for those wishing to take up or continue employment, reviewing overly restrictive or rigid labor market regulations, ensuring that wages reflect productivity rather than unwarranted seniority rules, as well as workplace interventions and skill development strategies that account for the strengths and needs of different age groups. Focus group interviews with older workers in Croatia, Poland, and Russia have shown the willingness of workers to work longer, at least part-time; but there is also considerable doubt that such opportunities are there. Workers become discouraged because employers are sometimes unwilling to hire older workers, citing concerns about their physical stamina, their ability to learn new skills, and their commitment to continued employment. The legal framework may not support part-time work, while the design of the tax and social benefits system, including pensions, often does not make (formal) work worthwhile and discourages longer working lives.

With regard to productivity, countries face two challenges. First, maintaining or increasing productivity in aging economies will entail substantial investments in the lifelong development of skills—technical, cognitive, and social-emotional. The skills mismatches and gaps that are evident in Europe's labor markets today must be overcome. Second, countries will need to find ways to tame the possible decline in productivity of some older workers. Recent evidence suggests that workplace adjustments, reassignments to age-specific tasks, and mixed-age teams are the most promising ways to do so. Opportunities for meaningful adult training or lifelong learning are very limited for older workers in most countries in the region. Moreover, such training, where it is available, has had disappointing results, suggesting that new methods of learning adapted for aging brains must be found.

The chapter highlights the importance of factoring in the labor market feedback effects of different types of reforms to address the pension financing dilemmas while maintaining adequate old-age protection. From the perspective of the individual, reforms that seek to improve the sustainability of pension systems can worsen the ratio of benefits received to contributions paid. As a result, workers who are either expecting or experiencing large-scale reforms will increasingly see contributions as taxes and not as savings with a reasonable future return. To the extent that these taxes discourage employment, it can become significantly more challenging to counter the demographically driven deterioration of the dependency ratio. The induced employment response may instead exacerbate demographic trends if the system is not carefully designed to preserve labor market incentives.

Most importantly, having more workers work longer and more productively is no substitute for reforming pension systems. Every additional worker, every additional hour and year worked, and every additional euro earned and contributed to the pension system will bring a short-term gain. But in the long run, it will not solve the financing dilemma of pension systems and in fact may make it worse, because the relationship between contributions and benefit accrual is fundamentally flawed. In other words, all these mitigating measures can ease the pain and spread out the costs of the necessary reforms over more people and generations; but as long as the pension system itself is not reformed, bringing more workers, more productive workers, and more contributions into the pension system will eventually drag it into deeper trouble.

Annex 6A Myths, Misperceptions, and Facts about Older Workers

Myth number 1: Workers, particularly at older ages, prefer to retire rather than continue working.

Fact: Most workers prefer to have the option of combining work and retirement, although in some countries attitudes and social norms do not favor longer working lives.

As already noted, the myth that workers in the region prefer to retire rather than continue working is unfounded. According to the results of a Eurobarometer (2012) survey on active aging in the EU-27 member states and five non-EU countries, most workers prefer to have the option of combining work and retirement. Around two-thirds of citizens across EU-27 and other participating countries find combining part-time work with a partial pension more appealing than full retirement. There is, however, significant variation across countries. Respondents in EU-15 member states were more likely than those in the EU-11 (69 percent vs. 52 percent) to find this option attractive. For instance, in Denmark, Estonia, Iceland, Latvia, and the United Kingdom, over half of respondents would like to continue working during retirement, while the opposite is true in most of Southern Europe, FYR Macedonia, and Turkey.

Furthermore, most citizens (61 percent) think people should be able to work past the official retirement age if they so desire. Similarly, a slight majority (53 percent) disagree with the entire notion of a compulsory retirement age. A higher proportion of respondents in EU-15 member states than in the EU-11 believe that older people should be able to continue working (64 percent vs. 49 percent). Well over half of respondents consider that the lack of opportunities to reduce work gradually is an important reason for stopping work at older ages; the highest proportions agreeing with this idea are found in Greece (82 percent), Hungary (81 percent), Belgium (79 percent), and Denmark (78 percent), while the lowest proportions are in Malta (61 percent), Lithuania (62 percent), and Estonia (63 percent). Moreover, when those currently employed are asked how long they expect to continue working, the majority of EU-27 respondents (59 percent) think they will carry on until they are in their sixties. Those aged 55 years and over expect to work until age 66, while those aged 15–24 only expect to work until 56.7 years.

Empirical evidence suggests that responding to these preferences for a more flexible approach to retirement would improve the quality of life in old age. Studies using longitudinal data for individuals aged 50+ living in the United States and cross-country European data found a similar significant negative effect of retirement on cognitive functioning (see, for instance, Bonsang, Adam, and Perelman 2012; Adam et al. 2007). Involuntary retirement has also been found to have adverse effects on the subjective well-being of pensioners, as they would prefer to work in order to consume more but are prevented from doing so (Bonsang and Klein 2012). Thus, reforms that foster LFP at older ages not only help ensure the sustainability of pension systems but may also lead to positive health benefits for older individuals.

In sum, the notion that older workers in the region are unwilling to have longer working lives is flawed. As noted in chapter 2, the expectation of retiring at age 65 came in with the social security system and employer-based pensions, but full retirement is not a universal goal for most workers. The majority of the population in pre-retirement age, and even those over 65, do not have health impediments that prevent them from working. Thanks to medical advances, the older population can enjoy good health, and in fact the elderly enjoy better-than-ever health status in Northern European and other OECD countries. Given the flexibility to choose, many would continue working longer in some fashion, perhaps changing the way they work but not stopping altogether. By doing so, they can also improve their health and well-being.

However, in several countries of Southern and Central Europe, attitudes and social norms do not seem to favor longer working lives. These norms are, of course, not immutable and may be related to policies and regulations affecting the suitability of employment at older ages, as well to unfounded perceptions about older workers' productivity, employability, and competition with younger workers.

Myth number 2: Older workers are less productive and are difficult to employ.

Fact: Most older workers can remain very productive over longer careers, yet many do face barriers in the workplace and when looking for work.

In reality, individuals and employers have mixed views about older workers. A vast majority of the respondents in the Eurobarometer (2012) survey perceive lack of skills for the modern workplace to be a strong obstacle that inhibits people 55 years and older from working. Many believe that older workers are less likely to be open to new ideas (57 percent) and up to date with new technology (41 percent) compared with younger workers. Perceptions tend to be polarized as far as how older workers compare to younger workers on flexibility and creativity—roughly one in three see each group as having an advantage.

However, when asked to compare the workplace qualities of older and younger workers, the vast majority of respondents actually believe that older ones have more advantages. For one thing, 38 percent see older workers as more productive than younger workers, while 41 percent see them as equally productive. Not surprisingly, virtually all respondents perceive older workers to be more experienced, and an overwhelming majority (80 percent or more) see them as either equal or superior to younger employees in terms of reliability, independent decision making, problem solving, handling stress, and working with other people.

Surveys of employers reveal that while they recognize strengths in older workers, many harbor negative views as well. In its report on aging and employment policies covering 21 countries, the OECD (2006) cites evidence that employers often have mixed views of older workers, including negative perceptions about their flexibility and ability to adapt to changes in technology and business. A 2008–09 survey of employers in France on management of employees over age 50 found that while employers' views about older workers have improved (compared to a 2001 survey), 30 to 40 percent of employers considered them less able to adapt to change and to new technologies, and over 20 percent saw them as more expensive, less healthy, and less mobile than younger workers. The interviews with focus groups of employers conducted in Croatia, Poland, and Russia for this report also reveal similar negative attitudes toward older workers in these countries: employers worry about their physical stamina, their ability to learn new things, and their commitment to continued employment. On the positive side, in all of these surveys a majority of employers considered older workers' greater work experience to be an asset, and they gave older employees an edge in qualities such as being reliable and having strong interpersonal skills.

A vast majority of the Eurobarometer survey respondents believe that negative perceptions of older employees among employers constitute an important barrier that keeps people 55 years and over from working. This belief that employer perceptions play an important role is stronger in the EU-11 than in the EU-15 countries (76 percent vs. 67 percent). Unfavorable employer perceptions are most widely seen (over 80 percent) as an important obstacle in Greece, Hungary, and Slovenia. Even at the other end of the scale, around 60 percent of respondents in Denmark, Iceland, and Sweden consider unfavorable employer perceptions to be important.

Are these ambivalent perceptions and attitudes supported by facts? Overall, the scientific evidence does not support the inevitability of a sharp fall in productivity with aging for all individuals. Numerous studies in occupational medicine, developmental psychology, and gerontology find that physical capacities (like muscle strength and eyesight) and mental capacities (like memory and cognitive ability) can start weakening as early as age 25.[22] However, such early onset is far from universal, and individual factors—chiefly exercise, training, and above all experience—can offset any age-specific declines in abilities until late in the working life. While some productivity-related capacities do diminish with age, the knowledge and capacity to understand and react to new situations can allow older workers to be equally, if not more, capable of taking on a variety of tasks where performance does not depend exclusively on physical prowess.

The micro-empirical literature on whether older workers are less productive is mixed. Studies with stronger designs either find no evidence that aging dampens labor productivity or find, at most, a slight fall to a level that is still above productivity in midlife and younger ages. There is also an increase in the variation in productivity levels at older ages.[23] For instance, recent studies using well-suited matched employer-worker panel data for Germany, the Netherlands, and Portugal fail to find a negative age-productivity effect.

A study by Börsch-Supan and Weiss (2011) of a Mercedes-Benz manufacturing plant in southern Germany is illustrative. The authors examine the relationship between the workers' age and their productivity in work teams using a unique panel data set that combines errors in the production process (a proxy for productivity) with detailed characteristics of workers in the plant, including the age composition of teams. Errors are rare, but when they are severe they can be quite costly for output, and there is little time to fix them. This leads to tense situations. While this work environment requires more physical strength, dexterity, and agility than many service sector jobs, experience and capacity to improvise and manage emotionally intense situations in a team are also vital. The authors, in fact, find that average productivity actually increases monotonically from ages 25 to 65. While older workers are slightly more likely to make errors, they make almost no severe errors. These results suggest that older workers compensate for any loss of physical abilities with an enhanced ability to grasp and focus on the vital aspects of tasks and difficult situations—an ability that comes with experience.

Although they are not corroborated by evidence, negative perceptions about the productivity or qualities of older workers can make it harder for them to find work. There is strong experimental evidence for discrimination in hiring against older workers, at least for entry-level jobs (Riach and Rich 2006, 2007a, 2007b). For instance, labor market experiments in France, Spain, and the United Kingdom sent out thousands of resumes for fictitious candidates to employers, with characteristics and qualifications the same except for age or work experience. A comparison of response rates found that older applicants were significantly less likely to be called for an interview.

In the EU survey on "intergenerational solidarity" (Eurobarometer 2009), age discrimination in the workplace or in the search for employment is the most frequent form of age discrimination reported by respondents. Around one in five had either personally experienced such discrimination (6 percent) or witnessed it (15 percent) in the two years preceding the survey. Interestingly, those aged 55 and over are somewhat less likely (16 percent) than young or middle-aged people (25 percent) to say they have personally experienced or witnessed work-related age discrimination. There is no gender difference. Overall, citizens in the EU-12 are more likely to report experiencing or witnessing work-related age discrimination than those in EU-15—respondents in Hungary, the Czech Republic, the Slovak Republic, and Turkey being the most likely (33 percent).[24]

Myth number 3: Older workers keep younger ones from finding jobs.

Fact: The "lump of labor" is nothing but a fallacy.

The long-standing public perception of a trade-off between employment of younger and older workers is commonly known as the lump-of-labor fallacy. In a Eurobarometer (2009) survey on intergenerational solidarity, covering the 27 EU countries, 56 percent of respondents said they thought that if older people worked longer there would be fewer jobs for young people. Respondents over age 55 were more likely to agree with this idea (57 percent) than respondents aged 15–24 (51 percent). There is also important variation across countries. Over two-thirds of respondents in Greece, Italy, Lithuania, Portugal, Romania, the Slovak Republic, and Slovenia believed in the lump of labor across ages, while only one in four respondents in Denmark and fewer than half of those in the Netherlands, Ireland, and the United Kingdom subscribed to this idea.

Although the lump-of-labor notion has been contradicted by both empirical observations and serious analysis of the data, it still permeates the policy debate about encouraging older workers to work longer. In fact, several pension reforms over the last three decades have been predicated explicitly on the argument that having fewer older workers in the labor market opens up more job opportunities for youth. However, time and again, the evidence has shown that if anything, the opposite is true. A comparison of employment rates of older individuals (aged 55–64) and unemployment of young people (aged 20–24) across countries actually yields a *negative* statistically significant relationship.

Gruber and Wise (2010) provide the most thorough analysis debunking claims of a trade-off between older workers and youth employment. Analyzing long time-series data from the 1960s to the 2000s in 12 OECD countries (including nine in Western Europe), they found in each country a strong positive correlation between employment of older (55–64) and younger (20–24) workers and even those in prime age. From panel cross-country regressions they found that a 1 percent increase in the employment of older persons is associated with a 0.91 percent *decrease* in the unemployment rate of youth. Moreover, results from within-country "natural experiment" comparisons in Denmark, France, and Germany—exploiting reforms that induced older workers to leave the labor force but were unrelated to the employment of youth—yield no evidence that reducing the employment of older persons provides more job opportunities for younger persons or that increasing the LFP of older persons keeps youth out of work.

The lump of labor across ages is indeed a fallacy. If anything, the weight of the evidence suggests that increasing the employment of older workers provides more job opportunities for youth and reduces their unemployment rate. As more workers of any age are employed, the growing segments of the economy tend to create more job opportunities for all workers, including youth. However, this positive dynamic may be hampered in economies with a sclerotic labor market, for instance, those with a dominant role for public sector employment that leads people to queue for government jobs.

Moreover, at the enterprise level there is some evidence of a complementarity between older and younger workers that positively affects firm productivity. Workers often work in teams and thereby affect one another's productivity. In the above-mentioned study by Börsch-Supan and Weiss (2011) in Germany, productivity of workers is measured jointly in a work team so that the results take into account the individual worker's contribution to his co-workers' productivity. Holding average age in a team constant, more experienced work teams (i.e., those with members of longer job tenure) are more productive. Hence, the productivity-enhancing effect of having more experienced workers translates into more productive teams. Another recent study by Göbel and Zwick (2009), using 1997–2005 matched employer-employee data for a representative sample of German enterprises, shows that establishments that use age-mixed working teams are characterized by higher productivity of both old and young employees.

These findings suggest that enterprises can adapt and reap the potential benefits of an aging workforce through the use of age-diverse working teams. Older and younger workers bring different strengths in their skills sets and experience. Older workers can use the tacit know-how and maturity derived from experience to effectively mentor younger workers, help teams focus on the vital aspects of a task, share tasks according to their strengths, and contribute to a better work climate. These aspects can be more important than the potential communication problems that may arise from different attitudes and aspirations across generations. In the 2009 Eurobarometer survey, roughly seven in 10 EU-27 citizens disagreed that companies that mostly employ young people perform better than those that employ an age-diverse workforce.

Summing up, the three myths about older workers—their alleged resistance to longer working lives, their low productivity, and their displacement of youth—lack a solid empirical basis. Once policy makers in the region move past these misperceptions, they can then confront real barriers that hinder the labor participation of older workers, as discussed in this chapter.

Annex 6B Modeling Direct and Feedback Effects of Reforms on Pension and Labor Market Outcomes

The analysis relies on a stylized overlapping-generations model, developed by Keuschnigg, Davoine, and Schuster (2013) for this report, that is able to capture the most salient features of pension reforms.[25] The approach has an explicit life-cycle structure to capture the dynamics of population aging and differentiate the labor market experiences (and retirement patterns) of different age groups and cohorts. It allows endogenous decision margins along several dimensions, including hours, participation, retirement, informality, education, and search effort while unemployed, thus capturing feedback effects on the labor market of pension, tax, and labor reforms. The explicit modeling of the informality/formality decision is an important innovation, given the role of the informal sector in transition economies. This extension allows us to assess the impact of reforms on pension expenditures and government revenue in a more realistic way. Figure 6A.1 shows a schematic representation of the individual and household decisions that the model accounts for.

The model also contains a stylized enterprise sector that makes production and investment decisions, and a government that sets tax and benefits parameters. The model is calibrated for Poland and the Slovak Republic using detailed information on three sectors:

- Government: redistribution and social protection policies, including benefit replacement rates of unemployment benefits and pensions, pension indexation, and tax rates.

- Households: labor supply responsiveness to financial (tax/benefit) incentives ("elasticities"), information on population size and

FIGURE 6B.1

Modeling Labor Market Feedbacks in Pension Reforms

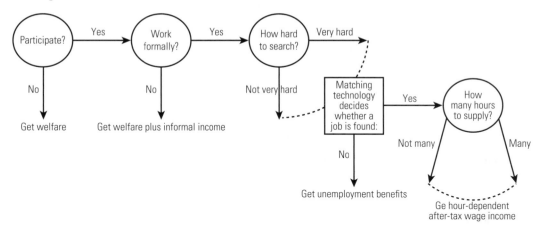

Source: Keuschnigg, Davoine, and Schuster 2013.

structure, incomes, labor market patterns, and savings rates by age group.

- Production: real interest rate, productivity and productivity growth, and substitution elasticity between capital and labor.

As some parameters are difficult to obtain, an effort was made to derive plausible values when data were unavailable for either of the two countries. Sensitivity analysis is conducted to assess the robustness of results to key parameters and assumptions.

While extremely useful for studying the impacts of reforms, the model has some important limitations. First, it does not model welfare (income) distribution explicitly, thus making it less suitable for poverty and income inequality analysis. Second, it assumes constant per capita (and per-age-group) health expenditures. And finally, simulations relied on a technical choice for balancing ("closing") the government budget through reductions in public consumption. This isolates the effect of aging and reforms, but again should be taken as an indication of the actual fiscal cost of aging in terms of reduced capacity to provide public goods and services.

Notes

1. Based on 2010 data from the International Labour Organization's ILOSTAT database. "OECD" refers to non-EU OECD countries; "Latin America and Asia" refers to non-OECD countries in these regions only.

2. The old-age dependency ratio is the number of those 65 or older per 100 people of working age: $(65+)/(15–64) \times 100$.

3. See Koettl (2008) for a detailed description of the methodology.

4. The survey covers 31,280 respondents aged 15 and above who were interviewed between September and November 2011.

5. Similar arguments have been made about the implications of women and immigrants joining the workforce, purportedly at the expense of male and native-born workers, respectively.

6. The Flash Eurobarometer survey on intergenerational solidarity covered more than 27,000 randomly selected citizens aged 15 and over in the 27 EU member states.

7. The countries are Belgium, Canada, Denmark, France, Germany, Italy, Japan, the Netherlands, Spain, Sweden, the United Kingdom, and the United States.

8. See Koettl and Weber (2012) for an exact definition and discussion of the FTR.

9. See, for example, Betcherman, Daysal, and Pagés (2008).

10. A recent study found that lower cognitive ability is associated with greater risk aversion and more pronounced impatience—factors known to affect old-age savings decisions (Dohmen et al. 2010).

11. For instance, Turner and Verma (2007) found that of those who were eligible to participate in 401(k) plans in the United States but did not, 40 percent explained that they could not afford to. Yet, when a sample of individuals was subject to automatic enrollment with a later option to opt out, they substantially increased their participation. Many allegedly income-constrained workers did not opt out, thus suggesting that for many, the contributions were, in fact, manageable.

12. Indeed, prominent authors warn that tax distortions that result from the financing needs of pay-as-you-go pensions are going to be the main channel through which aging will affect economic output. See Weil (2006).

13. Although a number of emerging middle-income economies have successfully carried out several reforms, including introduction of noncontributory pensions with broad coverage (Willmore 2007; Barr and Diamond 2009), empirical research has been constrained by lack of long time-series or natural experiments data that may allow isolation of causal effects. Examples of studies for middle-income countries are those documenting the effects of disincentives in South Africa (Bertrand, Mullainathan, and Miller 2003; Duflo 2003; Ardington, Case, and Hosegood 2009). In addition, a study by de Carvalho Filho (2008) shows that changes in pension eligibility rules and a doubling of minimum benefits for rural workers in Brazil reduced male labor supply by roughly 38 percentage points.

14. Betcherman (2012) provides a recent comprehensive review of the literature.

15. The EU enacted specific legislation requiring member states to prohibit age discrimination in employment. All member countries have now made it unlawful to discriminate in the labor market on grounds of age (among other factors).

16. See the recent review by Smith (2011). Jespersen, Munch, and Skipper (2008) provide a notable Danish example, while Raaum, Torp, and

Zhang (2002) do the same for Norway. Osikominu (2013) shows a more common situation, with only a very rudimentary comparison of costs and impacts.

17. See the evaluation of German training programs by Lechner, Miquel, and Wunsch (2007).

18. These results refer to the final "steady state," which in the model approximately corresponds to the year 2100. For much more detail on the modeling and results from a larger set of policy simulations considered, see Keuschnigg, Davoine, and Schuster (2013).

19. A counterfactual experiment in which pension indexation for retirees is doubled, on top of higher productivity, leads to a dampening of the increase in informality but a still modest improvement in the deficit.

20. Since informal earnings are untaxed, they grow faster than formal net earnings, making informal work more attractive (since pensions, part of the benefits of formality, grow less). The resulting increase in informality translates into higher consumption and also lowers contributions revenue.

21. See Skirbekk (2004) for a survey of the literature in various disciplines.

22. de Hek and van Vuuren (2011) provide a survey of the empirical literature.

23. Prejudice against older workers has led to the enactment of anti-discrimination legislation in many countries. The EU has enacted specific legislation requiring member states to prohibit age discrimination in employment. All member countries have now legislated to make it unlawful to discriminate in the labor market on grounds of age (or other factors).

24. The model is based on adaptations of the model developed by Fisher and Keuschnigg (2010) and Jaag, Keuschnigg, and Keuschnigg (2010).

References

Abowd, John M., John C. Haltiwanger, Julia Lane, Kevin L. McKinney, and L. Kristin Sandusky. 2007. "Technology and the Demand for Skill: An Analysis of Within and Between Firm Differences." IZA Discussion Paper 2707, Institute for the Study of Labor (IZA), Bonn, Germany.

Adam, Stéphane, Éric Bonsang, Sophie Germain, and Sergio Perelman. 2007. "Retraite, activités non professionnelles et vieillissement cognitif. Une exploration à partir des données de Share." *Economie et Statistique* 303: 83–96.

Ahituv, Avner, and Joseph Zeira. 2011. "Technical Progress and Early Retirement." *Economic Journal* (Royal Economic Society) 121 (551): 171–93.

Ardington, Cally, Anne Case, and Victoria Hosegood. 2009. "Labor Supply Responses to Large Social Transfers: Longitudinal Evidence from South Africa." *American Economic Journal: Applied Economics* 1 (1): 22–48.

Arias, Omar S., and Carolina Sánchez-Páramo. 2013. *Back to Work: Growing with Jobs in Europe and Central Asia*. Washington, DC: World Bank.

Autor, David, Frank Levy, and Richard J. Murnane. 2003. "The Skill Content of Recent Technological Change: An Empirical Exploration." *Quarterly Journal of Economics* 118 (4): 1279–1334.

Barr, Nicholas, and Peter Diamond. 2009. "Reforming Pensions: Principles, Analytical Errors and Policy Directions." *International Social Security Review* 62 (2): 5–29.

Bertrand, Marianne, Sendhil Mullainathan, and Douglas Miller. 2003. "Public Policy and Extended Families: Evidence from Pensions in South Africa." *World Bank Economic Review* 17 (1): 27–50.

Besharov, Douglas J., and Phoebe H. Cottingham, eds. 2011. *The Workforce Investment Act: Implementation Experiences and Evaluation Findings*. Kalamazoo, MI: W. E. Upjohn Institute for Employment Research.

Betcherman, Gordon. 2012. "Labor Market Institutions: A Review of the Literature." Background Paper for *World Development Report 2013*, World Bank, Washington, DC.

Betcherman, Gordon, N. Meltem Daysal, and Carmen Pagés. 2008. "Do Employment Subsidies Work? Evidence from Regionally Targeted Subsidies in Turkey." IZA Discussion Paper 3508, Institute for the Study of Labor (IZA), Bonn, Germany.

Bonsang, Eric, Stéphane Adam, and Sergio Perelman. 2012. "Does Retirement Affect Cognitive Functioning?" *Journal of Health Economics* 31 (3): 490–501.

Bonsang, Eric, and Tobias J. Klein. 2012. "Retirement and Subjective Well-Being." *Journal of Economic Behavior and Organization* 83 (3): 311–29.

Borghans, Lex, and Bas ter Weel. 2002. "Do Older Workers Have More Trouble Using a Computer than Younger Workers?" Research Memorandum 003, Research Centre for Education and the Labour Market (ROA), Maastricht University, the Netherlands.

Börsch-Supan, Axel H., and Matthias Weiss. 2011. "Productivity and Age: Evidence from Work Teams at the Assembly Line." MEA Discussion Paper 07148, Munich Center for the Economics of Aging (MEA), Max Planck Institute for Social Law and Social Policy, Munich.

Danzer, Alexander M. 2010. "Retirement Responses to a Generous Pension Reform: Evidence from a Natural Experiment in Eastern Europe." IZA Discussion Paper 4726, Institute for the Study of Labor (IZA), Bonn, Germany.

de Carvalho Filho, Irineu Evangelista. 2008. "Old-Age Benefits and Retirement Decisions of Rural Elderly in Brazil." *Journal of Development Economics* 86 (1): 129–46.

Deelen, Anja P., and Evangelia Bourmpoula. 2009. "Employment Protection Legislation: A Cross-Country Analysis Focusing on the Elderly." Paper presented at the European Association of Labour Economists (EALE) Annual Conference, Tallinn, Estonia, February 27.

de Hek, Paul, and Daniel van Vuuren. 2011. "Are Older Workers Overpaid? A Literature Review." *International Tax and Public Finance* 18 (4): 436–60.

Dohmen, Thomas, Armin Falk, David Huffman, and Uwe Sunde. 2010. "Are Risk Aversion and Impatience Related to Cognitive Ability?" *American Economic Review* 100 (3): 1238–60.

Duflo, Esther. 2003. "Grandmothers and Granddaughters: Old-Age Pensions and Intrahousehold Allocation in South Africa." *World Bank Economic Review* 17 (1): 1–25.

Eurobarometer. 2009. *Intergenerational Solidarity: Analytical Report.* Flash Eurobarometer 269. Brussels: European Commission.

———. 2012. *Active Ageing: Report.* Special Eurobarometer 378. Brussels: European Commission.

Eurofound (European Foundation for the Improvement of Living and Working Conditions). 2011. *Part-Time Work in Europe: European Company Survey 2009.* Dublin: Eurofound. http://www.eurofound.europa.eu /pubdocs/2010/86/en/3/EF1086EN.pdf.

Eurostat Statistics Database. European Commission, Brussels. http://epp. eurostat.ec.europa.eu/portal/page/portal/statistics/search_database.

Fisher, Walter H., and Christian Keuschnigg. 2010. "Pension Reform and Labor Market Incentives." *Journal of Population Economics* 23 (2): 769–803.

Gill, Indermit, and Martin Raiser. 2012. *Golden Growth: Restoring the Lustre of the European Economic Model.* Washington, DC: World Bank.

Göbel, Christian, and Thomas Zwick. 2009. "Age and Productivity: Evidence from Linked Employer Employee Data." ZEW Discussion Paper 09-020, Centre for European Economic Research (ZEW), Mannheim, Germany.

Gruber, Jonathan, and David A. Wise, eds. 1999. *Social Security and Retirement around the World.* Chicago, IL: University of Chicago Press.

———. 2004. *Social Security Programs and Retirement around the World: Micro-Estimation.* Chicago, IL: University of Chicago Press.

———. 2010. *Social Security Programs and Retirement around the World: The Relationship to Youth Employment.* Chicago, IL: University of Chicago Press.

Handel, J. Michael. 2012. "Trends in Job Skill Demands in OECD Countries." OECD Social, Employment, and Migration Working Paper 143, Organisation for Economic Co-operation and Development, Paris.

Hodin, Michael W., and Mark Hoffmann. 2011. "Snowbirds and Water Coolers: How Aging Populations Can Drive Economic Growth." *SAIS Review of International Affairs* 31 (2): 5–14.

Immervoll, Herwig, and Mark Pearson. 2009. "A Good Time for Making Work Pay? Taking Stock of In-Work Benefits and Related Measures across the OECD." OECD Social, Employment, and Migration Working Paper 81, Organisation for Economic Co-operation and Development, Paris.

Jaag, Christian, Christian Keuschnigg, and Mirela Keuschnigg. 2010. "Pension Reform, Retirement, and Life-Cycle Unemployment." *International Tax and Public Finance* 17 (5): 556–85.

Jespersen, Svend T., Jakob R. Munch, and Lars Skipper. 2008. "Costs and Benefits of Danish Active Labour Market Programmes." *Labour Economics* 15 (5): 859–84.

Johnson, Sandra, and Kathleen Taylor, eds. 2006. *The Neuroscience of Adult Learning.* New Directions for Adult and Continuing Education, no. 110. San Francisco, CA: Jossey-Bass.

Keuschnigg, Christian, Thomas Davoine, and Philip Schuster. 2013. "Aging and Pension Reform: A General Equilibrium Approach." Background Paper, World Bank, Washington, DC.

Koettl, Johannes. 2008. "Prospects for Management of Migration between Europe and the Middle East and North Africa: Demographic Trends, Labor Force Projections, and Implications for Policies of Immigration, Labor Markets, and Social Protection." Background Paper, World Bank, Washington, DC.

———. 2013. "Does Formal Work Pay in Serbia? The Role of Labor Taxes and Social Benefit Design in Providing Disincentives for Formal Work." In *Poverty and Exclusion in the Western Balkans: New Directions in Measurement and Policy,* edited by Caterina Ruggeri Laderchi and Sara Savastano, 133–54. New York: Springer.

Koettl, Johannes, and Michael Weber. 2012. "Does Formal Work Pay? The Role of Labor Taxation and Social Benefit Design in the New EU Member States." In *Informal Employment in Emerging and Transition Economies,* edited by Hartmut Lehmann and Konstantinos Tatsiramos, 167–204. Research in Labor Economics 34. Bingley, U.K.: Emerald.

Langot, François, and Eva Moreno-Galbis. 2008. "Does the Growth Process Discriminate against Older Workers?" IZA Discussion Paper 3841, Institute for the Study of Labor (IZA), Bonn, Germany.

Lechner, Michael, Ruth Miquel, Conny Wunsch. 2007. "The Curse and Blessing of Training the Unemployed in a Changing Economy: The Case of East Germany after Unification." *German Economic Review* 8 (4): 468–509.

Loch, Christoph H., Fabian J. Sting, Nikolaus Bauer, and Helmut Mauermann. 2010. "The Globe: How BMW Is Defusing the Demographic Time Bomb." *Harvard Business Review,* March.

Maestas, Nicole, and Julie Zissimopoulos. 2010. "How Longer Work Lives Ease the Crunch of Population Aging." *Journal of Economic Perspectives* 24 (1): 139–60.

Mazzonna, Fabrizio, and Franco Peracchi. 2012. "Ageing, Cognitive Abilities and Retirement." *European Economic Review* 56 (4): 691–710.

Neumark, David, and Joanne Song. 2012. "Barriers to Later Retirement: Increases in the Full Retirement Age, Age Discrimination, and the Physical Challenges of Work." Working Paper 2012-265, Michigan Retirement Research Center, University of Michigan, Ann Arbor, MI.

OECD (Organisation for Economic Co-operation and Development). 2006. *Live Longer, Work Longer.* Paris: OECD.

———. 2011. *Pensions at a Glance 2011: Retirement-Income Systems in OECD and G20 Countries.* Paris: OECD.

Osikominu, Aderonke. 2013. "Quick Job Entry or Long-Term Human Capital Development? The Dynamic Effects of Alternative Training Schemes." *Review of Economic Studies* 80 (1): 313–42.

Packard, Truman, Johannes Koettl, and Claudio E. Montenegro. 2012. *In from the Shadow: Integrating Europe's Informal Labor*. Washington, DC: World Bank.

Perry, Guillermo E., William F. Maloney, Omar S. Arias, Pablo Fajnzylber, Andrew D. Mason, and Jaime Saavedra-Chanduvi. 2007. *Informality: Exit and Exclusion*. Washington, DC: World Bank.

Raaum, Oddbjørn, Hege Torp, and Tao Zhang. 2002. "Do Individual Programme Effects Exceed the Costs? Norwegian Evidence on Long Run Effects of Labour Market Training." Memorandum 15/2002, Department of Economics, University of Oslo.

Riach, Peter A., and Judith Rich. 2006. "An Experimental Investigation of Age Discrimination in the French Labour Market." IZA Discussion Paper 2522, Institute for the Study of Labor (IZA), Bonn, Germany.

———. 2007a. "An Experimental Investigation of Age Discrimination in the Spanish Labour Market." IZA Discussion Paper 2654, Institute for the Study of Labor (IZA), Bonn, Germany.

———. 2007b. "An Experimental Investigation of Age Discrimination in the English Labor Market." IZA Discussion Paper 3029, Institute for the Study of Labor (IZA), Bonn, Germany.

Skirbekk, Vegard. 2004. "Age and Individual Productivity: A Literature Survey." In *Vienna Yearbook of Population Research 2004*, edited by G. Gustav Feichtinger, 133–53. Vienna: Verlag der Österreichischen Akademie der Wissenschaften.

Smith, Jeffrey. 2011. "Improving Impact Evaluation in Europe." In *The Workforce Investment Act: Implementation Experiences and Evaluation Findings*, edited by Douglas Besharov and Phoebe Cottingham, 473–94. Kalamazoo, MI: W. E. Upjohn Institute for Employment Research.

Turner, John A., and Satyendra Verma. 2007. "Why Some Workers Don't Take 401(k) Plan Offers: Inertia versus Economics." CeRP Working Paper 56, Center for Research on Pensions and Welfare Policies, Turin, Italy.

Weil, David N. 2006. "Population Aging." NBER Working Paper 12147, National Bureau of Economic Research, Cambridge, MA.

Willmore, Larry. 2007. "Universal Pensions for Developing Countries." *World Development* 35 (1): 24–51.

World Bank. World Development Indicators (database). http://data .worldbank.org/data-catalog/world-development-indicators.

CHAPTER 7

Lessons from Two Decades of Pension Reform and Policy Solutions for the Future

Introduction

Tackling the demographics of the inverting pyramid is a formidable task. Policy options exist, but few of them will be easy. Each country will have to make its own decision on which measures to adopt. Given the hard choices and differing country circumstances, each country will have to consider which options are easier for it to implement and which are impossibly difficult. Employing a mix of options may allow countries to make small changes rather than putting the full burden of adjustment on a single sweeping measure.

What Have We Learned from Reforms of the First Pillar?

Before looking at the policy options, it is worth reviewing some of the lessons from the two decades of pension reform already experienced by these countries. These lessons are concentrated in four main areas: (a) the limited impact of incentives on behavior, (b) the need to communicate what people should expect, (c) the need for policy consistency with regard to both the overall reform strategy and the measures required to make the strategy successful, and (d) the importance of a holistic approach to pension reform.

Limited Impact of Incentives

Contrary to expectations, neither improved incentives nor strengthened enforcement has led to full coverage of the labor force at pre-transition levels. The initial reforms had assumed a strong role for incentives and their impact on individual behavior. With contributor coverage falling during the transition from the whole labor force to only about half of the labor force on average, the original thinking had been that strong enforcement coupled with benefit formulas that tightly link future benefits to contributions would induce individuals back into formal labor markets. The evidence suggests that there has been some recovery in contributor coverage from the sharp initial drops in the early years of transition, but only to levels typical of other middle-income countries worldwide.

The lack of complete coverage has both short- and long-run implications. In the short run, countries should not expect to see rapid revenue growth from further increases in contributors. In the long run, there will be a smaller number of qualifying pensioners, which improves pension system finances, but there will also need to be some minimal old-age assistance provided to the noncovered elderly.

Similarly, reducing contribution rates has not provided sufficient incentive for formalization and has resulted in worsening pension system finances. Since some of the growth in informality stemmed from the very high contribution rates, it was hoped that reducing the rates would provide incentives for workers and employers to rejoin the formal labor market, which would improve pension system finances. While reducing contribution rates did improve the functioning of the labor markets and improve labor competitiveness, the increases in formalization were not sufficient to offset the decline in revenue from existing contributors. As a result, pension system finances have gotten worse, not better.

Incentives for postponing retirement have also been unable to induce individuals to work longer. The initial thinking was that if the pension system provided people sufficient incentives to keep working, they would choose to retire later, sparing governments from taking the painful political step of raising the retirement age. But the evidence suggests that people do not postpone retirement even with fairly high incentives. For example, in 2007, the notional interest rate in Latvia briefly reached 20 percent, suggesting that postponing retirement by an additional year would result in a 20 percent higher benefit throughout retirement. Nevertheless, people continued to retire at the earliest possible age. And going forward, with the limited financing available, countries will not be able to afford to provide incentives high enough to entice people to postpone retirement. These observations suggest that individual attitudes toward retirement are less influential than societal norms of the "right time to retire," and more efforts should be put into raising societal acceptance of longer working lives.

Incentives proved similarly ineffective in stemming the demographic decline. Generous family policies like two- or three-year maternity leaves, maternity cash benefits, and earlier retirement ages for women with many children did not result in substantially increased contributor cohorts in most countries. Rather, these policies increased social insurance expenditures and made it more difficult for young women to get jobs. The long maternity leaves also made it difficult for women to retain relevant skills, impeding their return to the workplace, and hindered the development of quality child care. The prolonged decline in fertility coupled with continued outmigration resulted in a very different demographic reality than what was assumed at the time of the initial pension reforms. This made some of the reforms that looked sustainable in the early transition appear increasingly unsustainable later.

The Need for Communication

A second area where the policy reforms made thus far have provided lessons is the need to communicate with the public and explain to people what they should expect. The initial intention was to enact reasonably strong reforms that would be automatically implemented based on developments in observable parameters, such as life expectancy and inflation. While linking parameters of the pension system to these external parameters should lead to a welcome consistency in pension policy, policy makers also adopted the automatic stabilization approach to avoid difficult political battles over where the retirement age and benefit levels should be in the long run. Meaningful public debate, aimed at convincing the population of the need for a rise in the retirement age and cuts in benefits, did not take place. As a result, when people saw reductions in benefits they started complaining and demanding that elements of the reforms be reversed. The subsequent changes undermined both the objectives and the underlying structure of the reforms, which did not have scope for unplanned ad hoc changes.

The application of starkly different retirement rules and benefits to adjacent cohorts also led to a feeling that the reforms were not fair. The logic behind the differences was clear: cohorts close to retirement had little time to adjust to new rules and benefit structures and thus needed to be protected, while those further away from retirement had time to adjust to the new rules and could face the full impact of the reforms. As a result, in many cases, the reforms applied to all those below a certain age at the time of the reform and not to those above that age. The problem was that individuals born on December 31 were often treated very differently from similar individuals born the next day, that is, on January 1 of the following calendar year. This differential treatment led to dissatisfaction with the reforms and to demands for reversals, again leading to ad hoc solutions. More gradual implementation of reforms, perhaps starting with small changes for even the oldest cohorts, with explanations to the public of why different cohorts were being treated differently, might help maintain the momentum of the reform path.

Part of the problem with tailoring benefits to cohorts was that the benefits of the oldest cohorts were kept largely fixed, even when unsustainable. Early in the reform process some countries missed the chance to restructure their unsustainable pension liabilities. Rather than explain to the public that older cohorts were being given more generous treatment because they had limited ability to adjust to the new rules, policy makers perpetuated the myth that older workers had "earned" these higher benefits. This sacrificed the opportunity to restructure some of the implicit pension liabilities by curbing early retirement, disallowing multiple benefits, and putting in place benefit ceilings. The one component of the reforms that did affect these older workers, indexation of benefits, was often not implemented as legislated.

While pensioners and workers were generally amenable to austerity when economic conditions were unfavorable, as soon as economic conditions improved, they began to demand rollbacks of the pension reforms. The public, in general, needs to understand that long-run demographics, and not just short-run economic conditions, require major changes to the pension system. There are limits to what the public system can provide, and there needs to be a broad public debate about what it will provide and the extent to which individuals will have to supplement that public provision. This should include discussions of public priorities for resource allocation—between categories of pensioners within the pension system (old age vs. disabled vs. survivors); between categories of elderly (those who did not contribute vs. those who contributed during full careers vs. those who contributed for the minimum number of years); between generations (current pensioners vs. future pensioners); and between pension spending and other spending. People need to realize that the burden of providing for old age in the future will have to be shared between the state and its citizens, and that this will require people to take a much more active approach toward retirement planning.

The Need for Policy Consistency

A third important lesson is the need for consistency in pension policy and in the follow-up measures required to make that policy successful. The region has benefited from a vibrant growth of democracy, with complete changes in government occurring in many of the countries as frequently as every four to five years. While democracy is a good thing, the installation of a new government has frequently been accompanied by repudiation of the policies enacted by the previous government. This constant shifting of policy has been unfavorable in a variety of contexts, but it has been particularly harmful in regard to pension policy.

Pensions represent a long-term contract between workers and the government. While it is acceptable that some parameters might need to change over the length of the contract in response to economic and demographic developments, huge and frequent policy shifts lead to worker perceptions that the government is not really providing any old-age security. This in turn undermines workers' willingness to contribute their limited earnings to such a system. Consistency is important not just in pension policy itself, but in other policies needed to make the pension system work. For example, the fiscal framework must remain consistent with the pension policy chosen. If there are transition costs to be financed, the fiscal policy needs to remain conservative enough to generate the resources to finance those costs. If retirement ages are rising, labor market policies need to support longer working careers.

Importance of a Holistic Intersectoral Approach

A final lesson is that pensions are part of a larger, holistic policy framework. Pension policy affects so much of the population and is so large fiscally that it touches a broad range of seemingly unrelated sectors. As a result, it requires a broad societal consensus on the way forward, with appropriate adjustments in multiple sectors.

Too often, pension policy is drafted by one ministry, with little input from other ministries. However, the success of that policy depends on factors that might not be under the control of the lead ministry. For example, later retirement ages might require increases in lifelong learning, which could fall under the purview of the education ministry. Issuing and regulating financial securities are functions that come under yet other ministries. Making the fiscal space for pensions clearly involves the finance ministry, tax authorities, and other ministries, all of which might have to adjust their budget envelopes. Even within the labor ministry, one reason that incentives have not worked as well as hoped in the pension area is that there are other rigidities in the labor market, unrelated to pensions, that prevent the labor market from being flexible. There needs to be a societal consensus on how old-age support will be provided and a coherent effort to make it happen once the decisions are made.

What Have We Learned from Experience with Second-Pillar Systems?

The more than 15-year experience with funded second-pillar systems has also provided lessons. The most important of these is the need for fiscal resources to pay for the transition costs, and to make space for the private, funded system, if the overall rate of pension contributions is not increased. As noted in chapter 4, many countries in Europe and Central Asia chose to borrow funds to pay for transition costs rather than paying for them by raising taxes or reducing other expenditures. The privatization revenues that were supposed to help offset the transition costs sometimes did not materialize, were insufficient to cover the costs, or were spent on other priorities. Interest on the borrowed funds accumulated quickly, which exacerbated fiscal pressures and led to unsustainable levels of debt. These fiscal pressures were the primary driving force that led some of the governments to reverse the second-pillar systems. This reversal temporarily relieves the fiscal pressure but leads to much larger fiscal liabilities in the longer run. Going forward, countries need to carefully plan financing to cover the fiscal costs of transition and to maintain a consistent policy framework so that future governments do not divert the resources meant to cover transition costs to other priorities.

The heavy reliance by government on borrowing to finance annual expenditures also adversely affects the pension funds' ability to diversify into other assets and the development of financial markets. Pension funds are often criticized for their heavy investment in government securities. The argument has been that since pension funds often invest in government securities, a funded system is really no different from a public system that depends on the government's ability to pay pensioners. But governments need to recognize that some of this investing in government debt comes from their own overreliance on borrowing. The more governments borrow, the higher the interest rates they pay for that debt, and if these government assets are considered safe or riskless, it is harder for pension funds to find other instruments with a similar risk-return profile. Governments also need to proactively assist in the development of financial markets. But when they rely on these pension funds for their own financing, development of the financial markets can threaten this financing, giving them less interest in further developing capital markets.

The institutional structure of the pension funds, adopted from Latin America, has turned out to be costly and is not necessarily producing the best results for workers. The original pension fund design consisted of multiple private pension fund administrators who provided both record keeping and portfolio management, each managing a single portfolio. Workers were expected to decide whether they wanted to join a private pension fund, and then expected to choose their pension fund administrator. A number of issues, including economies of scale in pension fund administration, the need for differing portfolios at different stages of the working life, and individuals' lack of sufficient knowledge or willingness to make choices, emerged to suggest that this might not be the optimal institutional design for a funded pension system.

Relatively small changes could lead to much better outcomes. Separating pension fund administration from portfolio management may result in lower-cost pension administration. In the pension fund administration industry, there are high costs of setting up the business, but relatively low costs of adding new participants. Pension fund administrators were generating high administrative costs by spending on advertising and salespeople to convince workers to join their pension funds. A single pension fund administrator could perform the record-keeping functions required at lower cost than multiple administrators.

Competition in portfolio management can help generate good returns for workers and provide individuals the flexibility to change portfolios over their life cycle. People at different stages of the life cycle have different investment needs. The appropriate pension portfolio for a young worker 30 years away from retirement looks very different from the portfolio of a person about to retire. The original design expected different pension fund administrators to offer different portfolios, but that did not happen. Instead, people of all ages were given the same portfolio. Active competition in portfolio management will help ensure the best risk-return mix for individuals and give them the flexibility to change their portfolios as they age.

In view of most people's reluctance to make complex choices, policy makers need to provide well-designed default options while still allowing individuals to make active choices if they wish to do so. The original design depended heavily on consumers making a series of decisions: whether to join a private pension fund, which of the many pension funds they should join, and if the fund offered multiple portfolios, which one they wanted. When they reached retirement, they were supposed to decide how they wanted their pension to be provided and who should provide the annuity. The competition arising from these individual choices, like competition in the market for toothpaste, was expected to generate the best returns for participants. In reality, most people were unwilling or unable to make these decisions. They let the system choose for them, or they made an initial choice and then left that arrangement in place through inertia despite evidence that there were better options available. The lesson from behavioral economics and from experience with private pension funds is that the default options need to be designed carefully to generate the best outcomes for most people. And the default options need to automatically apply to all individuals unless they choose to do something different.

Evidence from labor markets also suggests that it should be possible to keep workers working longer. Three findings stand out. First, not all workers want to retire as soon as they are eligible for a pension. Many would be willing to continue working, but they might prefer to work flexible hours or work part-time while drawing a partial pension. Second, older workers can remain productive throughout long working lives and are not necessarily less productive than younger workers. While certain physical abilities do decline, other capacities are enhanced by experience. Workplace adaptations to accommodate older workers and training geared toward older brains can raise productivity. However, employer prejudice against older workers is real, and rigidities in the labor market that require employers to pay older workers based on seniority and not productivity may also serve to reduce their employment opportunities. Third, continuing to employ older workers does not reduce employment opportunities for the young. Workers of different generations are not substitutes for each other, and there is evidence that increasing the employment of older workers does not increase youth unemployment; if anything, it may decrease it. When mixed-age teams work together, older workers are able to mentor younger workers, increasing the productivity of the whole work team.

Evidence from fiscal analysis suggests that raising revenue through consumption taxes might be more productive than raising revenue through alternative means. Some studies suggest, as noted in chapter 5, that consumption taxes have a positive impact on competitiveness and on growth. They are typically more broadly based than labor taxes, and the broader tax base means they generate similar revenues with lower tax rates and less distortion. Finally, given the intergenerational inequities in current pension systems, with the burden of benefit and retirement age adjustment falling largely on younger cohorts, consumption taxes allow for better intergenerational burden sharing as they affect all cohorts, while labor taxes again affect only younger cohorts.

Demographic Challenges Facing Countries of the Region

The policy choices available to each country depends on what its population pyramid looks like. In countries where the working-age population is still expanding, the population pyramid is in fact a pyramid, as shown in figure 1.1a (chapter 1). Even though coverage in the pension system might have expanded so much that the pension pyramid becomes almost identical to the population pyramid, this group of countries is continuing to bring in new contributors, who help pay liabilities of the elderly. In these countries the projected labor force in 2050 is expected to be larger than the labor force in 2010; thus their bars extend above the population stabilization line in figure 7.1. This group includes a few high-income countries, which continue to attract immigrants, along with the Young Countries, where fertility is still high. For these countries, the demographic challenge consists largely of increases in longevity—the easiest of the challenges to address. Linking retirement age to increases in longevity or reducing benefits through a formula like notional accounts might work in these cases as long as both economic growth and labor force growth are relatively steady.

The danger for these countries is that the factors that keep their population structure in a pyramid shape, high immigration and high fertility rates, could wane in the future. This could cause their population structure to change into a column or even an inverted pyramid. In the case of some of the Young Countries, while their

FIGURE 7.1

Projected Labor Force in 2050 Compared to Actual Labor Force in 2010, Selected European and Central Asian Economies

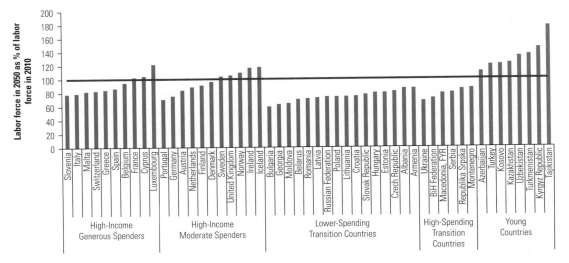

Source: United Nations population projections (UN 2011).
Note: The Federation of Bosnia-Herzegovina (BiH Federation) and Republika Srpska, which together make up the country of Bosnia and Herzegovina, have separate pension systems and are treated as separate data points in the figure.

population is projected to grow, the projections are based on historical migration patterns. As some of their neighboring countries begin to experience labor force shortages, Young Countries' emigration rates might begin to exceed historical patterns, and these countries might stop experiencing labor force growth, despite higher fertility rates. For the countries where the working-age population is expanding due to immigration it is also vital to ensure that the new residents can quickly accumulate human capital and reach the productivity levels of the domestically born population.

Countries whose labor force is no longer expanding have a columnar population structure. These countries can continue to expand the number of pension system contributors for a time by bringing in female workers, rural workers, and the self-employed. But once all workers in the country are in the system and have been in the system for 50 to 60 years, the country has no capacity to increase contributors further to help pay liabilities of the current elderly. The generosity of the pension system, which was built on the premise of a continuously expanding contributor base, will no longer be affordable, and these countries may need to return to the less generous pension system of the past. Alternatively, if they raise the retirement age sufficiently to return to the average retirement duration of only

15 years, which was the norm in the 1970s, they could both generate substantial numbers of older contributors and reduce the number of beneficiaries. This would allow them to maintain both the poverty prevention and income replacement functions of the pension system at levels similar to the benefits received today. Countries can then link the retirement age that results in a life expectancy of 15 years with further growth in life expectancy.

Countries where the working-age population is actually shrinking are experiencing the inverting pyramid. This group—the countries with bars below the line in figure 7.1—is large, and it includes some high-income, some middle-income, and some lower-income countries. The transition countries, in addition to the inverting population structure, also have been subject to premature pension system inverting as both unemployment and the rise of informal labor markets has reduced the formal labor force. They face the toughest choices. In addition to setting the duration of retirement at 15 years, as was common in the European pension systems of the 1970s, they may have to reexamine what kind of benefits they can afford to provide for old-age support. The difficulty for many of these countries is that they have already reduced the generosity of their benefits, and the gap between poverty-prevention benefits and average benefits is already quite narrow. Note that the red bubble countries in figure 1.2 (chapter 1) are relatively close to the origin and have already reduced benefit generosity. Here economic growth is especially needed, as it would allow a widening of the gap between poverty-prevention benefits and average benefits.

Expanding the Labor Force

Increasing the size of the labor force expands the policy choices available to all the countries. However, measures to increase fertility, while popular with governments, typically have limited impact on the size of the labor force, at least for several decades. The viable options therefore include (a) increasing labor force participation (LFP), especially at higher ages; (b) raising retirement ages until life expectancy at retirement is around 15 years; and (c) encouraging immigration.

Figure 7.2 shows the labor force as in figure 7.1, but in this figure the red bars show the labor force in 2050 if the LFP rates currently seen in the cohort aged 40–44 are extended until age 64. The blue bars above the red ones show the additional labor force gained if the LFP rates of the age 40–44 cohort are extended not just until age 64,

FIGURE 7.2

**Projected Labor Force in 2050 with Higher Participation at Older Ages Compared to Actual
Labor Force in 2010, Selected European and Central Asian Economies**

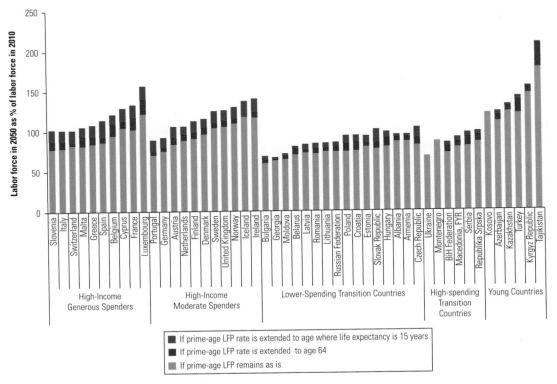

Source: United Nations population projections (UN 2011).
Note: The Federation of Bosnia-Herzegovina (BiH Federation) and Republika Srpska, which together make up the country of Bosnia and Herzegovina, have separate
pension systems and are treated as separate data points in the figure.

but until the age when life expectancy becomes 15 years in 2050.
Back in the 1970s, before the last wave of expansions in retirement
duration, retirement ages were commonly set at a level that, on average, provided pension income for the last 15 years of life. Therefore,
the last 15 years of life seems like a reasonable yardstick to define
"too old to work" for these higher-income societies. But extending
the LFP of the age 40–44 cohort until age 64 brings only two countries, Belgium and Denmark, into the group without the inverting
pyramid. By extending LFP further to the ages where only 15 years
of life expectancy remain, almost all of the high-income countries,
and a very few of the older transition countries, reach the point
where the pyramid is no longer inverting. Increased immigration
could push each of these labor force bars still higher.

The retirement ages at which life expectancy would be 15 years
in 2050 are shown in figure 7.3. For high-income countries, the

FIGURE 7.3

Effective Retirement Ages with Life Expectancy of 15 Years in 2050 Compared to Effective Retirement Age in 2010, Selected European and Central Asian Economies

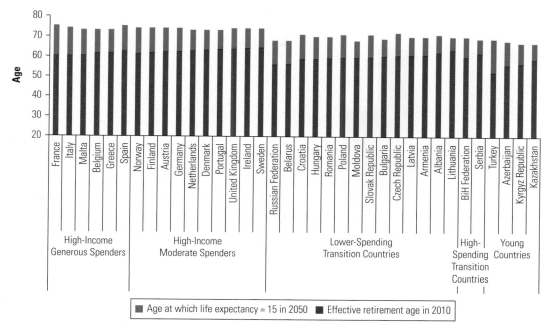

Source: Eurostat Statistics Database; country-provided data.

Note: The Federation of Bosnia-Herzegovina (BiH Federation) and Republika Srpska, which together make up the country of Bosnia and Herzegovina, have separate pension systems and are treated as separate data points in the figure.

retirement ages would have to be nearly 74 in 2050, while for transition and Young Countries, they would be close to 70. It would require an increase in the effective retirement age of about three months per calendar year, on average, between now and 2050 to achieve these retirement ages. It must be stressed that these increases are for the average effective, not statutory, retirement ages. If some people, such as miners or military service members, are allowed to retire early, everyone else will have to retire even later. Also, these increases in retirement ages will most likely have to be mandatory. Evidence has shown that raising benefits for workers who prolong their careers voluntarily does not persuade most people to do so, even when the incentives offered are very generous (as in Brazil and Latvia).

Can people work to such advanced ages? The evidence suggests that increasing life expectancy is associated with healthy aging. Health practitioners have compiled a list of "activities of daily living" and have studied the percentage of people in particular age groups who have difficulty completing at least one of these activities. The evidence from three European countries where some time series

FIGURE 7.4

Percentage of People Aged 65–74 Reporting Difficulty with One of the Activities of Daily Living in Denmark, Finland, and Sweden, 1980s and 2000s

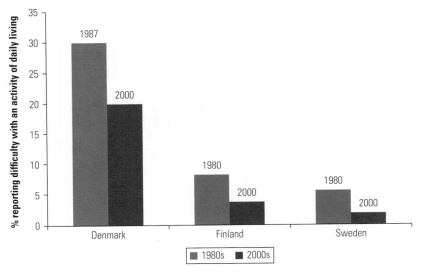

Source: Lafortune, Balestat, and the Disability Study Expert Group Members 2007.

is available suggests that the percentage of people in the 65–74 age group who report difficulties with at least one daily function has decreased over time, as shown in figure 7.4. The increase in life expectancy seems to translate largely into an increase in healthy years. Of course, not everyone will be healthy enough to work until these higher retirement ages, and those who cannot should of course be protected through the pension system.

LFP rates among those older than 65 are much higher in other parts of the world than in Europe, as shown in figure 7.5. This suggests that some of the low LFP rates in Europe and Central Asia arise not from the lack of ability to work, but from societal choices about when to provide a pension and when it is acceptable to stop working. LFP rates among those over age 65 are almost inversely related to life expectancy at that age. The highest LFP among older workers occurs in Sub-Saharan Africa, where life expectancy at age 65 was 12 years on average in 2010, while the lowest occurs in high-income countries of the Organisation for Economic Co-operation and Development (OECD), where life expectancy at 65 was 19 years. Life expectancy at age 65, well above the current effective retirement ages, averaged 14 years in the Europe and Central Asia region, the same as in East Asia and the Pacific, but with much lower LFP. Clearly, some of this is

FIGURE 7.5

Percentage of People over Age 65 in the Labor Force in Various World Regions, 2010

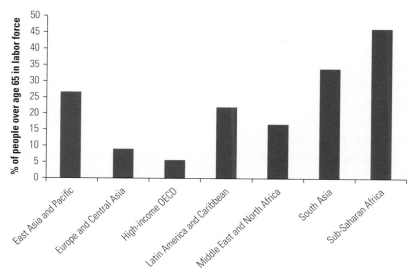

Source: Pallares-Miralles, Romero, and Whitehouse 2012.

a societal choice, but it is a choice that may not be affordable in the near future.

Immigration and productivity growth, if it does not translate into higher wages, can also help countries with the financing of old-age security. Countries where the labor force is projected to decline between 2010 and 2050, even with all of these changes, could consider filling the gap with immigrants. Even for the countries that can reach above 100 percent by raising retirement ages significantly, measures that increase immigration above what is already built into the United Nations population projections will allow a country to permit some earlier retirement. However, it should be noted that increasing immigration merely makes the system immature again and expands the pyramid. At some point, these immigrants will get old and will require pension benefits. But the immediate increase in revenues will help buy the system some time to accommodate more gradual adjustments. Productivity growth that does not translate into higher wages could also positively affect the pension system. Productivity growth that causes wages to rise, as is often the case, would not help in the medium term, since it would tend to raise benefit levels for those who experienced the higher wages.

Rethinking the Pension System and Prioritizing Spending

Faced with these challenging demographics, countries may be forced to rethink whether their pension system design will continue to provide the old-age security they want. Those countries where contributor growth is slowing and where the labor force falls below the 2010 level, even with increasing retirement ages, may need to reconsider what benefits they provide and to whom. Other countries might need to rethink their pension model, irrespective of their labor force growth, as the percentage of elderly who are not eligible for benefits begins to rise.

Countries typically enact modest reforms of their existing systems, but given the scope of the projected demographic change, it might be more useful to start by deciding where the country wants to be in 2050 and then deciding how to get there. Countries can first list the groups of people they want to protect through the pension system and try to quantify how many people are projected to be in each group by a long-run date like 2050. They can then define what benefits they want to pay each of these groups. Multiplying benefits by numbers of people will provide some measure of costs. The next step is to decide what budget envelope will be available to finance old-age and related security. To complete the calculations, countries will need to compare their estimated costs against their budget envelope to determine whether the proposed old-age security system is affordable. An example of such an exercise is shown in figure 7.6 and described below.

The first priority could be to make sure that all elderly receive at least a poverty-level benefit. We assume for this exercise that the average effective retirement age can be raised to 65 by 2050 from its current age, which is estimated to be 62 for high-income countries and 60 for transition countries, with the prime-age LFP rate extended through age 64. The absolute minimum that a country has to provide must be sufficient to keep all elderly, defined as those 65 and older, regardless of contribution history, out of poverty. The benefit level assumed in figure 7.6 is 20 percent of gross domestic product (GDP) per capita. The current poverty line is approximately at 20 percent of GDP per capita in lower-income countries, and a little lower in middle- and higher-income countries. Choosing 20 percent of GDP per capita instead of the absolute poverty line recognizes that poverty has both a relative and an absolute dimension. Countries are free to choose a different benefit level for this baseline benefit, but it should aim to cover the poverty line.

FIGURE 7.6

Example of the Cost of Financing Pension Priorities in 2050 with an Effective Retirement Age of 65, Selected European and Central Asian Economies

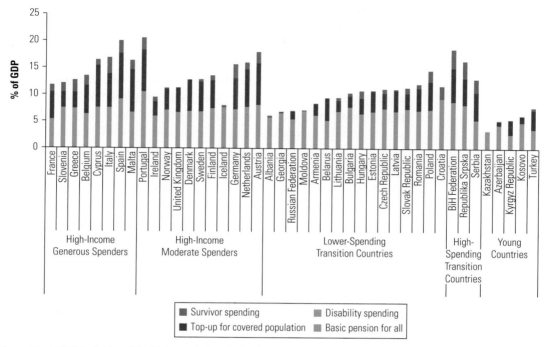

Sources: Eurostat Statistics Database; United Nations population projections (UN 2011); country-provided data.
Note: The Federation of Bosnia-Herzegovina (BiH Federation) and Republika Srpska, which together make up the country of Bosnia and Herzegovina, have separate pension systems and are treated as separate data points in the figure.

The bottom segment of each bar in figure 7.6 shows the cost of providing this baseline benefit to all elderly as a percentage of GDP. This bottom segment includes the cost of providing this baseline benefit for those who have paid contributions and for those who have not. Currently, in most transition countries, almost all elderly are covered under the contributory system; the few who are not covered sometimes receive social pensions administered by the pension system, sometimes receive social assistance, and sometimes receive nothing. In the future, as noted in chapter 3, there will be many more elderly without contributory pensions, and decisions will need to be made as to whether their benefits will be administered by the pension system or the social assistance system; in either case, this will be a cost for the government.

A second priority is to provide resources for those who are not healthy enough to work until retirement age. The second segment from the bottom in each bar represents the cost of disability payments. Some people will not be healthy enough to work until retirement age and will need government support. As we do not know how population health will evolve, we simply assume that the numbers of people receiving benefits and the benefit relative to average wage will remain roughly the same as they are today. This could be an underestimate, since older people are more likely to become disabled, and the numbers of people qualifying for disability benefits may increase as populations age. Similarly, increasing the effective retirement age means that some people who collect old-age pensions at the younger retirement ages of today may find themselves unable to work to higher ages and thus will need disability benefits. Nonetheless, improving health would tend to reduce the number of disabled. The second segment of the bar is based on the assumption that these three effects cancel each other out and disability spending relative to GDP remains about where it is today.

A third priority is to provide additional benefits for those who have contributed. In each bar the third segment from the bottom represents the cost of additional or top-up old-age benefits for these individuals. These are calculated by holding constant the current old-age benefit as a percentage of average wage, regardless of what the pension law would project, and subtracting the base-level benefit to these individuals, which was already included in the bottom segment. Benefits are provided only to those 65 or older and only to those in this age group who contributed.

Figure 7.6 shows this contributory benefit as a top-up to the base-level benefit for accounting purposes, but it may be administered differently. Many countries may prefer to combine this third segment together with the portion of the first segment that goes to contributors as the contributory pension, administered by the pension system. The remainder of the first segment might be called a social pension and might be administered by a different social agency. The advantage of combining the contributor and noncontributor base-level benefits, as figure 7.6 does, relates to the financing. As chapter 5 showed, taxes on a declining contributor base may not be sufficient to finance old-age security for contributors in the future and may need to be augmented by general revenue. Rather than financing the social pension through general revenue and then having to finance the deficit of the contributory system through general revenue, it might be cleaner to provide a base-level pension for everyone out of general revenue and then finance a smaller, additional benefit for contributors out of the smaller contribution revenue, with that top-up system being financially self-sustainable. However, these are implementation issues that countries can decide once the basic affordability decisions have been made.

A final priority is to provide benefits to surviving family members upon the death of the breadwinner. The top segment of each bar represents the cost of family and survivor pensions. As with disability pensions, the benefits as a percentage of average wage and the numbers of people receiving benefits are assumed to be roughly the same as they are today. Survivor benefits include benefits for widows and widowers and for orphans. Population aging suggests that the number of widows and widowers receiving benefits might increase, but the number of orphans might fall.

However, two factors suggest that overall survivor spending might decrease. First, higher LFP by women might lead to more women collecting their own pensions rather than survivor benefits, reducing the number of beneficiaries, given that the vast majority of spousal benefits go to women. Second, the level of additional benefit per survivor would be lower than today. At present, contributory old-age pensions average around 50 percent of GDP per capita. Survivor pensions are typically 60–70 percent of average old-age pensions, which would amount to 30–35 percent of GDP per capita. Since 20 percent of GDP per capita is already included in the bottom segment of the bar for all individuals over the age of 65, only the difference would need to be provided as survivor pensions.

If effective retirement ages rise to 65 and benefit generosity remains where it is today, pension spending will rise dramatically in many countries. In comparing projected 2050 spending in figure 7.6 to what countries are spending today, it becomes clear that spending in the future will be much higher; this is cause for concern, given that countries are already having trouble financing their pension systems. The High-Income Generous Spenders are today spending about 11 percent of GDP on pensions, while the High-Income Moderate Spenders are spending about 10 percent of GDP. Transition countries are spending on average 9 percent of GDP, while Young Countries spend only 5 percent of GDP. In 2050, by contrast, maintaining benefit levels similar to those shown in figure 7.6 will cost High-Income Generous Spenders on average 15 percent and High-Income Moderate Spenders on average 14 percent of GDP. Lower-Spending Transition Countries will average 10 percent of GDP, while the High-Spending Transition Countries will average 16 percent. Even the Young Countries will experience a modest increase from 5 percent of GDP to 6 percent.

What to do? Countries have a number of options. They can look for alternative fiscal resources to make the future spending requirements affordable; this may mean cutting other expenditure to make more fiscal room for pension spending and looking for other revenue sources, as suggested in chapter 5. They can revisit their pension spending priorities to see whether there is anything that can be reduced or eliminated. They can also look at increasing the labor force, either by raising retirement ages or by encouraging immigration. It should be noted that raising retirement ages affects both the expenditure and revenue sides of the pension balance, while immigration affects only the revenue side, and also increases long-term liabilities.

With respect to pension spending priorities, countries can evaluate all four components to look for potential cost savings. On the base-level benefit, there are a number of options. First, countries could means-test this benefit for noncontributors. The only major group likely to be excluded by a means test is nonworking spouses in middle- and higher-income households or spouses working in informal labor markets in middle- and higher-income households. In countries where coverage is moderate or high, suggesting there are few spouses in these categories, little is likely to be gained from means testing, particularly since administering a means test costs money.

The level of the benefit for noncontributors could be lower than 20 percent of GDP per capita, but again this will have a small impact on countries that have moderate to high coverage and few noncontributors. Typically, countries with low coverage are also lower-income, and this 20 percent of GDP per capita might be very close to the poverty line, which would make it difficult to cut. The age at which the benefit is available could also be raised for noncontributors.

An alternative approach would be to provide the base-level benefit at age 65 but raise the age for the contributory benefit. This would provide some income to contributors at 65 but would encourage them to continue in part-time work until they reach the age when they can receive their full benefit. For low-income individuals involved in physically demanding labor, who typically start work early in their lives, the base-level benefit might represent the majority of their benefit anyway and would allow them to retire after 45 years of contribution. For higher-income individuals who start work later and typically have less physically demanding jobs, receiving only the base-level benefit at 65 might encourage them to continue working.

Other countries might find that they can introduce better controls on disability spending. Countries spend widely varying amounts on disability, with differences in benefit levels and in definitions and practices. Definitions have been moving away from the inability to do the previous job or the percentage of the body that is impaired and now emphasize incapacity to perform any type of work. On the other hand, many countries have begun to include illnesses that rely on subjective assessments, such as mental illnesses and addictions, which are more prone to fraud. Countries can compare their spending to that of other countries in the region to determine whether they could realistically expect reforms in disability to save expenditure.

Still other countries might find that their contributor benefits can be reduced. On the top-up benefit to contributors, the question largely relates to the size of the benefit, since early retirement is assumed to have been largely eliminated. The inverting pyramid countries that provide sizable benefits above the base level might find that these benefits have to be reduced. Higher earnings-related benefits might be possible only through increased private savings, which can supplement the base-level benefit and the smaller earnings-related benefit.

It may also be possible to find some cost savings in survivor benefits. Some countries provide benefits to widows and widowers, well below the retirement age. While orphaned children do need to receive benefits and those benefits could enable a spouse to stay at home and care for the children, in general spouses below the retirement age should be encouraged to work.

A measure that might complement, or even substitute for, benefit reductions is an increase in the retirement age. Such a decision does not mean giving up all the gains in old-age security made during the twentieth century, but only returning countries to the benefit duration they offered in the 1970s, before the last expansion of social security took place. As noted in chapter 2, people used to expect benefits only for the last 15 years of life. Raising the retirement age is extremely powerful since it has a three-pronged impact: (a) it reduces total pension spending by limiting the number of beneficiaries; (b) it increases pension contribution revenue by increasing the number of people working who can pay contributions; and (c) by increasing the labor force, it also has a growth impact on GDP, which results in more noncontribution fiscal resources that can be used to support old-age security. If raising the retirement age is coupled with other policies, the duration of retirement can continue to be somewhat longer than 15 years.

If retirement ages are raised to the point where life expectancy equals 15 years, most countries will be able to spend about the same as they currently spend or less, as a percentage of GDP, and offer similar benefits to those offered today. In figure 7.7, High-Income Generous Spenders and High-Income Moderate Spenders

FIGURE 7.7

Cost of Pension Priorities in 2050 with Retirement Ages Where Life Expectancy Equals 15 Years, Selected European and Central Asian Economies

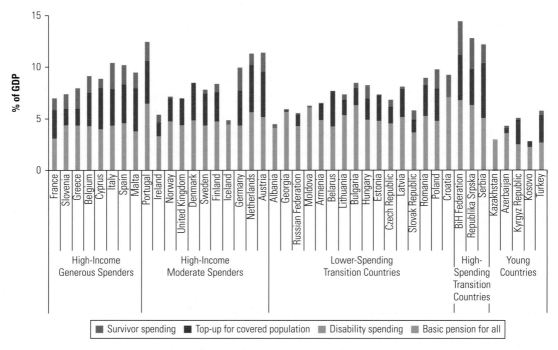

Sources: Eurostat Statistics Database; United Nations population projections (UN 2011); country-provided data.
Note: The Federation of Bosnia-Herzegovina (BiH Federation) and Republika Srpska, which together make up the country of Bosnia and Herzegovina, have separate pension systems and are treated as separate data points in the figure.

can provide benefits as generous as those that are provided today—that is, maintaining the same level of average benefit to average wage—while spending only 9 percent of GDP. This is significantly below the spending levels for these countries shown in figure 7.6. The Lower-Spending Transition Countries can provide the same generosity with only 7 percent of GDP. Young Countries will find that they need to spend only 4 percent of GDP on average in 2050. Only the High-Spending Transition Countries will still need to spend 13 percent of GDP, which is likely to still be unaffordable. These countries will have to make spending decisions in addition to increasing the retirement age.

Once a country has decided on a combination of benefit changes, retirement age increases, and changes to immigration policy, it must turn its attention to implementation and accompanying policy changes. The first issue is how to finance the chosen benefit mix. In countries where the contributory benefits are very close to the base-level benefit—whether because contributory benefits are low today or because choices were made to reduce contributory benefits in order to make the system fiscally sustainable—the country may be well advised to consider moving away from a contributory tax basis and toward general revenue. In countries where the contributory benefit is significantly higher than the base-level benefit, the country may consider financing the base-level benefit through general revenue while maintaining self-contained, contribution-based financing for the earnings-related contributory benefit. Providing earnings-related contributory benefits, with higher benefits for higher earners, from general revenue can be regressive, as is currently the case when pension deficits, which arise from higher benefits for higher earners, are financed from general revenues.

Adequacy of benefits will most likely require generation of private savings. While retirement savings are always desirable, they become especially important if average contributory benefits become close to the flat base-level benefit. In this case, there is very little room for differentiated benefits for higher earners. Wage earners will always want and expect to have their retirement income somehow relate to what they earned during their working years. If the public benefit that middle- and higher-income people receive becomes very low relative to their past earnings, there will be public pressure to raise the benefit level for everyone, which may be unaffordable. A better solution may be to help these individuals generate enough private savings to complement the lower public benefit and create a link to their previous earnings from private savings. The policies recommended in chapter 4, including automatic enrollment, well-designed default options, life-cycle portfolios, and a better institutional structure for pension funds, can help generate these retirement savings.

Retirement age changes will require complementary labor market policies. Even raising effective retirement ages to age 65, as was assumed in figure 7.6, will require active policies on the labor market side. Moving to the retirement ages of figure 7.7 will require even more proactive approaches. Early retirement practices need to be reevaluated and policies that couple part-time retirement with part-time work need to be instituted. Labor policies that allow discrimination against older workers, including pay structures that strictly relate pay to seniority, need to be discouraged. Older workers also need to have access to retraining opportunities designed to maximize their learning abilities and to workplace adaptations that can increase their productivity, as noted in chapter 6.

The bottom line is that countries will be able to provide old-age security despite the challenging demographics, but they will need to rethink the level of benefits they can provide and to whom.

They may also need to return to a duration of retirement closer to what they had in the 1970s, before increasing generosity lengthened the time most people spend in retirement.

References

Eurostat Statistics Database. European Commission, Brussels. http://epp .eurostat.ec.europa.eu/portal/page/portal/statistics/search_database.

Lafortune, Gaétan, Gaëlle Balestat, and the Disability Study Expert Group Members. 2007. "Trends in Severe Disability among Elderly People: Assessing the Evidence in 12 OECD Countries and the Future Implications." OECD Health Working Paper 26, Organisation for Economic Co-operation and Development, Paris.

Pallares-Miralles, Montserrat, Carolina Romero, and Edward Whitehouse. 2012. "International Patterns of Pension Provision II: A Worldwide Overview of Facts and Figures." Social Protection Discussion Paper 70319, World Bank, Washington, DC.

UN (United Nations). 2011. *World Population Prospects: The 2010 Revision.* New York: United Nations, Department of Economic and Social Affairs, Population Division. CD-ROM.